WELCOME TO LILY HILL...

...a quiet place where the breeze wanders through the vineyards and the rustling canopy of grape leaves casts dancing shadows across the hills. In the lull of midday, you can hear the noon whistle blow in town, five miles up the road. Take your time and stay awhile—you may catch a glimpse of the elves.

Here among the vines, Penny Kelly, the owner of Lily Hill Farm, meets a small group of elves who invite her to "find the nature of balance, rather than the balance in nature." Until now, Penny has never believed that elves, fairies, or any wee folk existed. She doubts her eyes and ears until, in a pivotal moment of blind trust, she makes a deal with them.

Over the next several years, as she struggles to hold up her end of the deal, the elves, the earth, and the elements teach her a series of powerful and challenging lessons that profoundly change her life—and will undeniably change yours, too.

About the Author

In early 1987, Penny Kelly and her husband, Jim, purchased fifty-seven acres of land, complete with a 100-year-old house, a dilapidated barn, and two small vineyards. At the time, they knew nothing about raising grapes.

Since then, they have remodeled the house into a rental property, and turned the barn into their home, office, and small learning center. They are in the process of restoring the soil, vineyards, and some of the natural habitat that had been lost. Since the encounters with the elves, they have decided to grow their own fruits, vegetables, herbs, and grains, and raise chickens and goats. In addition to her B.A., Penny has earned a degree in naturopathic medicine, and is working toward a Ph.D. in nutrition.

After a spontaneous "awakening of kundalini" in 1979, Penny found herself struggling with massive psychic abilities and overwhelming changes in perception and consciousness. Afraid she was losing her mind, she left her job as a tool and process engineer for the Chrysler Corporation, and returned to college to study the brain, consciousness, perception, intelligence, and related subjects. This led to her work as an educational consultant specializing in brain-compatible and accelerative teaching and learning techniques.

To Write to the Author

If you wish to contact the author or would like more information about this book, please write to the author in care of Llewellyn Worldwide, and we will forward your request. Both the author and the publisher appreciate hearing from you and learning of your enjoyment of this book and how it has helped you. Llewellyn Worldwide cannot guarantee that every letter written to the author can be answered, but all will be forwarded. Please write to:

Penny Kelly
℅ Llewellyn Worldwide
P.O. Box 64383, Dept. K382-4
St. Paul, MN 55164-0383, U.S.A.

Please enclose a self-addressed, stamped envelope for reply or $1.00 to cover costs.
If outside the U.S.A., enclose international postal reply coupon.

The Elves of Lily Hill Farm

A Partnership with Nature

Penny Kelly

1997
Llewellyn Publications
St. Paul, Minnesota, 55164-0383

Cover design: Anne Marie Garrison
Cover art: Stephanie Henderson
Interior design: Jessica Thoreson
Editing and layout: Laura Gudbaur
Project management: Amy Rost

Insert photos taken by Penny Kelly and Jim Jenzen, unless otherwise noted.

FIRST EDITION
Second Printing, 1997

Library of Congress Cataloging-in-Publication Data
        The elves of Lily Hill Farm: a partnership with nature / Penny
    Kelly.—1st ed.
        Includes bibliographical references and index.
        ISBN 1-56718-382-4 (pbk.)
        1. Elves.   2. Spirits.   3. Organic farming—Miscellanea.
    4. Organic gardening—Miscellanea.   5. Lily Hill Farm.   I. Title.
    BF1552.K46   1997
    133.1'4—dc21   96-52061
                                                                            CIP

Llewellyn Publications
A Division of Llewellyn Worldwide, Ltd.
P.O. Box 64383-0383
St. Paul, Minnesota 55164-0383
U.S.A.

ACKNOWLEDGMENTS

I would like to thank everyone who helped what at first seemed like an improbable idea to become a reality. I am eternally grateful to Nan Skovran at Llewellyn who first saw merit in the disconnected journal pages she received; to Jessica Thoreson and Amy Rost for shepherding the project through many editing tasks; and to Carl Llewellyn Weschke for his graciousness and the great common sense he brings to Llewellyn Publishing.

Thanks are also due to my parents, Hugh and Shirley Kelly; my daughters Kelly Anne and Penelope Wood; Chuck Reinert; Lad and Jana Hanka; and Rosana Rodriques. Each of them read and commented on the manuscript at various and difficult stages.

But special thanks go to my husband, Jim Jenzen, not only for his unhesitating acceptance of the elves and the difficult things they asked us to do, things that went against all conventional grape-growing wisdom, but also for his encouragement to write and rewrite…which meant he had the kitchen all to himself!

DEDICATION

*To Alvey, Mairlinna, and the many other forms of intelligent
life that exist and work to support human life.*

CONTENTS

INTRODUCTION

In the late seventies I was a tool and process engineer at Chrysler Corporation when, almost overnight, all kinds of strange and uncontrolled perceptual changes began happening to me. These changes were the start of over three long years of valiant struggle with both my body and my mind, while I was certain that I was going slowly insane. Most of the uncontrolled perceptions could only be called psychic experiences, but I had never had those kinds of perceptions before, nor did I know of anyone else who might have had such unusual experiences. I was not at all familiar with concepts such as clairvoyance or clairaudience, nor did I know anyone who was. I had neither read nor heard of anyone who claimed to be out of the body, or in two places at once. I did not believe in reincarnation, mostly because I didn't know anything about it beyond what the word suggested. In addition, communication had always been something that happened between me and other people who were alive and right in front of me, or by telephone, perhaps by letter. It is possible that if I had known anything about the subject of psychic experiences, this period of my life might have been a bit easier, less confusing, although it probably would have been just as frightening. I didn't know it at the time, but I was suffering from what was known as kundalini,* an ancient term for the sudden, massive awakening of consciousness with all of its powers, varieties of perception, and ability to enter other realms of existence. Even if I had known something about kundalini, the metaphysical realm, or the possibilities for experience beyond the immediate physical reality I was accustomed to, nothing would have prepared me for what I went through during this period.

The processes of this "awakening" resulted in such a wide variety of physical, mental, and emotional phenomena that every law of time, of space, of human capability and meaning that I had built my reality around was confronted, defied, and swept briskly away. It was as if I had stumbled through some door into a realm where none of the old rules of reality applied.

During that long, two-year period, in spite of extraordinary experiences, mushrooming psychic abilities, and the numerous physical difficulties brought on by kundalini, it never occurred to me to abandon myself to the spiritual fads that seemed to be popping up everywhere. Instead, I maintained my love of science, simply adding a deep spiritual component to it. I had little patience for people who declared that psychic experiences or abilities were crazy or nonexistent simply because they had not had such experiences or because there was no scientific research to prove them. Proof is not necessary in the realm of perception. I had even less patience for people who professed a syrupy spiritualism that dumped responsibility for everything into the lap of religion, who declared that science was irrelevant—even evil—or who believed that in order to be spiritual they had to give away all their money and become spineless, chanting doormats. I realized early that there could be no contradictions between science and spiritual experience—I had too much of each to discount one or the other. Contradiction would only seem to arise when there was incomplete observation and understanding at the scientific level, or incomplete experience at the spiritual level.

---

* My first book, *The Evolving Human*, tells the complete story of this awakening.

In honor of my respect for science and common sense, I maintained a healthy skepticism for anything with which I did not have a reasonable amount of experience. For this reason, I did not believe outright in elves and thought perhaps people who talked about fairies, angels, or nature spirits were lost in their imaginations or had been unable to leave childhood fantasies behind. However, in honor of my respect for the fields of metaphysics, parapsychology, true spiritual development, and all things psychic, I kept an open mind.

Twelve years after my first experiences with kundalini, in February of 1990, my husband and I were on a short vacation to Frankenmuth, Michigan, the town where we had been married seven years earlier. During the trip we went into Bronner's Christmas Shop and spent several delighted hours wandering through their Christmas wonderland.

In the course of this wandering, I happened to pick up and thumb through a small book. It was written by a professor who lived somewhere south, perhaps in the Carolinas. It seems to me that the good professor's dog had died inopportunely at Christmastime, and while he was out burying the dog, deeply mourning the loss of his furred friend, he happened to meet some elves.

I didn't read enough to know what the outcome of this meeting was. I didn't even want to know. Instead, upon skimming through bits of the professor's story I was aware of only one thought: how could someone as educated and respectable as a professor believe in elves? Perhaps it was only a story he'd made up. I put the book down and wandered over to other displays, never noting the title or the author's name.

After our trip to Frankenmuth and my brief scan through the book written by the professor, I found the subject of elves and fairies crossing my mind regularly. Perhaps my curiosity had flared because the professor had been exactly that—a professor, an educated mind. From the beginning of my experiences in the metaphysical realms, I had occasionally noticed the subject of elves and fairies from a distance, in books, articles, art, overhearing a chance conversation, or in greeting cards, but I never paid it much attention. With some effort, I stayed open, but I was definitely skeptical—to the point of being impatient and disdainful about the subject.

In late August of that same year, a young man who was rooming with us left on a trip to Africa and told me before he left that I was welcome to read any of his books while he was gone. One day while putting Brian's mail on his bookshelves, I knocked over a book titled *Agartha*. It was an odd title so I took the book down and thumbed through it curiously. Fifteen minutes later I was still standing there reading. I took him up on his offer and borrowed the book.

A couple of days later, I finished reading it and put it back on his shelf, caught in a circle of conflicting thoughts and feelings. Agartha was the name given to a woman who had developed some psychic abilities and although there were some similarities in the way my own and Agartha's psychic abilities had evolved, I felt she had gone too far in her claim to have contacted what she called nature spirits. In ten years of open-minded experiences and open-ended experiments with a wide variety of psychic abilities, I had little evidence to suggest that such things were real or worth investigating. Of course, I had never tried to contact elves or nature spirits either!

August ended, I went back to work as an education consultant, teacher, and would-be writer, but a month later found myself still thinking about Agartha and the idea of nature spirits. By this time, I had moved from complete disbelief, to the probability that Agartha had enhanced the story to make it interesting, then to a serious consideration of what it might mean if elves, fairies, and nature spirits really did exist, and finally to facing the possibility that I was acting like an ignorant know-it-all. Perhaps I was being introduced to another area in which I had much to learn. This last realization was difficult to swallow and for a short time I avoided the whole subject.

Curiosity filled me from time to time but I always ended up thinking that people who believed in elves or spirits were somehow unbalanced or childish or anything but normal. Then, one October day, extremely upset about Saddam Hussein's invasion of Kuwait and the fear that my son would be drawn into a war, I went for a walk....

CHAPTER 1 ❧

We were a month into autumn and more than two months into the confrontation with Iraq over their invasion of Kuwait. It was a fair day for a walk and by late afternoon, unable to concentrate, I was out the door with fears of war and visions of my only son as a soldier, pursuing me. Overhead was an overcast sky and the air was cool but reasonably dry so I headed along the lane toward the back of the farm. My cats, Jasmine and Gabriella—friends and companions for over ten years—followed, meowing plaintively when I got too far ahead of them.

I walked blindly, caught by the drama of what was happening in the Middle East, my mind careening from one awful possibility to the next, until my heart was pounding in a panic that we would all be swallowed in some stupid armed conflict because of Iraq's needy illusion that it didn't have enough—gold, oil, prestige, power, whatever. On and on the ugly scenes built themselves until the sheer ridiculousness of their content shocked me back to the present moment.

To keep the panic somewhere out on the edges of my mind, I dragged my eyes slowly and deliberately over the physical world around me, the world of grasses and grapes, of birds, breezes and rolling horizons. Gradually, the act of walking and the effort at mental self-discipline began to have some effect; a fragile calm settled over me, and I began to enjoy the walk.

Farther down the lane, I was passing the cornfield when thoughts of elves and nature spirits or whatever the small folk were called washed through my mind. I turned my attention elsewhere, judging elves and such to be imagination, but a few minutes later the curious thoughts returned. I had always thought that stories of elves were just that—stories. But provoked by the recent reading of a book that touched on the subject, and wanting to do something besides worry about war, I called out impulsively, first mentally, then aloud. Nothing happened and I felt silly, absurdly embarrassed in front of no one.

Hurrying away from my own foolishness, I reached the hill at the corner of the back vineyard. I had just begun to climb with reaching steps and deep breaths, unaware of the slope or my thoughts, when a seemingly distant chorus of voices in sing-song unison distracted me, brought me to full attention.

"May the road rise to meet ye!"

I was very surprised and stopped moving to listen closely. Nothing followed immediately except my own breath and a slow, defensive reaction.

"My imagination is playing tricks on me! That's just an old Irish poem, I've got some Irish in me and my mind is conjuring up voices of familiar things…."

I continued up the hill, trying to decide if I had really heard a chorus of voices or not when it dawned on me that because of the hill, the road really did appear to be rising, lifting itself to meet my feet. The ground seemed more vibrantly alive with every move of my legs; its touch offered more than just a spring to each step, it seemed to offer serenity and support.

The small chorus interrupted again, "May the sun be ever at yer back," and I was sure I had heard something this time. For no apparent reason, I recalled a time more than ten years earlier when I had been driving across the Great Plains, headed for Arizona with the hope of creating a whole new life. On through the late afternoon I drove, until evening when the lowering sun came across those treeless fields so brilliantly that I had to stop the car because I simply could not see the road or where I was going at all. It was while I sat there waiting for the sun to go down that I knew, intuitively, that I was not going to stay in Arizona. Looking back, the significance of this brief and now-distant moment seemed overwhelming. What a blessing it was to have the sun at one's back; how impossible things could become when you were so blinded by the pursuit of your personal visions that you were unable to see the path!

The chorus of voices chanted on, but now my heart was beginning to race in excitement; I was sure I was not just imagining things. Concerned with the validity of the voices, I missed the words of a line or two, catching only their final "And may ye find peace within." Peace, I needed it.

I reached the crest of the hill at the back of our farm and stood gazing over the countryside, wishing my house was up there instead of down by the road. My husband, Jim, and I had moved across the state and bought the fifty-seven-acre farm with its two small vineyards on Valentine's Day in 1987. For me it had been a home, a place to live, finally a place of our own. It had needed a lot of work and my immersion—in the remodeling of the ancient house and sagging barn, in the demands of two teens, and in efforts to revitalize my educational consulting business that had been pulled out by the roots when we moved—had been total.

During the first few years, I ignored the vineyards; they were a mystery anyway. It had fallen to Jim, who was already overworked between his job as a construction manager at Ameritech and the renewal of house and barn, to figure out what the grapes needed and how to take care of them.

Ernie, a neighbor from down the road, had visited us the first week we were here. Through introductions and a few cups of coffee we discovered that he had retired from making steel and building bridges to settle down and raise grapes here forty years earlier. Ernie knew everything about grapes—their care, bugs, diseases, propagation, necessary equipment—and the timing of all the activities related to these; he quickly became Jim's private coach and mentor. Together they had worked hard to restore our vineyards after years of absentee ownership and minimum care.

This year, however, Jim had been so consistently busy that vineyard work had gotten far behind and my help had been needed. I had learned to drive the tractor and to trim and shape new vines. Now I looked over the vineyards recalling how pleasant it had been to work among the vines for the first time this past spring and summer, and as I looked, I listened expectantly, hoping to hear something more from the small voices. But there was nothing.

I wandered around to the back side of the hill where it slid steeply down toward a tiny lake and wondered again if I had imagined the chorus of small voices. There were trees on that side of the hill, the north side, and I sat down in the tall grass right at the edge of the treeline, thinking I would try to meditate, still hoping to hear something more.

In the silence my mind drifted, refusing to stay still. The recent events in Kuwait lurched back into consciousness and the fear of a war between the U.S. and Iraq left me shuddering when the chorus of voices returned, thoroughly startling me.

"How can ye people look at yerselves and ignore the reality ye are creating? It's as if yer path toward war is some power dance that ye think will lead to economic gain and a higher standard of living. Ye are out of balance and yer standard of living is so close to a nightmare that we are sure ye must all be asleep!"

My mind split neatly along two lines, one a cool observer, the other in silent acknowledgment. For weeks, months even, I had been wondering if there were really such things as nature spirits or elves. Now here I was for the third time in the past half-hour with a chorus of voices talking all around me, and I still had not volunteered a single response. One side of me questioned the other—were the voices real or not? And where were they coming from? The other side of me, deeply caught in my worry about armed conflict and wondering how the world had gotten into such a mess, hung in distracted, worried silence.

The quiet remained unbroken in the minutes that passed; as if testing the reality of the voices, I waited to hear more, but when nothing else came, my mind drifted back to its worry about war in an imaginary future. It was filled with pictures of mothers like me sending their sons off to be maimed, of architecture and orchards mindlessly destroyed, of strange soldiers marching through my basil, and the possibility of nuclear weapons.

Tears, huge and bitter, tinged with mascara began to slide over my cheeks and fall freely into the small, grassy triangle formed by my crossed legs. Feeling angry with the whole world, I sobbed and cursed those who wanted war. I wished passionately for peace. In my mind I demanded it; at the same time I knew that there would be serious criticism for those who did not support the war.

Some time later, tired and with burning eyes, I sat, empty and quiet. In the dusk the countryside looked soft and beautiful. The breeze moved lightly across my wet face and I wished for peace all over the planet. As much as I wanted it, realistic consideration of the world made such wishes seem like futile fantasies. I found myself wondering if it would be possible to at least make our farm a wonderful, healing, safe and bountiful place to be. Off on the magic carpet of imagination I dreamed that it would never freeze here, that trees and flowers, plants, animals and people would live here and grow in perfect harmony, supporting and protecting one another. I pictured grapevines that produced hundreds of tons of grapes every year, herbs that replenished the soil, vegetables and fruits that cured sickness and disease, and humans that renewed themselves and their companions all over the earth until the forces that promoted war or worked against nature had been eliminated and the planet returned to an earlier, more pristine innocence.

Cutting into my reverie, a small voice, then another, and yet another, began to clamor all around me, asking, "Why do ye seek to control a specific balance in nature when it is far more important to find the nature of balance. One attempt is a closed operation and the other is open-ended."

"I don't know why we do what we do...," I said half-aloud, then sat there, realizing that I had finally answered the small voices. Only silence acknowledged me.

The cats had long since gone back to the house; the sun was headed down and I started the walk home, tired and cold, wondering how the "nature of balance" was different from the ecological principles I had once learned in a college science class, which talked about finding a way to protect, restore, and repair nature. Could we even begin to do such a thing? I considered the difficulties of telling people that we might be wiser to explore ecology and the idea of balance from a new perspective. Perhaps the nature of balance was some sort of higher law, but were there any practical higher laws and how did one go about communicating such laws—especially when it was obvious that so many people in the world were not listening? They were all caught in their present ruts, reaching for some future, or living in some past, out to get ahead or get revenge for something that had happened to their ancestors. I reached the back door of the house and went in to fix dinner, already forgetful about having heard the chorus of small voices, again caught in an emotional crossfire about the state of the world, her nations, and my son.

About ten days later, still thinking of my encounter with the tiny voices at the back of the farm, I went for another walk. It was very late in the afternoon and again overcast as I walked along the lane toward the back vineyard. I was pre-occupied with the idea of somehow contacting the elves, nature spirits or whatever I had heard, and I listened intently, eyes cast down as I walked, until I entered gradually a state of ever-enlarging consciousness.

For the first time, I became aware of the many other creatures besides myself who used the lane. There were deer prints that looked piquantly like broken hearts, rabbit prints in the sandy spots, and the small perfect hands of the raccoons. Dog and cat tracks wandered here and there, the Sanskrit patterns of bird feet started and stopped abruptly, and there were several prints that I didn't recognize at all. The tread of the tractor tires was a herringbone ribbon that stretched out ahead and behind me, and as I walked blackbirds whirled and cried over my head.

I walked past the corn on my right, amazed at how it towered over me and how loudly it rustled in the stiff afternoon breeze. Just to the left side of the lane the tall grasses whispered and nodded, and I felt awkwardly aware as I moved along. I was looking toward the ground but felt as if I was seeing in all directions until my eyes spied a large, flattened stone that appeared to have been recently pulled out of its resting spot and was kind of sitting up on its end in the middle of the lane.

An enthusiastic voice rang out, cutting across my consciousness, "Look underneath it and ye'll find the pot o' gold!" Without an ounce of hesitation I stopped, picked it up expectantly, and found myself staring at the wet, muddy underside of a rock. I looked at the empty hole it had come out of. There was nothing in it. It took a few moments for the reality of the situation to register. I had actually expected a pot of gold. I felt ridiculous!

Perhaps I was going overboard on the idea of elves. What was the matter with me? I thought about the old stories of elves and tried to remember what they had been about, but I had never really paid any attention. Maybe elves had nothing to do with pots of gold; in fact, it seemed like it was the rainbow that was connected to the legendary pot. Still, setting the rock back into the hole in a deliberately crooked position, I sent a loud challenge to any elves that might be listening or watching. "If you really exist, straighten this rock and put it back in the hole so it fits perfectly by the next time I walk by!" Then I stood up, brushing dirt from my hands and intending to continue walking toward the hill at the back of the farm.

"Aw, c'mon now, ask for something we can do. That business with the rock isn't even challenging. The tractor or the truck could roll over it and push it back in the hole and then how would ye know who or what set it right! Ask for something interesting!" It was the small chorus of voices complaining just like my teenagers.

Surprised, pleased, and momentarily at a loss for word or thought, I continued slowly along the lane, first sifting through an assortment of requests, then struggling with full-blown doubt, then returning to search my mind for decent or worthy requests. Nothing would come to me except the story of Aladdin's lamp and his three wishes—which I at first ignored. Then feeling suddenly bold and outrageous, I asked, "Could you give me three wishes?"

Immediately the voices replied, "And what would yer three wishes be?"

"Let there be peace, joy, and health here!"

The words resounded through the air like the wind chimes hanging outside my office door. I paused and tried to think of two more wishes, but at that exact moment, nothing else seemed important. Caught by a gripping anxiety, I was struck dumb. Neither would my tongue move nor could I even think of anything else to wish for; a three-in-one wish would have to be enough.

When there was no response to the declared wish, I started walking again, past the back vineyard on my way up the hill, moving smoothly over the peak until I found myself in a shallow dip on the far north side of the hill, close to the tree line. I stopped and stood there, my back to the trees, feet slightly apart, hands behind me, as if I were waiting expectantly for someone or something to respond to my wish. I was only there a short time when a single voice right beside me said, "What're ye doing?"

Startled, I jumped, practically off the ground. Stammering and a bit awkward I replied, "I, um…came to visit the elves. I'm…not…sure what to say or do…I just wondered if there's some way we can work together to make a better world." Actually, the thought hadn't even occurred to me until that very moment, but it seemed like a noble goal and a reasonable way to start a conversation.

"What would ye like us to do?" came the questioning response. I stood there for a moment, fumbling for an answer. I hadn't thought through this idea of contacting elves or nature spirits at all. I repeated my wish for peace, joy, and health here in this beautiful place. When there was no immediate response I added—hoping it would catch their attention—that I also wanted this farm, this earth, the dirt itself, right in this very spot, to find the nature of balance. Then in a rush of words unlocked from the speechlessness of only minutes before, I said that I wanted every square foot of this farm to have such a healthy effect on people that if someone got so much as half of their big toe over the property line, onto our land, the healing would begin. But as I tried to continue explaining what I wanted, I began to feel like I was asking for too much, and for things that were just not possible. I also felt foolish talking aloud and so fervently to someone or something I couldn't see.

An idea came to me. Drawing on my experiments with telepathy, I sat down cross-legged at the edge of the woods, closed my eyes, and began to create intense mental pictures of the farm as I wanted it to be, with images of loving people, joy, peace, plenty, health, laughter, and abundance—each carrying the essence of something so sweet my whole being ached.

I don't know how much time passed, but I was completely engrossed in the effort to communicate my wishes when my attention shifted back to where I was sitting. My eyes opened slightly and in some shock I gazed on another world. The hill appeared like a golden, glowing mountain with miniature fields and clearings and tiny paths that criss-crossed in many directions. There were tall weeds and short trees grouped around small thatched doors, and a soft, lingering "Oh-h!" rose unprompted from my middle to my lips. Everything glowed as if it were lighted from within, and I gazed at it for quite a long time. No matter in which direction I looked, I saw the golden, miniature world of the elves overlaid by a golden version of the reality I lived in. It was like nothing I had ever seen before.

The golden glow remained unchanging, and after a time, I decided to start walking again, even though I knew the whole vision might disappear. Slowly, not wanting to disturb the experience, I got up gingerly, and moved downhill. I could hear the small voices following me and somehow decided they really must be elves. Moving along the ends of the rows, I saw a few vines that made me wish I had brought my trimming shears and twine, but it was too early for shears. It had to get really cold first so all the sap dropped before any canes were trimmed from the vines. I didn't really know much about trimming anyway. I kept walking, thinking how much I had learned about grapes compared to three years ago—and yet how little I really knew.

When we had first bought the farm and began to learn from Ernie how to take care of grapes, I had been horrified at the powerful chemicals we had to spray on the vines to keep weeds under control or fungus, disease, and pests at bay; chemicals so potent we had to go in the house and close the windows and doors during spraying. When the actual spraying was done, we had not even been allowed to walk through the vineyards for a day or two. I had never seriously thought about doing anything different because I had never seriously thought about the vineyards; but now the idea of spraying poisons everywhere seemed ludicrous, crazy. I called out to the elves matter-of-factly, "What do we have to do to grow these grapes without having to spray chemicals everywhere? Can you help make them disease resistant? Is it possible to get eight to ten tons per acre every year?"

"Are ye sure eight to ten tons per acre is all ye want?" came a voice that made it difficult to tell whether it was a joke or a serious question, one that hinted at more by suggesting that my vision of what was possible was too limited.

Thinking of how often I had told my students that they were limiting themselves, I replied, "Well…how about twelve…no, make that…uh, fourteen tons per acre."

"Why not twenty?" came the small voice, which was immediately followed by a host of others echoing, "Yeah, that's more like it!… Make it twenty!… Let's go for twenty!… How 'bout it?… Yeah, twenty tons.…"

By then I was overwhelmed with disbelief. It just wasn't possible. Ernie was the best grower we knew. He used the same kind of trimming method we used—the Kniffen method—and consistently got six tons per acre in all sorts of weather and growing conditions. Eight was considered a bumper crop for Kniffen trimming and almost unheard of in these parts. Most vineyards, like us, averaged less than four tons an acre—whether they used the Kniffen method, the cordon system, or some other system for shaping vines along the trellis.

Doing some rough verbal math I said, "We have over thirteen acres of grapes if you put both vineyards together. The most we've ever gotten in a single year is seventy-seven tons total. That was in our first year and was probably beginner's luck along with the fact that the vines had been given marginal care until we came along. Our second year we got a mere thirty-six tons and the third year our crop was down to only seventeen tons. This year we harvested about thirty-four tons. At this point our average is around forty tons a year. Eight tons per acre would be more than a bumper crop for us and would give us one hundred and four tons in all. I could believe in a hundred tons of grapes. Would you go for one hundred tons?"

There was much discussion and argument among them for a moment, and then they agreed. "One hundred tons it will be! Ye do yer part and we'll do ours," they chorused.

"Okay," I said, snapping to attention, "show me what is possible, tell me what I can do to help."

"Walk yer land. Get to know it!" came their answer.

I hesitated for a long, uncertain moment. In my mind this did not seem like it would be of much use, but after a moment I thought, "Oh well, I'm the student here." So aloud I said, "Okay, I will. Is there anything else I could do?"

"Plant trees!" they cried in unison.

"Trees?" I said to myself. This seemed like a very odd prescription, but out loud I agreed amiably. Leaving the vineyard and heading west across the farm I wondered what on earth planting trees would do for the grapes. I also wondered what Ernie would say if I told him we had some new mentors to help us with our vineyard production and that they were elves or wee folk. He'd probably think we were unbalanced! I chuckled to myself.

The small voices followed me around the corner of the woods and downhill to the pond, an enchanting, secluded spot surrounded by gigantic fir trees some previous owner had planted in three concentric circles. "Hey," I called out, feeling somewhat rude at not knowing if the elves had names. "Do you think it would be a good idea to clean up around the pond, trimming and cutting back some of the trees?" I asked.

Again, there was much debate. Finally, the argument subsided and a demure female voice said, "Sure, go ahead. In fact, we would make some suggestions about yer pond. Jim has been worrying about where water would drain to if ye dug a pond in the front of the farm by the road. This is not the place for a pond. We can help ye, if, rather than a pond, ye put in a stream or creek."

Boggled at this, I did not respond. Then the whole chorus of voices began to call excitedly, "Come with us.... Come to the top of that hill.... Come on, come on...!"

When I reached the top they continued, "Look, carefully, at how the land slopes and curves. On this side of the lane the farm's water will drain naturally to the back of the farm. Why do ye think the pond back here exists with no effort to make it stay a pond or to maintain it?

"Now—ye will find a flowing well in that hill immediately to yer left. With planning and design, ye can tap that well and by digging a series of carefully placed shallow canals, ye can get the water to flow in a southeasterly direction from the north side of yer property all the way to the front and then around to a northwesterly direction, all the way to the natural pond at the back of yer property! See where it would flow on its way back, just this side of the cherry tree and right past the corner of the front vineyard, then on through the hills until it reaches the pond?"

I stood there, looking at the land, the hills, the rise and fall of the fields, amazed at the picture they were painting and the idea that it did look like it might work.

When I did not say anything right away, a single voice from the chorus piped up and said, "It would be some work. Ye would have to plant some trees up where ye were going to put the pond. These will help hold the soil. Ye would also have to put a small bridge in the lane. And all those stones and rocks ye keep looking for a place to dump can be used to line the stream...."

"I-I'll tell Jim," I stuttered, wondering if he would think I was crazy, or be disappointed about not having a pond up near the house. I had not really been in favor of a pond because it seemed like an engineering feat too big to deal with, but the idea of a flowing stream seemed ten times as complicated.

It was now well into dusk and I had been gone much longer than I had intended. I said good night and headed back down the hill, wondering about the individual voices that had spoken several times and if any of them had a name. These thoughts were interrupted by a small voice that echoed from quite a distance behind me, "My name is Alvey... call me Alvey...!"

In surprise I stopped, turned around, and looked toward the hills. The golden glow that had followed me to the pond was gone. "My name is Mairlinna," called the demure voice. "And I'm Kermots," shouted another.

"Good night, Alvey, good night Mairlinna and Kermots," I called, "and thank you... very much... all of you." I went back to the house and over the rest of the evening could not get the experiences of the day out of my mind. I kept thinking about the wish I had made for peace, joy, and health. Maybe I should have wished for something more exotic, like a vacation in Tahiti, or more practical, like a new roof on the house. After my first encounter with the small chorus of voices the previous week, I had gone to bed wondering if I had the guts to believe in them. Tonight, believing seemed like small stuff; the problem of acting on our agreement, of actually doing what they had asked, taking them seriously and acting as if they were real and that we had a deal— that was another matter. The terms were simple: one hundred tons of grapes in return for walking my land, but acting—and acting in good faith—was a monumental commitment.

CHAPTER 2 ❦

More than a month went by and not once did I think about going out to walk my land or get to know it. The opening of deer season in November reminded me that I wanted this place to be a safe haven for all the creatures of earth; that I had not even taken the first step toward that goal, a step which was no more demanding than putting on a hat, a coat, some boots, and going for a walk. But I was afraid of getting shot by some over-anxious deer hunter and put off any kind of walk.

December arrived and I was extremely busy. I had taken on a second job teaching at a local business college because I wanted extra money to buy a new sofa. Now, giving final exams to my students and grading piles of term papers, I wasn't sure the sofa was worth it; and the nagging voice that kept telling me to "just get out there and walk one time" had no patience for term papers and final deadlines. I continued to promise myself a quick stroll, and soon, but when the semester finally ended, it got very cold and snowy, the temperatures dropped into the single digits—and I again put off any kind of walk.

Christmas and the holidays rushed by, taking with them a large chunk of time and all my energy for walking. In the middle of January my forty-third birthday came and went leaving me with assorted feelings. I was too old to be believing in fairies, elves, and such. On the one hand, the whole idea of elves and walking my land seemed vague, or maybe useless. On the other, I kept telling myself I was going to do what the elves had suggested—but I didn't.

Jim, who had been quite interested in my account of meeting the elves, encouraged me to get out and walk around the farm just to see what happened. But I had set up an aggressive writing and editing schedule that stretched through all of January, February, and March. Definitely on the defense, I told him with considerable passion that every time I had a break from educational consulting or teaching and a chance to devote myself to writing, twenty other somethings needed to be done besides writing. I wanted out of educational consulting. I wanted to write. This time I was not going to let myself be distracted. Still, I kept promising myself that I was going for a walk—within a week, or as soon as I had written something significant—but neither happened, either the walk or the significant writing.

In mid-February Juan, our grape trimmer, arrived. He trimmed vines for us every year and always did an excellent job. He began trimming in the front vineyard and since Jim was gone more than he was home, I knew it was up to me to make sure Juan had everything he needed. It was the perfect reason to get out in the vineyard—but still I procrastinated.

Suddenly spring was less than three weeks away. I had been sitting, typing, writing for weeks, those damp chilly days that settle in your bones in the last weeks of winter and leave you feeling like an old sponge that's dried into some unnaturally curled position. I needed a break; and I needed to at least make a show of walking my land, so I finally put on hat and coat and went for a walk. It was cold, wet, and overcast, but the snow had melted, except for a few shadowed patches.

Once outside I wondered just exactly how one went about walking his or her land. Did I need to cover every square foot of the property? Probably not; but how much was enough, and did I need to follow a set pattern? How often? Was a special ritual necessary, or a general broadcast of my intention, something like "To Whom It May Concern: I am walking my land now."

First I worried that the elves might think I had forgotten all about them. Then it seemed quite possible that I had misunderstood the terms of our agreement, or that my entire encounter had been nothing but a figment. I walked along the lane alternating between a jovial pride that I had finally gotten out to walk my land, and feeling dubious about the whole business. Finally, close to the spot I had first spotted the flattened rock out of position, I put out a call to Alvey.

There was no response, and I didn't know what else to do so I kept going, past the back vineyard and up the hill at the back of the farm. I walked until I got to the spot by the woods where I had been sitting when everything turned golden the previous autumn. Again I called to Alvey, or any of his group, but still nothing happened.

After a short time, I began to feel upset, cold, and stupid standing there waiting for elves that probably didn't exist to come by and acknowledge my efforts to do something as vague as walk my land. With hands tucked in pockets and head down, I walked back over the hill toward the lane, intending to go back to the house. But as I neared the corner of the vineyard, a rising crescendo of tiny voices filled the hillside. I looked up and over toward the vines then stopped in shocked astonishment. There was almost no wind yet every vine was waving its arms, calling, "Come back!… Come back!… Come and work with us!… Remember when you came and took care of us last summer?… We enjoyed your presence…. Come back, please…. Please come and be with us again!…"

An ocean of memory swelled up, ferrying me back to the previous spring, an absolute novice trying to trim and shape some of the young vines, talking to them as if they were people, asking them what they needed in order to be healthy, to grow, and to produce excellent grapes. What an exquisite pleasure it had been to take off my shirt and work half-naked, the sun on my back as I had not felt it since probably six years of age. I had asked the vines not to scratch or poke me, and it seemed to me they understood, they were patient with me and my intent in spite of the fact I had no clear idea of what I was doing.

Amazed at how they continued to wave and to call, and forgetting to question how such a thing could be happening, I walked into the vineyard, gradually making my way toward the young vines in the back hollow that I had worked on so diligently last summer. They were beautifully shaped, and healthy, quite a contrast from the frozen-out, grotesque forms they had been when I started. I sat down under the trellis, suddenly a bundle of confusion, not caring about the wet ground, crying spontaneously in pleased relief at the results of my work. They wanted me to come back and work.

I recalled the profound contentment I had experienced in the vineyards the previous June. Never had I suspected that I could enjoy any kind of physical work so totally. Briefly, I wondered how I could find time to add vineyard work to a schedule that already seemed ridiculously scattered and short of time. I closed my eyes, engulfed in a deep sorrow that such pleasurable work was out of reach. I had a college degree, in fact, I taught at colleges. I had to make a living, but everyone knew this kind of manual work was for peasants. The tears continued, and I was ignorant of time until my nose began to run in earnest. I reached blindly toward my pocket for a tissue, blowing my nose loudly and wiping at my eyes. Then both eyes and mouth opened wide and round in surprise. The miniature, golden world I had observed the previous autumn surrounded me again.

Oblivious to the cold and wet, I sat under the trellis and looked intently about. This vineyard, which stretched partway up the hill, along with the crown of the hill and part of the woods, was the world of the elves. Again there were the small trees, clearings, paths crossing here and there leading to miniature doorways concealed in the tall grasses, hitching posts in yards and at apparent gathering places, smoke rising from hidden chimneys. Oddly, I knew that I had plunked myself into the middle of the community that they considered to be down in the valley, and that there were other neighborhoods of wee folk around the farm.

Something sweet gathered inside me, a scattered feeling disappeared, and a peaceful clarity settled around me. I had to find a way to put both educational consulting and writing aside; I wanted to work in the vineyards again this spring, even if just for a little while. Then an unvoiced awareness sunk fully into me. I not only wanted to work in the vineyards again this year, I needed to. I didn't understand it, and if someone had asked me to describe any part of what I was experiencing at the moment, I would have been unable. Neither did

I think to stop and ask myself what working in the vines might have to do with walking my land. I simply knew in my heart I had to do this. I got up hurriedly and called out to both vines and elves—in case they were listening—"Okay, I'll be back. I'll be happy to work with you. I will trim you myself!" Then I headed back home having a clear sense of direction and purpose.

Two days later after a marathon of typing and editing, I had brought my writing project to a reasonable conclusion. It needed editing, so I put it away for later. I cleaned up my office, paid the monthly bills, and finished the bookkeeping that went with the job. Then I called Jim who, as usual, was in Grand Rapids a good part of every week, and told him I'd finally gotten out to walk and make an effort to keep my agreement with the elves. I shared my experience of communicating with the vines and their invitation to come and work among them, then announced cheerily, "Juan is almost done with the front vineyard and we won't need him to do the back. I've decided to trim them myself."

Jim thought this was highly over-ambitious, since I had rarely trimmed anything other than an occasional young vine before. In an attitude of humorous despair he asked what on earth had happened to my writing career now, yet he seemed genuinely surprised that I had taken an interest in the vineyard and delighted that I wanted to help.

"Just work with Juan when you can, help him get the job done, don't try to do it all yourself," he advised me cautiously.

I was very resistant to having Juan trim when I had just promised the vines that I would come and work with them, but after several intense conversations in one day, Jim convinced me that six and a half acres was too much and spring was too close. Since the first twelve rows of the back vineyard were somewhat shorter than the rest of the rows, I chose those first twelve as mine to trim and announced to Juan that he should start at Row Thirteen when he got to the back vineyard. Then, I went to find some tools and a toolbelt so I would be ready to go out the next morning.

By the time my trimming shears were sharpened, my saw was oiled, and it was time to get ready for bed, I began to wonder if I knew what I was doing. I hated getting up early in the morning, and up to now I had trimmed a total of three adult vines—all with Ernie standing there watching, directing me. Since I had the bed to myself, I climbed in and decided to meditate for a bit and just picture myself doing a good job with the grapes. I dropped to a very relaxed state quickly, but found it hard to concentrate because I was so tired and so uncertain about trimming.

I was about to give it up and lay down to sleep when a powerful jolt shook me awake. I found myself out of the body, standing in the back vineyard at the east end of the first twelve rows, the ones I had decided were mine to trim. Facing me was a tall, slender man casually leaning with his elbow on one of the endposts. He had on a flannel shirt which was tucked neatly into a pair of jeans, and he wore a straw hat. His fingers were long and slim and his face seemed young, but he struck me as unimaginably old. Most shocking of all though, there seemed to be horns on his head under that hat, and he did not have feet—he had hooves!

This frightened me so badly that I instantly flipped back into the body. But I was only back in the bedroom a second when he seemed to draw me right back out to the vineyard again. We stood there.

"Um-m, hi… Who are you?" I asked finally, feeling curious and shaking visibly from the shock.

"You can call me Harvey," he said with a chuckle. "I heard you were going to work in your grapes and thought I might help you with your harvest!" He had placed a humorous emphasis on the "har" in both words then ended with a big grin.

I didn't know what to say and peered at him closer to see if those really were horns half-hidden by his hat.

"So you've been talking with the elves," he said in a matter-of-fact, yet conversational tone.

"Yeah," I replied, feeling like I had been born without a tongue or the capacity for intelligent conversation.

"Are you going to start trimming tomorrow?" he asked.

"Yeah," I said, sharply aware that my body was sitting stiffly in the bed and that I was standing here talking to a man with horns and no feet.

"Maybe I can guide you along… if you like?" he offered in a friendly way.

"Um… sure… that would be great. I've never trimmed on my own before." I was beginning to recover, even though my heart was still pounding at a brisk rate.

"Okay," he said, "I'll meet you in the vineyard tomorrow morning." And with that he was gone.

I slowly returned my attention to my body in the bedroom and sat there in unmoving shock for a time. Finally, shivering and stiff, I got up and went to the bathroom. Instead of going back to bed I got some paper and a pencil and made notes of what had happened. Then, even more greatly excited, I got back in bed and after what seemed like a long time, I went to sleep.

The next morning it was still dark when the alarm went off, and I was instantly awake, recalling the experience of the night before. I got up in slow motion and dressed, ate breakfast, then put on enough outdoor clothing to hopefully stay warm until noon. The toolbelt was too small with so many layers of clothing on. Awkwardly I took it off, adjusted it, and put it back on. It still didn't fit. Off again, another adjustment, and back on. I felt like a swollen mummy strung with the tools that would assist my entry into the next world. There was the door. "Don't think," I warned myself and out I went into the frosty dawn, toward the back vineyard to trim grapes.

It was not an easy walk. Doubt and argument raced through my head. What was I doing out here in the freezing morning, setting out to trim grapes when I had never done so before? Ernie had given me a few demonstrations so that I would understand the basic criteria for hiring trimmers, but I really didn't know much about it at all. I was college-educated; this was not the kind of work I was supposed to do. I could be comfortable and warm back in my office or my kitchen. I should be writing. I might ruin the vines altogether by chopping them all to heck. There must be something wrong with me to suddenly decide to work in the grapes—especially when the decision was based on what other people might think was a delusion. And then I was at the first row of grapes.

I stood there looking at that first vine forever and nearly jumped out of my skeleton when Harvey appeared quietly to my right and said, "Let's begin."

I stepped up to a vine that seemed to tower over me and said, "Okay, you guide me, I'll just cut where you tell me." But I was paralyzed. I was sure that I would cut off something I shouldn't or that I would ruin the vine.

"Cut here," he prodded. "Leave that… take this off… and this… leave that extra long for now until you've got most of the excess out of the way… remember the things Ernie has taught you, too… get your saw and cut this back to eliminate disease. What we are aiming for is almost twice the number of buds and canes that you would normally leave. Instead of sixty to ninety buds, you want 100 to 140. Generally speaking, you should separate your vineyards into sections and trim some sections for a very heavy crop one year, and trim the others for a light crop. The next year you will alternate the sections. The heavy crop puts a demand on the root system and the plant's response is to put energy into a bigger root system. After the heavy crop is harvested, you will allow the plant to take a little break the following year and trim it for a light crop.

"After about five years of alternating demand and good feeding, an excellent root system will be built up and your vines will be able to support a consistently heavy crop of grapes and still reach the sugar levels of 16 percent or above. Of course, you will have to take care of diseases and pests as needed, but after the root system has enlarged you will find that the plant is a little more able to resist freezing and some diseases."

We worked intently on the first three vines and when we moved to the fourth I looked at my watch. It was after 10:30 A.M. Over two hours had gone by and I had only trimmed three vines! My heart dropped in discouragement. At one vine every half hour, and sixty vines in the row, it would take me almost a week to do one row. It would take me three months to finish my twelve rows! My respect for Juan grew by leaps and bounds.

We worked until noon and finally, cold and sore, I told Harvey I needed some lunch and a short break. He said I was doing fine and that he would see me later. I headed up to the house, he disappeared.

I restored myself with a sandwich and a cup of hot tea, worrying about how slow I was and wondering how I would explain my sudden diversion into grape farming if we ended up with a very poor crop and low tonnage. How would I feel if I let go of other projects that consistently made money and there was a bad freeze in the grapes? Or we got hailed out? After only one morning's experience I realized that if I was going to keep my commitment to trim those twelve rows, I would have to let go of almost all other work. Letting go of the other things I did to make money only seemed like a good idea when I believed that we could get a good crop.

Lunch was over and there were no reassuring answers; it was time to go back out in the grapes. I pulled on the boots, sweaters, and coats, wishing there was some kind of harvest guarantee. When I got to the back vineyard Harvey did not appear and I worked alone for the rest of the day. When the day was over and I left to go back to the house in the gathering dusk, I had finished a total of ten vines. I ate supper, cleaned up the kitchen, and went to bed, exhausted.

CHAPTER 3

Three days had passed since I started trimming in the grapes. The weather had gotten colder, making the job less and less appealing, and Row One was not even half done. I could hardly move my hands, but I kept at it, determined to keep going and to complete as many rows as I could. The elves came by to visit, but I was so weary I greeted them almost absentmindedly while continuing to trim. I was afraid if I stopped for any reason I might not go back to it. Even though I couldn't see them, I could hear them clearly and they seemed to be watching me work for a moment.

"Yer going to have a nice crop on those vines," one of them said. "Better make sure the posts are in the ground good and solid and that the trellis is in good shape. Be a shame to come out here one morning and find yer crop on the ground!" Then off they went. I told Jim about these comments and we decided to go to the time, effort, and expense of replacing the upper and lower wires in the front vineyard and the lower wire in the back vineyard.

At the end of that first week I had finished trimming my first row of grapes. My hands were red and sore, my back ached constantly, my face was rough and chapped, and my hair was awful. I did not see Harvey after the first day, but Ernie heard that I had decided to trim my own grapes and stopped by once or twice to give me some pointers and cheer me on. I think he found it hard to believe that I was willing to go out in the vineyard and do manual labor; he expected me to give up at any minute. So did I, but somehow I kept going.

At the beginning of the week it had taken me over forty-five minutes to trim one vine. Over the week I had slowly progressed to one vine every twelve minutes but I was hoping to do better still. I wanted to be able to trim an entire vine every five minutes.

Some of the things Ernie had taught me a couple of years earlier regarding the hows and whys of trimming began to come back and for the first time made good sense. Even so, the actual experience of trimming raised more questions than ever and I went back to him again and again, asking for more detail. He listened patiently to my long descriptions of individual vines or watched as I tried to draw a picture of some condition I had observed. He often asked me what I thought, and patted me on the back with a "That's right, good choice!" when I told him what I had done in each situation. Then he would offer one or two more alternatives that I could consider the next time that situation came up.

Juan had long since finished the front vineyard and was working with me in the back. He trimmed a row and a half every single day in a relaxed manner that seemed effortless. I was in awe of his ability and stamina. One morning we arrived in the vineyard at the same time and he stopped by to chat.

"You're leaving an awful lot of wood on those vines. You're gonna kill them plants. Either that or the crop will be so heavy the vines will tear. You might wreck your vines," he observed, sounding concerned.

I explained a little of what I was trying to do. When I finished explaining he said nothing, but he shook his head as if he was sure I didn't know what I was doing and when he had gone I was quite upset. Was it realistic or wise for me to be following the directions of some elves and an apparition named Harvey?

A few days later Ernie came over to look at my trimming job. He immediately got out his shears and went after that first row of vines.

"Too much wood left on these vines, too much wood!" he muttered as he quickly reduced the first vine to four thin canes.

I stood there in agony and didn't know what to say. Finally, I offered a lame explanation, "But Ernie, I want a lot of wood on them. I'm experimenting with them."

He continued to trim, his hearing aid apparently turned down. I continued to agonize. Finally, I said I would go over them again, trimming them back a little more. Fortunately, he only fiddled with the first four vines and then he had to go.

"The trimming should be completed by the time the first dandelion shows up," he told me as he left. "When the dandelion appears, the sap in the vines is rising. But you have a little time yet."

I continued to spend my days trimming and began to think positively about my deal with the elves for one hundred tons of grapes. Since they had only asked me to walk my land and I was doing a little more than they had asked, I found myself wondering if the crop would be even better than one hundred tons. Gradually, I began to wonder what else we could do to help the vines produce a super crop.

When I brought this up to Jim, he suggested I talk to the elves about a few of our general agricultural practices in the vineyard so I took the Pumpkin, an old remodeled golf cart painted bright orange, and headed toward the hill at the back of the farm. After parking the Pumpkin on top of what I now referred to as Golden Mountain, I went to sit on the back side of the hill, along the edge of the woods. I called to Alvey, then Kermots, and Mairlinna. After a short time I heard them coming and for a split second wondered why I had seen their world and heard their voices but hadn't seen any individual elves at all. I wondered what they looked like, but then we were greeting one another and I was caught up in the commotion and excitement they seemed to generate.

They congratulated me for my work in the vineyard and I asked them how they were. They answered that all was well except when I brought that noisy, clattering, smoke-breathing machine out to their homes. I apologized for the Pumpkin and quickly brought up the first question. Should we spray a pre-emergent chemical on the weeds to keep them down, thus reducing the number of later weed sprays?

Gasps of horror and vehement protests met what I thought was a sensitive, sensible question. "No sprays, no poisons!" they insisted. "What are ye trying to do to this poor earth?"

"Well, what are we going to do about the weeds?" I asked. My pride in asking thoughtful questions had quickly faded.

"What weeds?" they questioned.

"The weeds... you know, the weeds in the vineyard!" I replied. Certainly they had to know what weeds were.

After a few moments without a response it occurred to me that we could just as easily hook up the tiller and till the weeds under instead of spraying. "Well, I guess we can always till them in, or use the spider,"[1] I mused, half to myself.

"Too much destruction!" they declared, startling me and leaving me at a loss for options.

"But how are we going to keep weeds under control?" I asked in an exasperated tone. "We have to do something!"

"That's right, ye really ought to do something to get those ideas about weeds under control!" came their sharp response. It was clear, and even understandable, why they were against spraying chemicals of any kind, but it was beyond me as to why they seemed hesitant to condone mechanical weed control such as disking, tilling, or spidering with the tractor.

"I think you're being unrealistic," I complained. "We can't have weeds in the vineyards or they'll take all the nutrients that should go to the grapes. We have to deal with the weeds or they'll overrun everything! Couldn't you put up with our sprays and tilling if we promised to do it only when we absolutely have to?"

"Well... if ye think it's absolutely necessary to spray... then ye'll probably have to spray... but, please, only when ye think it's necessary to save yer crop," they gave in grudgingly.

---

1 The "spider" is a common usage term for a mechanical hoe. Like an arm with eight metal fingers that spin in a circle, it attaches to a tractor and is used to remove weeds between vines as the tractor moves along the row.

"I promise—only when we have to." I agreed with relief. "After all, what other options do we have, unless you guys know some magic!"

"That's it—magic!" they chorused together. "We'll use magic to keep the weeds away. Then ye won't need to spray."

"You can keep the weeds down? How?" I was definitely skeptical.

"It's easy!..." they chorused, "Yea, we certainly can! We can do it! Weeds are no problem for us," came the barrage of reassurances followed by the babble of everyone talking at once.

I couldn't understand a word, and when I interrupted with a "Hey, just a minute!" they fell silent instantly.

"I can't understand you when you all talk at once," I informed them. "Now what were you saying—how were you going to keep the weeds down?"

The babble broke out again and nothing was understandable. I interrupted a second time, but in the end all that I got was their promise to help keep the weeds down as much as possible, and they were certainly vague about how that would happen. Highly doubtful about the feasibility of trusting weed control to them, I went on to the next question.

"We have bats in our barn loft and we want to remodel the loft and use it. We have built several bat houses and would like to know where is the best place to hang them. And how can we get the bats to leave the barn and move to the bat houses?" I asked.

They seemed to think this question was on the ridiculous side. "Put the bat houses wherever ye want the bats to live. Just make sure they get lots of sun. And there's no need to ask them to leave the loft before ye start. As ye remodel—they'll leave. They don't care for fluorescent lighting and all that electronic activity!"

Jim and I were prone to working at night, well into the hours past midnight, and I could easily imagine bats fluttering around us as we tried to repair the roof, put in electricity, or hang drywall. I was afraid they would get in my hair, especially since it would surely be standing on end the minute I saw one. I wanted them out before we started and Jim wanted them out before they had babies. Bats eat lots of insects and we wanted as many as possible to stay on the farm. We did not want to feel responsible for any dead bat babies or mourning mothers, but Alvey and his group reassured me that chasing them out of the loft at this time was premature.

"Okay then, just a couple more questions," I went on. "We have this mole that is ruining our yard. We don't want him around and I wondered if there's some way to get him to leave. Would it be all right to spray diazinon to kill the grubs since that's what he lives on? And if we don't spray, how can we deal with both the mole and the June bugs?"

Again, there was a great deal of protest and pleading not to spray. "If ye'll just spend a bit of time re-thinking how perfect that yard of yers really has to be, we'll do our best to keep the June bugs to a minimum," they promised. "And as for the mole, all ye have to do is ask him to leave. He'll go, just talk to him. But please, don't be a-sprayin'."

I was dubious but said I would try it and after a few more minutes of conversation I got up to leave. Apologizing again for the noise and smoke of the Pumpkin, I went back to the house, wondering how one went about talking to a mole.

Nearly three weeks had passed and I was now trimming in Row Four when Dean, our neighbor from up the road to the east, came by. He helped trim a vine or two while we laughed about how slowly I was going. He said that was all right, anything new was bound to take time to learn. I felt pretty good when he left, but the weather was getting quite warm. Each day it was more obvious that I was never going to finish all twelve rows in time for the buds to open.

By the last weekend of March I had finished four rows of grapes, started the fifth, and had reached an average speed of one vine every nine, maybe ten, minutes. Sometimes I did not even have to think about what I was doing. I went into some kind of automatic mode and could trim the small-to-medium-sized vines in only six minutes. Ernie was now coming by regularly and asking if I was "going to finish in time." Jim was also struggling to manage both his job and the replacement of the top wire on the trellis. Finally, we knew we had to get some help.

Ray, Jim's dad, came from across the state to help put in new end-posts and take down the old top wires. Then, Ernie came over a day or two later and helped Jim put up the new top wires.

When my mom and dad—both still recovering from my father's bout with colon cancer—came down to help over the Easter weekend, I kept a watchful eye on Dad. He and Jim worked over the entire three-day holiday putting new bottom wires on the trellis in the front vineyard. Additional help also arrived in the form of my son, Nathan, and his friend, Steve, who came across the state for the weekend and helped take down old bottom wires. Mom and I went along the rows, tying floppy young vines up to the trellis and out of the way of the tractor tires. Then, in an operation called "picking up stumps," we started picking up trunks of dead or diseased vines that had been cut out from the rows in the front vineyard. We piled the stumps in big piles, set them afire, and warmed ourselves while they burned. When everyone left to go home, we were all tired. It had been a strenuous holiday.

The next morning, Easter Monday, Ernie came by again, still checking on how I was doing. It was the first day of April and painfully obvious that I had recently begun Row Five but he asked me politely how many rows I'd trimmed since I started. When I told him "only four rows in almost four weeks" he offered to help and I took his offer gratefully. We agreed that he would trim the last six rows of the twelve I had originally set out to do, while I finished the two remaining, Rows Five and Six. He left to finish some business he had to take care of, but he came back shortly after lunch, shears in hand, and we worked until nearly 6:00 P.M. When he left to go home that first night, he had finished almost an entire row.

On Wednesday of that same week I offered to make him a sandwich and invited him in to have lunch with me. We talked while we ate and since he was usually open-minded I told him I had a secret to tell him if he promised not to tell anyone.

"Sure, I won't tell," he said, so I told him I had met some elves on our farm, that I had been working with them and that they had promised me a good crop.

"Elves?" he said. "What do you mean?"

"You know... elves, wee folk, little people!" I replied.

"You mean someone short?" he asked humorously.

"Yes!" I told him, laughing, "very short, maybe not even two feet!"

"Who is it?" he said. "Is it that midget that used to live over on the other side of Lawton, almost to Paw Paw?"

"No, Ernie, I'm talking about elves," I told him. But his face went blank and he started talking about the midget who used to live near Paw Paw. At that moment, I realized he probably couldn't deal with the subject of elves and I was embarrassed. I probably sounded silly or crazy to him. So, when he was finished talking about the midget, I changed the subject.

On Friday morning, five days after Ernie started helping me, we finished trimming the last few vines. Ernie finished the last of his six rows and still ended up helping me trim the last half-dozen vines in Row Six. It was done! Juan had finished the other forty-two rows days ago. I was so relieved that it was over. As we left the back vineyard and headed toward the house for something to eat, I noticed the first dandelion of the season.

"Look, Ernie, we're done just in time. There's the first dandelion!"

"Yep," he nodded, "better hurry and get them tied. Once the sap is up the buds are not far behind and you don't want to damage buds while tying them to the trellis."

My relief was short; we had to start tying the canes to the trellis immediately. I decided to ask Juan to help us tie, but the weather gave everyone a needed break for several days.

By the end of the next week, I finished picking up stumps from the back vineyard, I took soil samples to the Extension Office for testing, and I had another visit from Harvey. He appeared as I was coming out of the front vineyard, and we walked for a while.

We talked about the farm in general and I asked him about planting the new vineyard next year. He approved the location and said it was our decision as to whether to plant the vines running north and south rather than east and west, but he suggested with some passion that we first concentrate on planting fruit trees along the southern edge of the existing vineyard. He led the way to the southeast corner of the woods and pointed to where the rows of fruit trees should be planted. He explained that a mixture of pears, peaches, and plums would provide a necessary type of companionship to the grapes. He said something about their patterns of light being complementary and reinforcing one another. He also pointed out that the elves would be quite pleased at these trees, as they were always in favor of more trees.

Although this struck me as a nice idea, I said to him, "But what will we do with the fruit? There wouldn't be enough fruit to sell to a juice company or winery, so what would we do with it?"

He looked at me quizzically and said, "You have a whole planet full of people that are hungry and you don't know what to do with it? People love fruit! They would love to have fruit grown without poisonous chemicals, and they would benefit from the healing properties of this particular fruit. Give it away if you don't know what to do with it!"

"But how would we do that? How would people even know it was here?" I asked, unable to comprehend just giving away baskets of pears, peaches, and plums.

"Put an ad in the paper, post a notice at the grocery store, put an ad on the radio, tell people to come and get it. There are lots of ways," he said.

"But they'll think we are crazy!" I said, trying to keep the protest out of my voice.

"There is a plan," was all he said, and disappeared.

Over the next week I thought about Harvey's advice, his mention of complementary light patterns, and his comments about giving fruit away. When I was unable to settle things in my mind, I went for a walk one evening, hoping to find the elves. I wanted to ask them if fruit trees would qualify for their blessing or if we should plant some particular kinds of trees. They had asked me to think about how perfect our yard had to be and this raised some questions about cutting the grass. Also, the mole was still tunneling his way freely through that same grass and I had not been able to get any sort of response to my efforts to get him to go away or dig elsewhere.

As it turned out, I wasn't able to raise a response from anywhere—the elves and Harvey included. I came home disappointed and continued to stew. Sometime that night I happened to remember a bit of information I had heard about a dozen years earlier. It was about a garden in Scotland that grew some very large vegetables and had something to do with elves. At the time I first heard the story, I was mildly curious but not enough to look into it further. Now, I resolved to see if I could find out something about it even though quite a while had passed since then.

A few days later I was at a bookstore up in Richland and asked the owner if she had heard about the place in Scotland. She had; she said it was called Findhorn and pointed to a shelf in the far corner of the bookshop. I couldn't find the exact book I had heard about, but I did find one called *The Findhorn*

Garden and purchased it. I drove home all excited about planting my flowers, fruit trees, and vegetables, anxious to read my new book, and hoping I would get some pointers on working with the elves.

CHAPTER 4 ✌

April was more than two-thirds gone, and we were heavily into vine-yard and garden work. I was trying to find a few days to visit my parents in the northern part of the state when my son called me from the Detroit area. Nathan wanted some help in getting himself and his educational records together so that he could graduate from high school in June. So, instead of going north, I ended up driving east across the state early on a warm Wednesday morning. To my surprise and pleasure, Harvey joined me for part of the trip, simply appearing in the passenger seat beside me.

We talked about many things, especially the farm. He expanded a little on the picture of the farm the elves had first painted in my mind the previous October when they described the way we could tap an underground well and

create a small flowing stream through our property. At that time they also suggested we take out a small corner of the front vineyard which was quite low in
production and allow the small stream to flow through that area. But Harvey
said we should not be in too much of a hurry to remove the grapevines down in
the front hollow, in spite of the fact that they often froze. He said it would be
much wiser to allow at least a few years for the expanded vibrations and new
care program to build up those particular vines. He said elves were always anxious to get more trees and water, that these things were like treasure to them.

When I told him we had been searching for a name for the farm for over
a year and finally came up with Lily Hill Farm, he said he thought it was an
excellent name. When he told me we would learn to communicate with all the
energy sources available by learning from others who were already doing so, I
wondered who these others might be, but didn't get a chance to ask. We were
almost to Detroit when Harvey suddenly announced that he had to leave. He
made a sad comment about the state of general energy in Detroit and said that
learning not to form such big cities would be one of the hardest lessons of our
time, and then he was gone. I drove on to meet my son and went to several
meetings with him, but for the rest of that day Harvey's comments hung in the
forefront of my mind, coloring my thoughts and my whole awareness.

Upon returning from the trip to Detroit, I had a momentary slow-down
in my schedule and finally found time to read *The Findhorn Garden*. When I finished it the hair on the back of my neck was still curling upwards in shock. In
the book, someone who was familiar with the Findhorn Garden reported several
meetings and conversations with a tall, slim man who simply appeared and disappeared—just like Harvey. And the tall, slim man had hooves instead of feet—
just like Harvey! Except the tall, slim man with hooves was named Pan instead
of Harvey! I got out my desk encyclopedia and looked up Pan and sure enough,
he was listed as a creature from Greek mythology, a god of fertility.

For days I was both frightened and excited. I had no real idea of what it
all meant or how I should think about it, yet I felt validated by what I had read.
Secretly, I was certain that somehow we were going to have an experience just
like the people at Findhorn. In my mind I could see our grapes, each one as big
as a peach, luscious and juicy and sweet, the vines straining to hold them, the
trellis sagging with the weight of so much fruit, the total harvest was well over
one hundred tons of grapes. The world would be transformed in the realization
that we could produce enough food for everyone and somehow it was better
tasting as well as better for you.

Inspired, I decided to try to contact some of the nature spirits, devas, or elementals and other beings discussed in the Findhorn book. The obvious possibility that I had been missing myriads of life- and energy-forms that could be observed or communicated with was overwhelming and humbling. Immediately I set out to contact the Great Mole. The Findhorn people had trouble with their moles and had talked to them just like Alvey had suggested. If they could do it, then it must be possible—and I could easily copy their methods.

Four days later I had not succeeded in contacting anything—not the Great Mole, the mole deva, or even the barest essence of the little fellow who was mightily trenching through our yard and garden. I was discouraged. I had not been able to raise anything that I recognized as a response. Finally, I decided to just put my message out there on some sort of etheric bulletin board and see what happened. The message was blunt: "To the mole or moles living on Lily Hill Farm in Lawton, Michigan, PLEASE MOVE!"

After that I tried to contact several of the vegetable and flower devas, then some version of what I thought a nature spirit might be, and finally any elementals or fairies that might be around. There was no success in getting a response from any of these either. Keen disappointment, combined with a recurrence of doubts about the whole business of elves and devas, spun a sense of vague anxiousness that suspended itself in the corners of my mind. What if it was all just my imagination? For a time, I even had doubts about Findhorn. What if it had all been just imagination? But it couldn't have been imagination—as evidence they had forty-pound cabbages for everyone to see and eat, and roses that bloomed in the snow.

Within a few days, a returning sense of balance and perspective brought the thought that perhaps I was too excited about the whole thing. It still wasn't really clear to me just exactly what a deva or an elemental was. Would I even recognize one if it did respond? How would I know if a deva was answering me when I was so excited I could hardly concentrate? And what if my mind just made up a response because I wanted one? The proof, I decided, was in the pudding—either we would get one hundred tons of grapes or we wouldn't. Meantime, I told myself there was no need to fret. For the time being, I left off any attempts to contact the beings I had read about, partly because I had other things to do, and partly to save face.

❧❦☙

May arrived. Spring evenings were warmer, longer, and invited us to come out-side. Jim and I took the truck and a couple of handsaws and went to the back of the farm to trim the trees at the west end of the back vineyard. We worked until dark trimming the lowest branches off the trees, pulling the wild vines down, and cutting back the brush. It never occurred to either of us that we were doing anything other than cleaning up our property. But the result was a group of very upset elves.

Jim was unloading the brush into the fire pile and I had just finished putting away our tools. I was about to go in for the night when the elves came right to the back of the house. Although they tried to be polite it was obvious they felt invaded and threatened.

"What're ye planning to do in that spot?" they asked judiciously.

"Nothing... other than trim... and shape it up so it looks neat," I answered.

"Would ye be so kind as to leave it alone?" they asked in their best English.

"Well, I guess so, I mean, sure, if it's important to you," I said.

"It's important!" they chorused. "And if it's not asking too much, would ye be willing to leave the west side of the pond alone as well? Ye can do what ye like all around it but for a corner of the west. We would surely be grateful," they promised, nodding at one another.

Suddenly, I realized that for the first time I was seeing them! What a shock! They were short, perhaps two feet tall, with an assortment of baggy clothes and hats. A few of them carried sticks or some kind of handled instru-ments and all of them looked both aged and ageless. Mairlinna had on an ankle-length skirt, wore some kind of wrapper or shawl, and had a braid of sandy-colored hair that fell down her back and reached right to her skirt hem. Alvey had on baggy trousers, a large, beat-up hat with a feather in it, and some kind of cape-like jacket. Their shoes were mismatched, their ears were extremely large, their noses quite round yet with a slight hook, and they had short chins with wide smiles.

My stomach dropped and my heart stopped beating for a few minutes while I stared and they laughed in a good-natured way.

"Ye look like ye've seen a spirit or something!" they said.

"I can see you!" I spouted.

"It's nigh time," they retorted, and we all laughed.

Returning to the subject of their visit, they said they would just like to have a bit of land that was theirs without worrying about who would move in or come tearing things up. I promised that we would not touch the corner they were in and we'd be happy to leave the bushes and branches on the west side of the pond as well. I mentioned that Jim and I were interested in buying some of the wooded land immediately behind us and if we did, they would have even more protected areas to roam in.

Suddenly very attentive, glancing back and forth at one another, they asked if I wanted them to influence the man who owned the property.

"He would be happy to sell to ye," they promised.

With an almost guilty shock at what they were implying I immediately said, "Oh no, please! We're not ready to buy anything yet anyway. We have a huge debt to pay as a result of my attempts to publish a newsletter for educators. It will take us several years to pay it off."

"Are ye sure?" they said with raised eyebrows, and chuckling merrily, they turned and headed toward the lane singing, "One hundred ton o' grape on the vine, one hundred ton o' grape..." to the tune of "Ninety-nine Bottles of Beer on the Wall." I could only stare after them as the familiar feeling of sparkling joy I always experienced when they were around surrounded and filled me. I found myself humming the old beer bottle tune with the new words for the rest of the evening.

The next day I was at work in my office when there was a brief knock on the door. To my surprise it was the elves again! I invited them in and they gathered in a small knot at the side of my desk, standing and seriously attentive while Alvey, Mairlinna and Kermots took turns talking. When they left I sat, buried in thought for a long time. With earnest tones and faces they had asked me to consider a plan that would "develop Lily Hill." They talked in some detail about this development, what it would require, and what it would include. They said that we should finish remodeling our barn; that I should consider teaching more classes in how to develop intuition, how to accomplish body maintenance and healing through correct diet, and how to communicate with the intelligences that were the essence of various animals and plants. They wanted me to encourage others to work with elves and nature spirits to rebalance their lives and to grow all kinds of fruits and vegetables that were wonderfully delicious and healthy. The picture they painted of Lily Hill was filled with gardens of all kinds; gardens overflowing with vegetables, herbs, flowers, fruits, trees, grasses, and even a few specialty items in a greenhouse or two.

Bluntly, they advised me, "Write, yes, go ahead and write. But write materials that you can use in your classes. Write materials for your own use.

Forget trying to write that book about the fellow from the sixties. Stay away from political writing. As far as the world is concerned, write the kinds of things that will teach the nature of balance to others.

"First produce materials, booklets, stories, and things for the people who will come here. If it happens to also work for the mass markets of the industrial and commercial world, that's okay. But be careful, that world is coming undone in some deep changes. We will show you the new way to work, to feed yourself and to exist," they said.

They described the finished barn, remodeled to be as comfortable as a home, where many who were interested in a more balanced and healthy way of living would come to learn and to heal. They told me to take my time creating Lily Hill Farm, and take time to get myself ready, not to rush things or to start before I was organized.

They told me we should make space not only for teaching, but for massage therapy and the preparation of good food. They went on to say that music was also a very useful teaching and healing tool and that we should plan a space for healing with music. In fact, they emphasized that music and its frequencies would become a key component in everything we did here.

They urged me to plant many more kinds of trees and herbs and flowers and to experiment with them in every way I could think of. They gently prodded me to find a way to work openly in what they referred to as "the world of the psyche" and to bring that information into what they called the common reality.

Finally, with a few more remarks about expanding my herb garden and experimenting with vegetables, they went their way. Later, I told Jim about their visit and what they had said. We talked for a while and I realized that while we could develop Lily Hill Farm and teach some of the things they suggested, I was concerned about how much work it all seemed to be. I had always wanted to write, I liked my privacy, I loved my solitude, and one lifetime did not seem to be long enough to accomplish what they were describing! Still, it was an idea that we agreed to think about, at least initially.

By the middle of the first full week in May, there was a considerable amount of new growth on the vines and we were busy every minute. A load of lime, ordered by Jim and delivered by Ted Wolsey's company, had been dumped near the barn and was waiting to be spread in the vineyards. But as soon as the lime arrived, we began to have second thoughts about using it. Jim began pressing me to talk to the elves again, this time about fertilizers. He also wanted to do a little selective weed spraying where the brambles, sassafras, and virginia creeper were getting out of hand. After the elves' impassioned plea to avoid spraying and several of our other vineyard practices, we were becoming reluctant to take any kind of action without some kind of consent, or at least the courtesy of informing them in advance.

It was a bright Wednesday afternoon and I decided it was time to make another effort to contact nature spirits or devas and let them know about the lime and the need to begin our annual fungicide-, pesticide-, herbicide-spray program. A rule-of-thumb spray program usually started with a fungicide, like Mancozeb or Dithane, for problems like phomopsis,[2] then went quickly to pesticides, like Lannate or Lorsban, for cutworm and leafhopper. As the season progressed, more fungicides, like Nova, Bayleton, and Ridomil, were sprayed routinely, every ten to fourteen days, to prevent black rot, powdery mildew, and downy mildew.[3] And there were always at least two, usually three, and sometimes four, herbicide combinations that went on over the growing season. An early spray of Roundup and Princep (simazine), sprayed to kill perennial weeds and prevent their seeds from germinating, was usually followed four to six weeks later by sprays like Gramoxone (paraquat)and Karmex, used to burn stubborn weeds off. We didn't like to use such heavy poisons any more than the elves did, but we did want to harvest a decent crop!

Getting myself into a calm, meditative state, I sent out mental calls to any grape devas, or the nature spirits in charge of the grapes and waited patiently. When nothing that I could call a nature spirit or a deva answered, I simply repeated the messages and left them out there on my etheric bulletin board. Later that day I tried again, but nothing answered.

---

2   At the time, I did not know what phomopsis was, but I heard growers talk about it frequently. Later I learned it was a fungus that damaged the canes of the grapevine and infected the stem of the fruit cluster. Fruit development proceeded normally, but the fungus caused the fruit to fall off the vine too easily as it ripened.

3   Black rot is another type of fungus. It causes the grape berries to turn black and mummify into hard, bitter fruit. The mildews are the same as the stuff that appears in the warm, wet corners of your bath or shower. Both downy and powdery mildew are the result of bacteria growing in warm, humid environments.

Disappointed at the lack of response, I decided to try the elves. It seemed that they, too, deserved a little bit of warning that we were planning to spread lime and spray. When there was no immediate answer from them either, I went back to work.

Ernie had been over a couple of times since the beginning of May, urging us to spray to prevent phomopsis. The spray that controlled phomopsis was very powerful and could only be applied in spring, before bloom, so it was now—or not at all.

On Thursday, the day after my efforts to contact both elves and devas, Jim asked me several times, "Should we spray? What did the elves say? Did you contact the devas yet? What should we do? The weeds are getting really high and it doesn't look like the elves are doing anything about it." He was obviously upset about being caught between Ernie—who sprayed our vineyards for us and wanted to begin our usual spray program right away—and the wishes of a group of elves he couldn't see or hear.

The next evening was Friday, and Ernie came by for the third time since the beginning of the month. Earlier that day, I had again tried to notify vines, elves, nature spirits, devas, and anyone else I could think of that we were going to spray, but there was still no response, and Jim and I were still dragging our feet about a decision. Finally, we broke down and told Ernie to go ahead, begin the spraying. He nodded in relief and said he would be by in a few days with the first fungicide if the wind and weather were right.

I put out another mental call to the elves late Friday evening, and while I was putting away my tools, the entire group showed up, acting more boisterous than usual. I told them about the lime that was going to be spread and they were suddenly serious. They asked when it was going to be added to the soil and seemed fairly tolerant of the idea. But when I told them it was time to begin the season's spray program, a storm of protest rose around me.

"Oh no, please no! Don't be a-sprayin' that poisonous juice again," they argued. "What good can ye possibly believe ye're doing?"

"I don't know exactly what phomopsis is, but Ernie says it's important to get rid of it and we can only spray for it now—before bloom. And the weeds are nearly to our knees, we need to do something!" The memory of Jim's frustration ran through me and I felt like I was pleading for some vague permission.

They put their heads together for a moment and there was a murmur of voices around the circle. Finally, in grumbling acceptance they said, "Well, then, follow yer usual practices, but give us lots of notice when ye're about to spray—at least a couple of days to make sure everyone is ready."

"No problem," I said, "Ernie is going to be spraying a fungicide in a couple of days; it depends on the weather and how much wind we have, so do whatever you have to in order to avoid a hassle and discomfort. I don't want any sick or disillusioned elves on my conscience. The weed spray will probably be sometime next week. I'll let you know."

"All right," they mumbled, obviously disappointed.

Not sure what else to say, I changed the subject to what I was going to put in my garden, and after a brief conversation I was ready to say good night.

But they were not quite ready to go. They asked when I was coming out to visit them. I hadn't thought of visiting them in the same way that I would go to visit my friend Anna, so I hesitated. Seeing my hesitation they urged me with even greater persuasion to come and visit. I told them I would be attending a writers' conference at the university on Thursday through Saturday, but said I would try to find some time by Sunday. They urged me to come as soon as possible, saying they had something to show me. Then they were gone.

Shortly after sun-up the next morning, much to my horror, Ernie drove in on his tractor, spray rig in tow, and the couple of days' notice I had promised turned out to be the few hours between dusk and dawn. Sick at the thought that some small creature would become ill or suffer because of our spraying, I wondered how we were going to continue working with elves and devas. Ernie said he'd be here in a couple of days. I said I'd give a few days' notice. Neither of us did what we said we were going to do. Maybe we all had a lot to learn about communication. We either didn't say what we meant, didn't mean what we said, or didn't do what we said we were going to.

CHAPTER 5 🙰

I drove home from the writers' conference at supper time on Saturday. After a simple meal of muffins and tea, I cleaned up the kitchen and decided to make the visit the elves had suggested. I told Jim where I was going and walked down the lane toward the back of the farm. I wasn't sure just where to meet them, or how one behaved as a guest of elves, especially when it was right here on my own farm.

But did the farm really belong to me? What about all the other creatures who lived here? Was my claim to ownership more righteous because I paid taxes? Could I really do anything I wanted with this fifty-seven acres just because I had a piece of paper that said it was mine? For a moment I imagined the confusion that would be generated if a group of raccoons and deer, or birds and garter snakes showed up in court with papers of their own and sued for ownership based on a prior claim. The idea of animals holding paperwork seemed ridiculous, but only for a moment, after which it seemed just as ridiculous for humans to run around waving papers and claiming ownership—all backed by some higher authority called the court of law. Such thoughts left me vaguely unsettled, and I had no answers to such dilemmas, but lately I was most uncomfortable thinking of the farm as mine, or as mine and Jim's.

I was moving along the back vineyard, planning to go to the backside of Golden Mountain, when I made an impromptu detour through the grapes to say hello to the vines and see how they were doing. They were past bud stage and doing well. I moved through the rows thinking that we had withstood the recent cold snap extraordinarily well and that the new growth seemed completely unaffected.

Leaving the vineyard, I continued on up Golden Mountain, went over the crest, and sat down on the other side near the woods in the place where I had first seen the elfin world.

"Hello! Hello!" I called, "Alvey, I've come to visit! Kermots! Mairlinna! I'm here! Would you like to visit?"

Immediately, I heard them coming. They gathered around me and there was the usual commotion of nodding and shuffling as we said our hellos and exchanged wishes for good health and luck, something they seemed to do as a ritual of general courtesy each time we met. After what I thought was a reasonable amount of time, I asked Alvey what they wanted to show me.

There was some silence and then the chorus of voices began in astonishment. "Ye mean ye didn't see!"

"See what?" I asked.

"She didn't see.... She didn't even notice.... Begorra!" came the responses.

"Gosh, I'm sorry," I said feeling somehow upset. "Tell me, what did I miss?" I asked apologetically.

"What do we do with her?... She didn't see..... She walked right through it and didn't even notice!..." they continued to bemoan my ignorance to one another.

"What!? What was it!" I exclaimed, embarrassed at what seemed to be a gross oversight on my part.

"A hundred tons o' grapes!" they cried in unison. "Ye walked right through a hundred tons o' grapes!"

"Ohh-h-h! Oh yes!" I said. I had forgotten all about the specifics of our agreement the previous fall. I had been too caught up in the experiences of becoming a practicing grape farmer rather than raising them from a distance like I'd done the first few years we were here. Before this year I had rarely gotten my hands dirty. Now, I was so busy trying to absorb what I needed to know about grapes in general that the goal—one hundred tons of grapes—had slipped into the background. Suddenly, I was delighted.

"Really?" I asked the excited voices around me, "Do we really have a hundred tons of grapes?"

"Yup.... Or durn close.... Maybe over that.... A hundred and one by my estimate... good crop...." they continued to rattle off numbers and exclamations of success.

"So now what happens?" I asked excitedly. "Do we count our chickens before they're hatched?"

They looked at me as if lost. I heard someone say, "Chickens? What's chickens got to do with it?"

I had to chuckle. "Never mind," I said. "Is there anything we can do to make sure that all those grapes will actually end up at Welch's?"

"Next we call in the bees!" they exclaimed. "Bloom time will be coming up and we'll need all the bees we can get."

I promised them if they would call in the bees, I would bury long arms,[4] which was a method of starting new vines in the bare places under the trellis. I also said I would continue shaping the young vines so they were straight and strong. After a bit more conversation, I said good night and left, feeling pleasantly satisfied all the way home.

The writers' conference had given a real boost to my resolution to live the writer's life, and I came home determined to thresh unnecessary appointments

---

4   Sometimes called "setting drops," burying long arms is a method of replacing old or missing grapevines by taking an extra-long cane down to the ground, burying a length of it that includes at least three buds in the ground, then running the remainder of the cane back up to the trellis and tying it in place. In about two years the young cane will have roots growing from where the buds were; you can cut it away from the mother vine, and you have a healthy new vine living on its own.

and meetings out of my life so I could continue working on my manuscript, *The Evolving Human.* Instead, I found myself powerfully drawn to work in my perennial garden, planting bulbs and flowers, pulling weeds and raking out old leaves. But what started out as one of my beloved springtime tasks turned into an emotional pit of uncertainty and guilt.

My sensitivity to animals and plants as purposeful beings had been increasing steadily as a result of having met Alvey and his group. I had tried communicating with a few plants besides my grapevines and found that many responded by putting out a sweet, unusual smell. Now, down on my hands and knees pulling weeds with an air of vigorous nonchalance, I was suddenly aware that many of them seemed to be hanging on to the earth for dear life and were unwilling to go. I slowed down with some dismay, wondering what to do, if anything. When hoeing or turning over the soil along the edge of the flower bed, I felt bad each time I discovered an earthworm cut in half and writhing in gruesome pain.

I began calling out to the devas for help, pleading with them to intercede for me with the worms. "Tell them to move so I can get this garden planted," I begged. But reluctant plants and murdered worms continued to be the result.

The longer I worked, the more irritated I became, first with the plants and worms, then with the devas, and then with myself. "I told them to move," I thought defensively, time after time.

Finally, I sat down, treading an ocean of frustrated feelings and thoughts. "What is the matter?" I wondered. "Why doesn't the communication thing with plants and animals work for me like it had seemed to work for the people at Findhorn?

A very soft and gentle voice spoke up, "This will never work if you intend to just give orders and drop off messages. To work with us there must be two-way communication."

"Who is speaking?" I inquired in guilty surprise.

"The Deva of the Lilies," she replied quietly.

My mind tumbled about, feeling at once chastened and rewarded. She was unexpected but not unwelcome and after a moment's reaction I said, "Umm-m-m, okay then, of course, it has to be two-way. I've been asking these earthworms to move out of the way and these weeds to relinquish their spot so I can plant my garden, but I haven't gotten any kind of response from anyone—until now—when you spoke up."

"Two-way communication occurs when you are asking the plants to respond to you—not just telling them what you want. And, you will get a response when you are truly willing to hear and to respond to what they have to say. Simply wait, and listen, until they have communicated their willingness to cooperate. Then it is all right to go on with your garden planting," she said.

"But I need to plant this garden today! According to the moon sign tables, today is one of the best planting days this month!" I said, still feeling defensive.

"What you might have done was to come out here a day or two before you intended to begin planting and communicate your plans to the creatures already living here. Then, today would have been much easier," she suggested.

"A day or two! That takes much more planning than I ever have time for!" I felt a surge of resistance at having to be responsible for what seemed like an increasing number of communication protocols.

"Well, if you continue as you are, you will also continue to have injured worms, weeds that fight you, and lilies that find it difficult to prosper."

Wanting to cooperate but feeling in a hurry to get things planted and move on to my next project, I immediately announced to all earthworms, weeds, and other living things that I wanted to plant the garden today and tomorrow. I asked them if they would agree to this, then I took a short break to give them time to cooperate. The Lily Deva had disappeared. I got no recognizable response or answer from worms or plants, and so continued to work as quickly and carefully as possible.

But the results were the same—miserable weeds and injured earthworms. I worked steadily, wrapped in a mist of private misery over the clumsy way I was going about gardening. I had always loved planting and cultivating, and never before had I experienced anything but a sense of pleasure and accomplishment in doing so. I found myself wishing I had never heard of devas; I wanted weeds and worms to return to their former status of unimportant, unintelligible forms. The frustration turned to anger, the anger to guilt, and the guilt brought a barrage of defenses against my own ignorance.

My mind was a confusion of questions without answers. How did we all come to act so callously superior to the other living things around us? How did one go about judging which plants should live and which should die? Why were some plants considered desirable and others just weeds? If there were other forms of life and intelligence that we could communicate with, why were we so ignorant of the possibilities and benefits of doing so... and so lacking in the skills of listening and responding to those communications? Was I imagining all this, or was the world simply brimming with life and intelligent messages that we never paid attention to?

When the day ended I was exhausted—physically, mentally and emotionally. I intended to go to bed early to get some extra sleep, but when I turned out the lights, the entire room lit up with a green glow. There was green everywhere, around my hands, around my head and shoulders, around the bed and the furniture. The air was suffused with a lovely green light, and I could see patterns of deeper green all around, whether my eyes were open or closed.

I climbed onto the bed and sat, still as a drugstore Indian, staring at all the green forms moving around the room. Almost an hour later, still not knowing what to make of it all, I lay down, closed my eyes and rolled over intending to go to sleep, but my head bumped into something. I opened my eyes to discover with great amazement that I was lying under a huge toadstool. I looked at it for a while, wondering if this was how the story of Alice in Wonderland had been inspired, and then, too tired to even wonder any more, drifted off to sleep.

CHAPTER 6 &

The next day was long and hot, and I again spent all of it working in my perennial garden—but things were much different than the day before. The weeds seemed less tenacious and by grasping each one gently, asking it to let go and give up its location, I could hardly believe how easily they released their hold on the earth. There were no earthworms cut in half or writhing in agony and several robins followed my progress from the lowest branches of the pines just overhead, dropping down only a few feet away to nab seeds or morsels that looked tasty.

One of the Wolsey men came over with his equipment to spread the lime in the vineyard. When he arrived, I waved and pointed toward the pile of lime at the rear of the barn, and after that paid little attention to him. He unloaded a tractor from its trailer bed and then began filling a spreader box with the lime. Back and forth he went, from the lime pile to the vineyard.

After several trips he drove his tractor around to the front of the barn where I was working and announced that the biggest swarm of bees he had ever seen in his life was clustered on the trellis and one of the vines in the back vineyard. He said he thought if I was into bee farming or knew anyone who was, we could go get the swarm and have a nice addition to our bee stock.

I shook my head and said I wasn't into bees and the only person I knew of who was lived out in Minnesota. He drove off and it didn't dawn on me until much later that those might be the bees called in by the elves!

Late in the afternoon I put away my garden tools and went inside to do some office work, even though I hated being indoors on such a beautiful day. The need to spend time at my desk filled me with frustration, and I found myself thinking hard about my career, again.

Sixteen years earlier, when a difficult marriage had ended and I was left with four young children, I set out to be a doctor, my life-long dream. But it wasn't long before I realized that a lone woman with four young children simply didn't have the time, the energy, the financial resources, or the physical and emotional supports that it would take to make it through four years of pre-med classes, four years of medical school, and another three or four years of internship and residency. So, even though I had discovered a love of English, reading, writing, art, design, and poetry, I set my cap for a degree as an engineer, knowing that it was immediate good money with lots of options for smart women who were interested in moving up the corporate ladder.

After only three years of college, I landed a great job with Chrysler Corporation. But two years into my career as a tool and process engineer, I left my position abruptly. The extraordinarily powerful effects of kundalini left me practically hiding in my home for two years, struggling to get my mind back into some semblance of ordinary perceptual operation and my body under some reliable physiological control.

By the time I had learned to manage the new perceptual abilities that kundalini bestows, I was forced to acknowledge that I had become a fairly versatile psychic. Determined to figure out what had happened to me and why, I went back to school to study the brain and the mind, perception and consciousness, cognition, and intelligence. As my expertise in these areas of the brain/mind grew, it led gradually and without plan to my work as an educational consultant. Driven by a deep understanding of how the brain was meant to develop and learn, I taught courses on brain structure and function to teachers and school administrators. I became an expert at teaching teachers how to use brain-compatible and accelerative teaching and learning methods. My love of writing and science led me into teaching things as varied as English and college writing courses, science, and computers for gifted sixth-graders, office automation and desktop publishing for business professionals. I began developing specialty courses for corporations and set up whole learning centers. I was also lecturing to master's level teaching students.

At first in adult education programs, and later in my own home-based learning center, I also began teaching people how to develop and use high degrees of intuition; using my psychic abilities I started mentoring business students at the local community college who were interested in opening their own business. On the side, I saw a continuous stream of people who came for personal consulting because they had heard of my psychic abilities. But I kept this as much to the background as possible. I was an educational consultant, and it made me a living. But through all of this I had fallen deeply in love with writing.

I was awash in thought about how impossible any serious transition was—whether to writing or to developing Lily Hill Farm—when the elves again came to visit. It was a pleasant surprise.

"Thank ye for agreeing to think about developing Lily Hill Farm," they told me. "We know ye wanted other things and would have chosen a more scholarly path, but someone has to be there for the awakened ones. Just because they will reach a more aware level of development does not mean they will no longer need teachers, guides, or healers, and ye are wise in these ways."

I said nothing. Instead I thought about my career. It was something I had been struggling with for years and they seemed to know it.

"Ye can consider this farm yer market area," they cheerfully interrupted my thoughts. "Yer work will proceed, bit by bit, one seminar, one client, one group of students at a time. Ye are needlessly concerned about yer reputation where psychic ability is concerned, but do not worry. It will all come together and yer work in the development of the human mind will be of great value."

"Thank you," was my doubtful response.

"And would ye do us a favor?" they asked as they began to disperse. "Could ye get that lime ye just had spread all over the vineyards worked into the ground as soon as ye can. If ye don't ye'll be unbalancing the whole vineyard, causing a powerful lot of inconvenience and illness to the bugs, birds, mice, and other creatures who live on the land."

With that they were gone. There was a wonderfully sweet smell in the air, yet I was left with a sinking feeling that everything we tried to do to improve things for ourselves was like a stick in the eye of nature.

The following day was again long and hot, and I again spent every waking moment in my flower garden. Only when the sun went down and it was too dark to see any more did I even think about quitting. When I did, I was tired to the bone. By 11:00 P.M. I had showered, crawled gratefully into bed, and was nearly asleep when a form appeared in the bedroom right over me and announced that she was the Lily Deva. And then another form appeared. It was another deva, then another. The need for sleep disappeared. I sat up wide awake, full of energy, and they came—in a long procession, one deva after the next, some in silent curiosity, others with suggestions, others as if in mild reproach. For some reason, I recognized many of them on sight; others I neither recognized nor did they say their name.

Those who looked as if they were mildly upset or reproachful were mostly weeds that I had pulled or hoed out roughly. I told them I hated to cause pain or trouble but didn't really know how to call them or get in contact with each one when I wanted to weed the garden and plant something else in their place.

Several weeds suggested I could communicate with the "overlight angel" and tell her what I was planning, if I was comfortable working with such energies. They said this overlight angel would let each of them know what we were trying to do, and would also help us work together much better.

I had read about the possible existence of an overlight angel in the book about the Findhorn Garden, but, as usual, I dismissed the idea as someone else's construction. I had a basic distrust of those who tried to extend the idea of hierarchies into every area of life. They were too much like corporate power structures, and the concept of an overlight angel[5] had seemed too close to the idea of an overseer, thus I hadn't even considered trying to contact such a form

---

5 Upon re-reading *The Findhorn Garden* several years later, I discovered that the term "overlight angel" was sometimes used in place of Landscape Angel or Landscape Deva, a deva that I had met and talked with several times.

of spirit or intelligence myself. Now, I decided that there must be some kind of primary pattern of intelligence for each form in nature and what it was called was irrelevant. I made a mental note to learn to contact the primary form and direct my messages to it consistently. Then, I told the weeds they were welcome to grow in other places—the fields, the woods, or out by the road, but the nutrients and space in the gardens were really for other plants that were invited to live there.

The Lily Deva then reappeared and said how pleased the lilies were to be the namesake and the symbol for our farm. She said we would not be disappointed, that lilies were hardy, easy to grow, that they multiplied quickly—just like the awakened ones would—and they renewed their blossoms almost daily during bloom time.

The Moonflower Deva appeared and said nothing other than to let me know who she was. Immediately following her a number of others appeared, also silent, peering at me. I watched the long procession of forms and at one point said, "You know, I just don't know what to say or how to deal with all of you! Am I supposed to be doing something other than just watching?"

The Gladiolus Deva appeared at that moment and replied that there were few humans awake enough to acknowledge the plant and animal spirits. She said that when one (human) was available, they (the nature spirits) all wanted a chance to communicate. "And some nature spirits are more attuned to humans than others—just like some people are more tuned in to us than others are," she pointed out "although it is much easier to get a nature spirit to waken and begin communicating than it is to get humans to start the same process!"

When the Strawberry Deva appeared, she told me that the plants I had received were quite anxious to be planted. "Plant us!" she said.

"But according to my moon sign charts, tomorrow and the next day are not good planting days. Friday and Saturday are the next good days for planting," I told her.

"How would you like to be tied with a rubber band, wrapped in a plastic bag and stuck in a refrigerator?" was the reply. "Plant us anyway. I promise we'll grow," she insisted.

One by one, dozens of other devas came and went leaving good wishes, messages and words of encouragement. I had long since gotten up and gone down to the living room to take notes, trying to draw the patterns of color and light that formed each deva. It was now 3:15 A.M.

In the quiet dimness of the living room, I suddenly remembered Harvey and wondered if he had anything to do with the appearance of the devas. I called him and almost immediately the lights dimmed seriously then flickered, giving me the feeling that he was there, but I couldn't see him or hear him. For good measure I thanked him for anything he had done to facilitate my initiation into the world of plant devas or nature spirits and other intelligences.

The lights flickered again and I was sure he was listening, but for some reason wasn't showing himself. Ever doubtful, I said, "Let me know if you are really here." Immediately and all at once the furnace came on, the refrigerator came on, the water softener came on, the pump came on and there was a loud knocking sound in the woodstove pipe.

I nearly jumped off the sofa! "Okay, okay! You're here!" I said. It occurred to me that I was always asking for proof or help and never seemed to have anything to give in return, so I invited Harvey to give thanks with me. I closed my eyes and, not sure what to expect, was quite gratified to find that I was in a world of golden-white light so brilliant that I felt I could stay there forever. After a while he said, "Come with me, I want to show you something."

Not sure what to expect, I was startled when a huge, noisy housefly appeared out of nowhere even though it was really too early in the year and too cool for houseflies. By now I was certain it was Harvey and that wherever we were going it had something to do with this fly. Somewhat disgruntled, since I had a distaste for flies, I asked sarcastically, "Do I have to become a fly, too?"

At this the huge fly swung around and dived at me kamikazi-style, missing my nose by inches. This frightened me so much that I swung my arm at the fly and jumped off the sofa, dumping papers and pen onto the floor. Rattled, I apologized for my reaction and Harvey replied, "Maybe you're not ready for this!"

I agreed and said, "I guess not. I think I'm tired now, maybe I should go to bed. It's quite late."

He bid me a cheerful goodnight, and I went back upstairs to go to bed. It was nearly 4:00 A.M. but once in bed I was again wide awake and surrounded by devas, nature spirits, and their gentle communications. Instead of trying to communicate in return, I just watched, awed by their many forms and colors.

Gradually, the nature spirits disappeared, and I found myself looking at a world of lines. They were beautiful threads of luminous light, pulsing gently. In varying tints of red, blue, green, yellow, violet, pink, and white, they were coming out of every direction and seemed to be going in every direction.

I simply observed. No thoughts entered my head, no questions or ideas crossed my mind at all. I was completely caught up in wondrous gazing. Then, amidst the light, I saw a large, luminous bird. It seemed to consist of nothing other than clouds of the gossamer light I had been looking at. It turned pink, then blue, then green, then yellow, and finally a glowing white.

The luminous bird had eyes like pools of fire, and I gazed into them steadily. We just looked at one another for quite some time as if the bird were part of my mind, I were part of its awareness, and nothing but love and peace existed between us, no questions, no needs. Lovely colors and patterns of light changed shape around it, but it remained for a long time.

Gradually, the bird faded and the lines of color began to take on the appearance of a kaleidoscope with new, ever-changing geometric patterns. They were beautiful beyond description. The colors were so intensely brilliant and so uniquely arranged that I watched almost breathlessly. Sometimes the patterns were reminiscent of places or things in the physical world, sometimes they suggested amorphous shapes, but mostly they were simply exquisite patterns formed of basic shapes.

After what seemed a long time I found myself trying to capture some of the patterns in memory, thinking what wonderful images they would make for an artist to reproduce, wondering what kind of medium could be used to convey the same brilliance and luminosity. But the more I tried to imprint the lovely colors and patterns, the more I became aware of being tired. I rolled over and looked at the clock. It was 5:20 A.M., and finally, I slept.

CHAPTER 7

It was a beautiful, sunny Sunday and I was walking from my office in the barn back to the house when a bee stung me on the arm. Highly irritated at such an aggressive, thoughtless act, I swore and swung a hand at the bee. It flew off slowly, not the least bit aware of the hand that swung past it, my outrage, or the curses heaped upon it. Feeling wronged, I called out to the Bee Deva. No one answered although I listened carefully for one of their usually soft, gentle voices all the while I made a paste of baking soda and water which I dabbed on my arm.

I made a cup of tea and sat down to relax with it, wondering why I had been stung. It was the first time in years. Gradually, as I relaxed, a form appeared, announcing herself as the spirit of the bee, and commenting that I looked well, a comment that struck me as ironic.

"A bee just stung me!" I complained, sounding like a child tattling on someone. "Why did he do that! I wasn't threatening or bothering him!"

"Why do you complain?" she asked.

"I thought plants and animals were sensitive to people and only gave you trouble if they were threatened," I said crossly.

"Do you think that all plants and animals are the same?" she inquired politely. "We have our unenlightened, our troublemakers, and our fearful ones, too. And, what makes you think that every bee or bug or tree is waiting to talk or to communicate with you?" With that she faded away, leaving me feeling infinitely more humble.

May was two-thirds over, spring was in full bloom, and the weeds in the vineyard were growing like gangbusters. Jim had asked me ten times since the beginning of the month, "Should we spray the weeds with some kind of herbicide? Have you talked to the elves? Would they agree? They finally said we could spray a fungicide for phomopsis, why wouldn't they agree to a herbicide for weeds?" He continued to fuss and worry. I offered to till the weeds under but Jim seemed to think it was ridiculous to spend all that time, energy, diesel fuel, or tractor-tiller-wear-and-tear when all we had to do was one quick spray and we would be done with weeds for half the growing season. I said nothing in response to this logic. It seemed to make sense, but I wondered what people had done before such powerful herbicides had come on the market. Finally, with many misgivings, we decided to spray and I told him I would notify the elves.

On a brief walk I headed straight to the back of the farm, sending out mental messages to Alvey and the entire group of elves. There was no immediate answer, so I walked back to the barn and later, after I closed up for the night and was walking back to the house, there they were in the north driveway, under the cherry tree. There was a cheerful greeting, and without wasting time I told them Jim wanted to know if it was okay to spray the weeds in the vineyards. After some effort to talk me out of it, followed by a cross-examination in which they seemed to be trying to determine how necessary I thought this weed spray was, they said grudgingly that we could go ahead.

I complained slightly to them that Jim was driving me crazy worrying about spraying this or that and they informed me that I had not communicated clearly with him. They said he did not seem to understand that it was okay to follow our usual agricultural practices for the first couple of years, but with the full intention of eliminating all harmful sprays.

According to them, if we kept at it, we would learn other methods for dealing with insect, fungus, and weed problems—including how to communicate directly with the weeds. The first step was to make us aware that we could do so, the second step was to increase our sensitivity to the need for new information and frequent communication. The power and quality of the communication would be the third thing we would learn, and the fourth would be how to use that power in a way that was best for all concerned. I could not see what use it would be to communicate with weeds, but I took them at their word and said nothing, assuming there was something I did not quite grasp yet.

"Meanwhile," they advised, "keep going with yer usual vineyard practices to supplement yer belief system until ye're successful with the new, much easier and less expensive ways."

"We're still having trouble with the moles, too," I told them. "Would it be okay to spray just around the house?"

This raised a storm of protest. "No sprays there, please, not around the house," they cried. "Ye kill the bugs, or contaminate them, the moles and the birds eat the bugs and get sick. The result is no critters, and instead of getting rid of yer problem, ye have increased it because ye destroyed yer natural predators. The goal is not to get rid of animals and insects, it is to keep them from taking over. Ye must learn to share with them. The real problem is one of balance, remember? Rather than sprays, put yer money into the birdhouses we talked about, plant trees and finish yer lily pond so an abundance of creatures will be supported. Spend time learning to talk to the mole. But please, no sprays!"

I needed time to think about all this. When they had gone I settled myself quietly in the porch swing, determined to relax and concentrate on communicating with that cussed mole. Taking time to carefully clear everything from my mind, I reached the point of quiet emptiness. In deep concentration, I called to the spirit of the moles or the natural essence of all moles. I was just about to try to visualize the little fellow who was living in our yard when a huge mole, as big as a dinosaur, materialized and came toward me, his every step shaking and rumbling through the earth. Repressing a moment of panic, I met him eye-to-eye and after a moment, asked quietly if he would ask the mole who was living in our yard to please move out to the field.

There was no animosity from the big mole, but he looked at me squarely and asked, "Why do you want us to move? Where do you expect us to go? Humans keep pushing nature around as if they were alone on the planet. Why should we cooperate with that kind of attitude?"

Somewhat taken aback, I tried to defuse his attitude by lightly skirting the questions he raised. "Well, um, you would be welcome to live in the fields, just don't ruin my grass and flowers."

"Of course! And then, when you decide to start tearing up the fields, where shall we go from there? How long will it be until you come pushing us out again?" With that he turned around and lumbered away. Again, the whole earth shook with each of his steps. I was dumbfounded. I spent the rest of the evening trying to deal with the sense of human superiority that I'd grown up with. Were we any better or more deserving than moles?

For the last two weeks of May and the first week of June, we worked long hours on our house. It was nearly one hundred years old when we bought it, and it needed everything from new wiring and plumbing to new walls and floor joists. We also finished building a small lily pond in the back yard. Then a string of business commitments found me on the road, and when I was finally free to return home, I was feeling that I had been neglecting the grapes, the elves, the devas, and any nature spirits who lived on our property.

After arriving home late on a Saturday night tired and worn out, I was brushing my teeth when I heard someone knocking at the back door. I thought nothing of it and continued brushing thinking Jim would answer the door. But a few minutes later the knocking was repeated. I went to the head of the stairs and called to Jim, "Is someone at the door?"

"No, I didn't hear anyone," he answered. I went back to the bedroom to continue getting ready for bed. Shortly, the pounding on the door began again. I went to the stairs and called to Jim, "Someone is knocking on the door!"

He got up, went to the back door and opened it. "No one's there," he called up the stairs and sat down again. The knocking began again, so I put on my robe, went downstairs and went to the door. I didn't see anyone either and went back upstairs, but as soon as I got to my room, the pounding commenced again. I went back downstairs and this time went outside to stand on the sidewalk and look around. From across the driveway came the sound of small voices, and to my surprise there stood the elves.

"Good evening," they said decorously.

"Well, good evening!" I returned, "Would you like to come in?" At first they stood there, unsure, and then they pointed at the barn. I went to get my keys and returned to the driveway motioning them to follow me. Once inside my office they all moved to a single chair and sat down—in, on, and around that one chair—leaning, jostling and crowding one another, forming what looked like a large pile of elves! The picture they made was almost hilarious. They complimented us on the completion of the lily pond, saying we had done a very nice job. They also appreciated the small trees I had spared by transplanting them out of my flower garden and encouraged me to plant more trees.

Earlier in the week, Jim and I had written down several questions for them, so I went briefly back to the house to find my notes. When I returned, the sight of them still sitting in one large heap made me burst out laughing. Swept along on a cloud of evanescent joy, I was aware without thinking that their presence so easily renewed my energy and that we had never really celebrated just being together. Forgetting my questions, I asked spontaneously if they would like to hold hands and just give thanks for everything. We joined hands in silence, and I closed my eyes for a bit. When I opened them, the room was filled with light. It was the same kind of golden-white light I had first experienced on Golden Mountain. After we let go of hands, there was a tremendous clearing of throats, which made me chuckle.

I told them Jim was going to mow the headlands after I finished with the spider, and then we planned to go through the vineyard and disk the soil. In sharp contrast to the remaining glow that hung in the room, groans and moans greeted my announcement, and Alvey, ever the spokesman, grimaced dramatically.

"Why do ye keep undoing our excavation sites?" he asked. "And where can we store our treasures? Every time we put them someplace, somebody comes along and messes up the land making it hard to find them next time we need them!"

I wondered what they meant by their treasures and felt a tad guilty. One hundred and eighty degrees from the joy of their presence, this nagging feeling of not doing something quite right was something I'd felt all too often since my first awareness of elves and devas and nature spirits. I recalled the comment of the Lily Deva. "It has to be two-way communication," she had said. Perhaps they would have to adapt some of their ways just as we humans would. Feeling guilty and getting upset had accomplished nothing so far.

"Alvey," I ventured, "our grapes need to be tended and cultivated just as your treasures need to be excavated and stored away. Perhaps we must all learn new ways if we are going to work together. Maybe if we are open we will discover ways that work better than either of us imagined."

It was very quiet in the room. Feeling as if some other force were speaking, I continued, "I have learned so much about you and your ways, about the devas and nature spirits! What once seemed odd or strange now seems as down-to-earth as daffodils in spring and paydays on Friday. I feel a love for all of you that would have seemed absolutely ridiculous a year ago. It took me a long time to believe in you, but now you're an important part of my life. Don't you suppose that if many humans felt this way about you, you would begin to understand what humans need to survive and we could all support one another somehow?"

The silence deepened. After what seemed like eternity they stirred among themselves, seeming embarrassed at the declaration of love and the suggestion that we all had something to learn.

"Why didn't ye believe in us before," Kermots finally asked. "After all, we tried to save ye from that disastrous affair ten years ago."

At first I wasn't sure what they were talking about. Then it came to me and it was my turn to sit in frozen silence. In the midst of all my troubles with kundalini, I had been madly in love with a man whom I intended to marry. We bought a house together and lived there, at first quite happily. One Saturday morning, we were awakened before dawn by the alarm clock I had forgotten to turn off for the weekend. Unable to go back to sleep, Ben went downstairs as it was our Saturday morning habit that he would make a cup of coffee for himself and some tea for me, then bring them both back upstairs where we would sit, looking over the bay, drinking the warm brew and talking a bit.

As usual, I was still lying in bed, enjoying the luxury of having Ben make tea, as well as the fact that I didn't have to get up and go to work that day, when I heard a small voice say, "There she is...."

Turning my head and opening my eyes, I found myself looking at three small elves peeking around the door into the bedroom. Without a moment's hesitation they rushed into the room and over to the bed, picked me up bodily and started to carry me out the door! Having never seen such creatures before, having never believed in elves or fairies at all, and caught in an engulfing shock somewhere between terror and disbelief, I panicked.

Kicking and squirming, I tried to get free, but they had a grip like iron and refused to let go. I fought harder, becoming almost wild. They had me half out of bed and it looked like they were actually going to get me out the door when I began screaming hysterically. I could hear Ben running up the stairs yelling, "Good God, Penelope, what's the matter!" In a flash the elves were gone and I was left half out of bed, shaking and breathing heavily as the fear subsided.

As Ben came in the room I cried out, "Some elves just tried to carry me out the door…," but he only laughed in disgusted disbelief, shook his head, and without a word, went back down to get the coffee and tea.

By the time he returned, I had composed myself. "I'm sure I was awake," I told Ben. "But it must have been some kind of dream… or my imagination…."

In spite of the intensity of the experience, it had raised no curiosity about elves. I refused to alter or expand my belief system even a little bit, and as far as I was concerned, elves were still creatures of myth and legend.

Soon thereafter, I discovered Ben had begun to drink and was involved with another woman. The business deal we had put together fell apart—yet still I hung onto him, clinging to the hope that he would forget her and love only me once again. I was sure that if I could just be patient we would live as happily as if nothing had ever gone wrong. Eventually, the whole affair ended disastrously and I lost everything—Ben, the house, the children, and the business.

Now, ten years later, I was risking my next year's income on an agreement with some elves. I not only believed in them, I had whole conversations and visits with them. I even had a deal with them—and it all seemed so normal.

My reverie ended. "Well, I believe in you now," I smiled apologetically. Then, trying to lighten the mood, I said, "I believe in you enough to ask you to intercede for me with the great Master Mole, or whatever he's called."

They pointed out that it would probably do more good if I made the effort to contact him again myself. "After all, he owes ye a favor now."

"He does? For what?" I asked.

"Because ye stopped that stray dog from torturing and killing the little mole that was living on the east side of the yard. He'll be more disposed to listen to ye. Try him, ye'll see!"

I agreed to try one more time.

As if by an unseen signal, we all got up to leave, me for the house, they for the back of the farm. It occurred to me that they had come looking for me, but I had done most of the talking. I had hardly given them a chance to say anything. "By the way, Alvey, was there something you wanted to tell me?" I asked belatedly.

"Just wanted to suggest that ye might get together all of yer notes of our conversations and meetings. Get them organized and typed before any more time goes by and ye start forgetting the details. After all, ye wanted to write!" he answered. Then they were gone.

I stood staring after them and knew that somehow something was truly changed. I had believed that they wanted to help, that they were interested in what I wanted and in the success of what we did here on the farm. Now the belief reached a deeper level. It was moving from my head into the realms of my heart. I had gone from thinking it was all a fantasy, to being hopeful, to a curious sort of respect, to a solid knowing.

Since our first meeting, I had thought of them as part of the generally unseen world, the world of spirits and intelligences. I always believed that those forms of life were far superior. It was true that we humans had much to learn, but it hadn't occurred to me that we might also have something to teach. Or, that the results of this teaching-learning relationship might make everyone's reality a little bit sweeter—ours and theirs.

It was the last half of June and getting hotter every day. I got up early one morning to go and work in my perennial garden before the heat became uncomfortable. I was busy pulling weeds and cultivating the soil around the flowers when I noticed that the mole was now digging his tunnels all the way out to the front of the yard. I stood there looking at the raised areas, assessing how many flowers would die, their roots hanging from the ceilings of the mole tunnels, drying out and unable to get water or nutrients. In the yard, the grass above the tunnels was yellow and prickly. I had not sat down and formally tried to contact the Great Master Mole again, but I had constantly been thinking how much I wanted the moles to move out back to the fields.

As I stood there staring at the little fellow's work and his results, a voice echoed like chimes through my head and I heard, "Just give us a little more time. We're working our way down the yard and will soon be in the field. We're going to the field across the road as well as out back." That was all.

I stared at the mole tracings with new eyes! The moles were moving to the fields! They were doing as I had asked! For some reason I had expected the response to my request to be an instant yes or no along with immediate and humble compliance. Since the mole was still doing his damage, I assumed the answer was no. It had never occurred to me to allow some time for the little fellows to pack up, close up old tunnels and dig their way to a new home elsewhere. I thought about how long it would take me to actually get out of my house if I decided right that morning to move. Even if I took action immediately, six months would be an overly optimistic goal.

But they were going! They were on their way to a new home in the fields across the road. Others were going out back. I was so grateful that I actually began to worry about things like how they would get safely across the road. And since they were moving to Dean's field, what if the worries of the Great Master Mole came true and the moles got plowed and cultivated out of that home too?

In the end, I was content to know that they were moving to places where they could live in peace. I was again struck by the realization that I was getting what I had asked for. In a world where instant gratification was expected, and the speed of the response was the measure of one's power, getting a couple of moles to leave one's yard, perhaps by the end of the summer, might be considered a ridiculous measuring stick of success. Even so, I was pleased.

I continued working in my perennial garden, my mind focused intently on what the elves referred to as the common reality. It was clear that there were far fewer limits to what we could ask for than what we currently accepted. Clint, one of my best friends, always said that people loved their limitations and built their lives carefully inside those limits. I had always thought that I had gone beyond the limitations others took for granted, but it was turning out that I had constructed a number of limitations too! Not only did I live comfortably within their walls, I had not questioned them or even tested whether they were real or not.

CHAPTER 8 ❧

It was the first morning in July. Jim and I woke up quite early and lay in bed for some time, enjoying the cool morning air, talking about the farm, the grapes, the garden, and the number of things we were trying to get done. Since the weather had been very hot and dry, with no rain for more than three weeks, we gradually got around to the subject of rain.

I had done a little rain prayer several times the previous week, but not even a hint of a cloud or the much-needed moisture had appeared in response, and dust swirled around our feet whenever we walked through the garden or the vineyard. I was barely able to keep up with the watering demands of the young vegetables in the garden, the perennials in the flower gardens, the newly planted grass, the fruit trees, and the young trees we planted last fall. A number of times rain had been forecast for our area, but it had not fallen up on the Lawton Ridge where Lily Hill Farm was located.

After a lengthy discussion, we eventually got around to each other and started to make love. It occurred to me that we could add a little punch to our rain prayer if we made love with the energy devoted to producing rain. I suggested to Jim that we use the lovemaking as a little old-fashioned rain dance and try to bring a little rain this way. He laughed and made some funny comment, and we continued without much interruption. But as the lovemaking proceeded to its climax, I imagined myself as a puddle of water and Jim as the wind who scooped me up into the sky and then, suspended over the farm as a million droplets of water, I showered the farm with the much-needed rainfall.

That afternoon the sky clouded over and the rain just poured. Thunder and lightning provided a little summer drama and I couldn't help chuckling at the idea that we had done a good job making rain that morning!

Several days later, I wondered if we had done too good a job with the rainmaking business. Showers and thundershowers had been coming and going at odd hours of the day and night ever since our rain dance and most of the storms had been on the violent side. It had been very hot as well, into the nineties on the thermometer, leaving us to bake in the hot, stuffy house. Every night I had opened the windows wide to help cool things off as much as possible, but had been forced to get up again in the middle of the night to close them when the winds picked up and more rain started.

For the third morning in a row I found myself awakened at 5:00 A.M. by the sound of thunder coming closer and closer. I crawled out of bed half-awake to close the windows, wishing I didn't have to close them completely since that would cut off the cool pre-dawn breezes. So, I left each window open an inch or so, knowing that if it got really bad I'd have to get up again and close them the rest of the way.

Just as I crawled back in bed, the wind started to pick up and it started to sprinkle. I lay there, only half-awake and wanting to go back to the familiar nothingness of sleep, yet hoping the storm wouldn't get too bad because I didn't want to get up again and I didn't want to close the windows all the way. But the wind continued to build until it sounded like a gale and the rain began to come down furiously.

I lay there for a sleepy moment, thinking I had better get up immediately or I'd have to mop up windowsills and floors. A picture of the furious wind and pelting rain on delicate flowers and young vegetables appeared in my mind and I worried that they would be injured by the storm. Without forethought I called out to the wind, "Wind... Wind... Ms. or Mr. Wind... easy, easy, easy, please. Be gentle on my grapes and flowers..." Immediately the wind died down to a light breeze. The rain was still coming down hard so I called out to the water elementals, "Water... Miss Water... steady, not so hard, just wash the grapes and flowers carefully... be gentle... like a steady, even shower..." Immediately the downpour slackened to a gentle cascade.

"Oh my gosh!" I thought, still lying there in bed. "That was easy!"

If I hadn't been so foggy with sleep I think I would have been astounded. Instead, I was simply grateful that I didn't have to get up again. I thought about the story of Jesus and the way he quieted storms on the water. He had been asleep at first too. Maybe you had to be not fully awake and in that sort of in-between stage when one foot is in each world and all things are possible. I thought about waking Jim and telling him what had just happened, but figured he had missed the real action and a re-telling just wouldn't have the same impact.

Since the elements seemed to be listening and responding so well, I made one more call, this one to the earth. "Earth... Mother Earth... feed my plants and sweeten my grapes... please drink this rain and use it to carry nutrients to my vegetables and flowers...." Then I lay there, hoping that the earth would respond as well as the wind and rain had. I wondered if I dared go back to sleep or if it was necessary to stay awake and continue to monitor or manage such things. What if it started to pour again as soon as I drifted off? In the end I went back to sleep, grateful for the immediate response I had gotten and the fact I didn't have to get up and close the windows all the way.

Over breakfast of that same day, I told Jim about my experience with the wind and the rain in the early morning hours and he was somewhat impressed. Even I considered the immediate response of the weather as a rather unusual event. With his usual, practical approach, he made some comment that perhaps we might never have to worry about the weather again, if we could learn to communicate with it properly.

The rest of the day was bright and beautiful and for supper we decided to eat outside at the picnic table. We finished eating rather late. Afterward, I was moving back and forth between kitchen and picnic table, cleaning up. On my last trip out of the house toward the remains on the picnic table, I noticed Jim standing stock still, looking up at the sky. A slim, sickle-shaped cloud the color of mars black curved through the otherwise bright blue sky above us.

"Look at that unusual cloud!" he said. "I don't think I've ever seen a cloud like that before." I hadn't either and just looked at it, a long, dark, slender feather curving up out of the southwest with clear blue sky on either side of it. We could hear thunder rumble and see lightning flash among its few folds, and yet the sun was shining brilliantly in the west, on its way toward the evening horizon.

As the black, sickle-shaped cloud positioned itself directly over our house, a most unsettling feeling ran through me. Quickly the thunder and lightning intensified, and within minutes it began to sprinkle. I went in the house to close windows and was upstairs when Jim came running in shouting for me. "Pen, it's hailing, call the hail gods, call the elves… quick, do something!" After my success story with the morning's weather he obviously thought I could fix any weather immediately, including the hail!

My stomach sank as I thought about the damage even fifteen seconds of hail could do to our grapes and I immediately called out to the water elementals. I begged them to stop the hail, but when there was no immediate response as there had been that morning, I called to the Grape Deva, telling her to "Pull the leaves over the grapes, quick, hold them tight, shelter the grape berries…."

Then it was back to the water elementals. "Please, no ice, only water… melt the ice, only water… please, stop the hail…" Standing at the window in the upstairs hallway I watched the hail pour for another minute then finally melt into rain. Somewhat relieved I went back downstairs and out into the screenhouse. The rain continued to pour from the dark cloud as it passed directly over us, the sky was still clear and blue on either side of it, and the sun continued to shine as it headed for a sensational sunset. I stood there watching the sunset through the rain, feeling cheated and angry that the hail had to drop on our vineyard. In fact, it appeared that the hail and rain had passed deliberately over our farm and nowhere else.

Several hours later, it was time to go to bed, but I was still so upset that I could not relax. I decided I just had to talk to the water elementals and ask why they had dropped the hail on our farm. So, I settled myself in a meditative position on the bed and called out to them. Soon, a form appeared before me and, still upset, I started in passionately, "It is not good to drop ice on tender young fruits and vegetables! Only water should be allowed during the growing season! You can drop ice balls or hail on mature forests, open fields, on roads, parking lots, grass, or your own bodies of water—your lakes, oceans and streams—but not on young plants, please! At this stage of growth bring only gentle rains."

Without waiting for a reply I called to the wind and when the familiar form appeared I vehemently told him almost the same thing. "It is not good to carry ice balls over tender young plants and then blow them forcefully to the earth! You create much suffering and damage! Carry the hail to mature forests perhaps, although trees have their limits too... or take them to open fields, rocky hills and mountains, roads and parking lots, grass or streams, lakes and oceans. Always be careful of the size of the ice balls! And don't drop any on young vegetation at all!" There was a moment of silence as I caught up to myself.

"But we enjoy many forms, sizes, and kinds of expression!" It was the water elemental speaking.

I was surprised. I had not really been expecting an answer because I was so upset and had dispensed with the rules of two-way communication. Before that morning, I had never tried formally to communicate with any of the weather elements and was still quite surprised at the response I'd gotten. Some small part of me still thought it must be a fluke or a coincidence.

With a great internal effort I worked to find some way to appreciate their response to my call and to tone down my negativity. After a long minute I replied, "Yes, it's wonderful to be able to create and enjoy many forms and effects and stuff like that. It's just that some forms are more appropriate at certain times and places. Hail and high winds are fine in the autumn when the crops have been harvested. Or in the winter, or in the early spring before buds begin to open. Rains and mists are best in spring, summer, and autumn. Snow is beautiful in winter, but large hail is very harmful to us here. I would ask you to create nothing larger than one-half-inch balls of ice, at the most, if you are going to be dropping them on young plants and trees. Of course they could be larger if you wanted to pour them back into some deserted areas of rock or ocean. That would be okay, you know...."

"We appreciate your wishes. We would really like to work together with humans, but no one bothers to give us any feedback or to communicate with us at all. We had no idea that we were causing difficulties," they both said rather graciously.

"But I am willing to work with you... you and the others of your kind. I appreciate so much the way you have responded." I wanted very much to continue learning to work with these forms, and it had never even crossed my mind that perhaps they didn't know hail was bad for blossoming flowers and growing fruits. My next thought was that maybe hail had a very important purpose I'd never considered. Suddenly, I was discouraged at how many levels of subtlety and awareness there were.

My thoughts were interrupted by the voices of the wind and the water. "Talk with us, let us know what you desire, we will be happy to cooperate," they echoed together. And then they faded.

It occurred to me that I should have asked for hail no larger than one-quarter of an inch, maybe smaller, where plants and animals were concerned, but it was dark, quiet, and there was no further response to my belated request.

Thunder and lightning were approaching again, and I found myself listening to it and feeling swamped with emotion. The more I discovered, the more overwhelmed I felt. I already had great difficulty keeping up with the demands of my life. Was I now going to be responsible for managing things like wind and rain, watching out for hail and other troublesome forms of the elements? Wasn't managing a farm, a business, and a household enough? Instead of a nicely coordinated matrix of nature and humanity, I could see only a huge web of increasing complexity engulfing me.

I did not have the guts to go out and look at the hail damage in the vineyard until nearly a week had gone by. Jim had given me a preliminary report right after the long, black cloud of hail hit us. "It doesn't look too bad out there, Pen, only about 1 percent damage I'd say."

I disagreed the minute I started along the first row. Several times in the past we had been hit by hail, and Ernie had taught me how to estimate the damage. This looked more like 5 to 10 percent of the crop was seriously damaged. There was also a tremendous amount of leaf damage and this could interfere with the vines' ability to make sugar as the grape berries ripened. I felt really discouraged.

I had not been out in the vineyard or gone out to walk my land for a couple of weeks because it had been just plain too hot. But now, with cooler weather and a sense of worry about the outcome of this year's crop, I went back to the house, got my shears and gloves and started work on Row Twenty-nine in the front vineyard. I cut out suckers and shaped the young plants, enjoying the work, the sun, and the communication with the vines. They seemed to be glad to see me and I felt twinges of guilt at having concentrated on office work just because it was air-conditioned.

For the rest of the day and the next few days, I had the grapes constantly on my mind. I was back in my office again, this time feeling that I needed to keep at least some semblance of my consulting business going. I disliked the amount of phone work, paperwork, and attention to detail that were required to keep in touch with various clients and follow up on contracts. I wanted to be out in the vineyard, or in my garden, or working among my flowers, but I felt I should back up my deal with the elves in case something went wrong. I sent messages to the vines, telling them I loved them and that I was thinking of them, but I knew it was not the same as walking through the vineyards, being with them and working on them. At moments when I felt especially guilty or pulled in too many directions, I excused my procrastination with the thought, "Well, Alvey and I never really discussed how many times I had to walk my land, he just said to walk it. Who knows? Maybe even once or twice is enough…?"

The rain was a tremendous stimulant for the weeds in the vineyard. Within a short time it was obvious they were enjoying an unlicensed growth spurt. Jim began to carry on about the weeds again, especially the marestail. Marestail is a tall weed that refuses to be affected by ordinary weed sprays because of its coat of fine hairs that prevent droplets of weed spray from getting directly onto the surface of the leaves and stem. The kinds of weed spray that would have killed the marestail would have also killed the vines, so we were stuck. If the marestail continued unchecked, it would be five feet tall or more at harvest time and its seeds would get into the grapes. Welch could refuse to take the crop and we could be faced with disaster.

So, after much cajoling from Jim to "talk to the elves, the weed people, somebody" I sat down and made an attempt to go straight to the nature spirit of the marestail.

After taking a long time just to quiet my own internal turmoil, I called out to the marestail. Nothing happened. I waited. I called again, working to create a clear picture of the marestail so she would know I wanted to talk to her. Finally, my created picture disappeared and was replaced by a delicate form in the colors that surrounded me.

I asked if she was the nature spirit of the marestail, but received no direct answer. When there was no denial after a second inquiry I simply assumed she was the one I wanted to talk to, so I said, rather bluntly, "I am calling to you to ask if you would be willing to leave our vineyard."

At this announcement she seemed to fade a bit, and I wondered if she was going to faint. A helpless regret snaked through the back of my mind and I was uncomfortable at having obviously caused her some distress. She faded so dramatically I thought she was going to disappear.

"Oh, don't go yet, please! You are welcome in the other areas of the farm, but your presence in our vineyards threatens our grape crop and we just don't know what to do. Please, can we talk about this?"

She continued to alternate between a fading and a brightening sort of action. It reminded me of some scene out of *Star Trek* or something. But then she stabilized and gazed at me steadily.

"Jim and I need to take some kind of action, but we don't want to do anything without your cooperation and understanding. When the grape harvester comes along to harvest each row of grapes, it shakes the trellis which knocks the grapes onto a conveyor. The conveyor then carries them into a large bulk box. If the dried seeds on the tops of your plants also fall into the conveyor and end up in the box, our buyer will not accept them. It's not that we hate you or wish you harm. It's just that we want to make sure our grapes are clean and not mixed with bits of leaves and seeds. Do you see?"

She continued to gaze, still saying nothing, so I asked again, "What could we do that would be the least uncomfortable for you?"

After a long time she offered, "We could slow our growth, perhaps."

"But many of the marestail plants are already three feet high and anything over two feet is high enough to get into the grape harvester conveyors."

"Well... we would be willing to fall over at the first frost," she said.

"But the grapes will be harvested by the time we have a frost," I told her, "and the marestail directly under the grapes would be protected by the canopy of grape leaves so they would be the last to be touched by the frost. The marestail plants directly under the trellis are the ones causing problems," I said, trying not to sound argumentative.

"Are you sure?" she asked.

I wasn't clear just what she was asking me about. Was she referring to the frost, the protected position of the marestail directly under the trellis, or the fact that they were the worst part of our problem. I didn't know, but all her offers seemed to be aimed at finishing out the growing season for marestail if at all possible. I wondered if she was going to be totally against any kind of action that might interrupt their life span.

Before I could say anything further, she offered to dry out and not grow any more, but our experience with the weeds so far this year had left me too doubtful to accept that kind of alternative. I decided that perhaps I needed to introduce the options that I thought were necessary.

"We have a couple of choices at our end of things. One is to spray with something that will burn off the plant above the ground—but you would have to agree to let this type of weed spray affect you. The other is to cut back the weeds under the vines by hand, although this would be an awful lot of work. Either way, we just don't want to take any action without your understanding. And we would really like to do these things at a time when you would be most cooperative and would suffer the least. In other words, we would like the most effect for the least amount of chemicals, labor, and pain—for both of us."

She was very quiet again. Finally, she said that they would be most vulnerable and least uncomfortable if sprayed just before the new moon. "We sleep then and our defenses are down," she said. "It will be like dying in our sleep."

I winced a bit at her blunt acceptance of "dying in our sleep," and it was my turn to be quiet. I felt a plan had to be agreed upon, so I said to her, "Would it be okay if we tilled or mowed the center of the rows, then did a regular weed spray to remove all the weeds. After this, the only weeds left standing would be the marestail directly under the trellis. If we then cut back the marestail using a hedge trimmer or string trimmer, or, if we can't get the help and instead decided to follow the tilling immediately with a very light spray directly under the trellis, would you cooperate and not regain your height?"

She nodded gently and said, "Wait one month until the next new moon, call us two days before, we will all say goodbye." Then she faded.

I felt tired and exhausted. It seemed like I had done nothing but deal with elves, nature spirits, devas, or elementals for months. It wasn't difficult to communicate with them, and they seemed willing to be of help in any way that they could, but somehow their perception of reality seemed different from mine in a major way. I realized I kept trying to get them to understand how we did things and bend to meet the restrictions of the world we lived in; but they were somehow either resistant to this or unable to comprehend the difficulties we lived with. I knew it was not likely they were playing dumb, and yet my efforts to inform them of what I thought was basic and obvious to any form of intelligence seemed to fall far short of being understood. I usually ended up feeling that our agricultural practices and the reasoning I was trying to get across to them sounded stupidly ridiculous or lacked simple common sense.

I went to bed wondering why life seemed to be so complicated lately. After reading the story of the Findhorn Garden, I had come to feel that perhaps something special was happening here. It seemed that the connection to the elves and nature spirits was a gift of some kind. But, if the chance to work with elves, devas, and other unseen forms of intelligence was a gift, why were we working so hard? Why didn't we have some kind of special protection against mistakes and misunderstanding, or a dispensation from difficulty?

CHAPTER 9

It was the first week of August and nearly a month had gone by since the hail storm. Except for a bit of work on the day I had assessed the hail damage, I had not been out—either to work in the vineyards or to walk my land—since June. How had two months gone by so quickly? I felt uneasy; I was not keeping my end of the bargain with the elves very well. They had asked me to walk my land, and with excuse after excuse I kept telling myself I would do it tomorrow.

Earlier in the spring, when the elves had visited my office to ask if I would consider developing Lily Hill Farm, I had casually responded that it sounded like a neat idea and much more appealing than going back to educational consulting. With a too-fervent combination of sympathy and eagerness, they offered to "make sure I didn't have to." I had laughed then, amused at their efforts to get me to develop Lily Hill.

When that first seminar was canceled in May, I thought nothing of it. Cancellations were rare but not unheard of, and I was enjoying my work in the vineyard.

When the second seminar was canceled in June, I was surprised, but still thought nothing of it.

The third seminar was canceled in July, and in the end, everything I had scheduled that summer was canceled. I was no longer amused. After spending March, April, and May working in the vineyards, I suddenly realized that I had not brought in any money and did not have any prospect of doing so in the immediate future. I was out over ten thousand dollars and was sure that the elves had something to do with the cancellations, but every time I called on them intending to discuss the matter, they seemed to be too busy to talk.

Upset about the canceled contracts and suddenly worried that we were not going to get one hundred tons of grapes, I made a panicky decision to put energy into replacing the lost income and went to work feverishly making contacts among schools and educators.

"What was the matter with me?" I asked myself over and over. "Why had it seemed so easy last spring to go out in the vineyard and work in its wonderful magic? What had made me think I could just overlook a much-needed income over the course of summer?"

Since it was so unbearably hot outside, it had not been too difficult to go back to the cool relief of an office and my work as an educational consultant— but I did so with only half a heart. I didn't really feel I had the energy to keep dealing with schools, teachers, and the mess in our educational system.

By the middle of August, I was absolutely miserable. I knew a review of one's life was necessary once in a while, but I was so terribly disappointed in myself that I fell into a deep pit of self-pity and remained mired there, reflecting on the events that had led to my misery. The previous autumn I had made a deal with the elves to walk my land in return for one hundred tons of grapes. It had seemed an almost too-simple agreement when we made it. I tried to carry my end, but fell prey to my usual habit of great enthusiasm at first, then less and less energy into the project.

As I looked back over the past ten months, I realized I had been in an escalating career crisis. After working for years to establish myself as an educational consultant, I felt that I had thrown it all away to devote myself to writing. For two whole months—January and February of this year—I had written, working steadily on one book intended for the students taking my classes in intuition, and planning a second book about a friend who had been quite a radical in the sixties. In March I abandoned both projects and suddenly took to working in the vineyard. When the weather got hot and uncomfortable I abandoned the vineyard and went back to working in the office where I was forced to face the canceled seminars and loss of income.

Now my career crisis reached the frenzy level. I had serious stomach upsets, diarrhea, and a flare-up of my hiatal hernia—all of which contributed to my wretchedness and pain. I was tense, sleepless, tired, and generally harassed by the demands of the office and the people I had always dealt with so smoothly and effortlessly.

Life had always offered me many alternatives and I had always tried to sample them all. I had always been anxious to make more money, to find the right path, to create a better world. The choices danced before me—mother, engineer, educational consultant, writer and author of great books, healer, intuitive, technological wizard, teacher, mentor, guide, and endless other possibilities.

When the elves entered my life, they served up another choice—the chance to experience communicating with a new assortment of living things, with the plants, animals, and forces in the world of nature. These experiences included, but were not limited to, other forms of communication besides the obvious ones; an opportunity to see what happens when the very real power of clear and simple love was projected to a whole range of critters and forms of life; ongoing experimentation with consciousness and the mind in their effects on plants; a systematic exploration of hidden skills and abilities in the human being; the sensible and practical use of these abilities to aid us in getting the necessities of life—food, clothing, shelter, relationships and joy; and the possibility that we could learn to create miracles. These were some of the things that I had believed in and been teaching for years. Now I was being offered a chance to demonstrate them in living flesh, or rather, living stems, leaves, and fruit.

When Alvey and his group began to encourage me to develop Lily Hill, they had made it seem that the farm could become a heaven on earth, a paradise of abundance where everything lived in beauty, peace, and balance. It would be a place to demonstrate what is possible upon the earth when humans, plants, animals, and minerals lived as one in loving communication.

Over the summer, other people and their chosen projects had also continued to appear. Mary and her educational software project, Stan and the Multi-Cultural/Academic Excellence Program for Kalamazoo Public Schools, Duane and the building of high-tech research equipment for brain/mind applications—these were only the most persistent in asking for some of my time.

There I stood, caught between the peace and promise of Lily Hill Farm and the old dreams of fame and fortune, success and power, material satisfaction and personal pleasure.

I tried to talk to Jim about how I was feeling trapped between two choices, but words failed to convey the depth of my confusion and the pain of my disillusionment with myself. The sheer intensity of the conflict and the power of my own feelings forced me to look at the real motives behind my actions.

"What was I really doing, and why was I choosing to do it?" I asked myself. After agreeing to work with Mary and with Stan and Duane, and after taking on clients who wanted information, students who wanted more classes and personalized teaching, and others who just wanted a piece of my time, I was a wreck. I felt I was coming apart.

"What has real meaning? What is my path? And what if, in the overall scheme of things, I discover I am doing all the right things for all the wrong reasons?" I cried and cross-examined myself for days. When I asked for guidance, I got the same answer every time, "All paths are equal and lead to the same goal."

But all paths did not feel equal. It had been only a short time since I decided to return to educational consulting and already I was fragmented. I had no center, no anchor, no bearings, and no sense of what was right or wrong for me. I lacked the certainty of purpose I had when I got up and went out to the vineyard every morning.

I knew it was fear of not enough money that had pushed me to leave the farm suddenly in the background and return to consulting, but somehow the feeling that I was doing something worthwhile had been left behind as well.

Logically, I told myself I could be of greater service by giving myself to the world of education. The world of elves, fairies, and magical plants would sound like a farce to anyone out there in the real world, the world beyond Lily Hill Farm. It seemed reasonable to think that I could have a greater impact on a wider scale by plunging myself further into the educational research and development that might help enlighten the world about the damage we were doing to children by taking them away from parents at too-tender ages, putting them in nurseries and public or private school classrooms, giving them little other than paper and pencil to work with. The great need of the young human brain to be included in the everyday fabric of life and to have hands-on experience with all of reality was being overlooked and short-circuited. Already the result was several generations of learning-disabled children who became seriously under-abled adults.

Yet, in the withering light of that same clear perspective, I could see how aggressive and self-seeking I was. I still longed for wealth and recognition. I looked forward to the power and personal satisfaction I would have by offering the world its avenue to advanced education. I would save the world from itself and succeed where all else had failed.

How ignorant and selfish I suddenly felt, and how sick it made me to realize that perhaps I did not know how to make an unselfish decision. What good would it do me to save the world if I lost myself in the process? I had always wanted to do so much and at that moment it all appeared to be so hollow, just a scheme for glory.

Now, I found myself facing a deep truth about myself I had long ago run away from. Back when I was eighteen, I couldn't wait to get out of my family home—away from the dull farmers who made up the bulk of my family and friends, away from the backward, old-fashioned rituals of a small town far removed from the action and excitement of big cities. How harshly I had judged them, those farmers, those friends. It was now clear that I just wanted to think I was better than they.

"I never planned to own a farm, I just wanted a house of my own," I moaned. "How did I end up with this farm and this crisis over what to do with my life?" My former judgment of farmers now made me cringe in agonized embarrassment. How ironic it seemed that I should have to choose between all the fancy, college-educated dreams I nurtured all these years—and one farm called Lily Hill.

My ignorance had come full circle. I was face to face with a choice I had never intended—to explore the gift of the farm and learn what is possible when humans, plants, and animals work together or to satisfy the old dreams of money, power, and glory. Choosing to work on the farm, to experiment with and possibly expand the old limits of reality in ways that might benefit others, to discover new ways to use the great powers and abilities of the mind—all seemed to conspire to force me to retract my earlier critical judgments of family and farm life.

"What if others begin to look on me as just another dull farmer?" I fretted to myself. "Or perhaps farming is just an excuse to avoid dealing with the incessant demands of my educational consulting business and escape the rest of the world? Worse, what if peace, health, bounty and balance end up being no more evident here than anyplace else on earth?" There were no guarantees and now I was at the bottom line.

I had wanted more than anything to learn, to progress, to evolve in my existence here. Almost as strongly, perhaps even more powerfully, on occasion I had wished to help the seething mass of humanity along the way. Now it looked as if a large part of that goal was really quite self-serving. Logically, I assumed that living in the Christ-mind would have its material benefits, like success, recognition, and financial security. In my heart, I knew that these last things were not enough by themselves. I knew myself at least well enough to know that if the work did not spring from my heart I would not stick to it for long.

It was time to choose a path. But the two paths presented to me could not have been more difficult than if I had deliberately selected ghosts from my past and spirits from my future, then told them to challenge me and all my assumptions about life and how to live it. I cried for a week.

In the end, I decided I simply had to develop Lily Hill. But I left the decision hanging there, without any idea of what to do, where to begin, or how I was going to make a living at it. For the moment, I just could not trust that I would be taken care of financially. I struggled on with the educational consulting.

Toward the end of August it was time to take a sampling of our grapes up to the Welch plant for sugar testing. After the dew had dried on a warm sunny morning, I went out and picked about twenty clusters of grapes. It was a lovely day, and I found myself missing the work in the vineyard terribly. As I went along the rows, inspecting the vines I had personally worked on, I was gratified to see that they were healthy and well-formed.

I went down Row Twenty-four in the back vineyard to look at the few vines that I had tried to shape last year when I was truly a novice. They looked so good that I rejoiced for a moment. It was going to be a great crop and an amazing harvest.

Then doubt clouded over and through me again. How did I know that this wasn't just a chance good year, one of those years when things just sort of go right for everyone? After all, everyone seemed to be having a good year.

A voice from the top of the hill rolled down to me, "What did ye want—for everyone else to have a bad year and yers to be great?" There stood Alvey and his companions beaming down at me.

"Well, not really, well... maybe yes... I mean, I don't want other people to have a bad year, I just figured that my crop would somehow be bigger and better than everyone else's. Otherwise it's just going to look like everyone is having a good year and I won't have any proof that you're worth it... I mean, working with you is worth it... I mean, that it really makes a difference to work with you..." I ended kind of lamely.

"Tsk! Tsk!" they said, moving down the hill toward me. "You can't ask for something to be good for ye and bad for anyone else. That's how ye don't get what ye ask for!"

"But how will I know if I've really accomplished anything unusual? How do I know it just didn't happen to be a good year in general?" I asked. "From what I hear, everyone is having a great crop!"

"Did ye expect to have sunshine and gentle breezes here at Lily Hill while farmers all around ye suffered frost and clouds, or hail and drought?" Alvey inquired.

"Well, not exactly," I answered, still doubtful about how I was going to prove that working with Alvey and his group could make a real difference in the total crop harvested.

"Look at it this way," said Alvey. "Ye decided to work with us, with the elements of wind and rain and sun, with the Grape Deva, and anyone else ye thought would have a positive influence on your grape crop. If even one person works with us, everyone around that person will also benefit! Yer neighbors up here on the ridge will have a great year right along with ye. Think what could be accomplished if ten people decided to work with us. The positive effects would be even more widespread. Imagine if every farmer in the Michigan Fruit

Belt[6] worked together with us! There would be a massive improvement in production and quality of fruit! Ye would be able to feed half the world with what ye produce right here in the Fruit Belt!" With that they turned and marched up over the hill and out of sight.

---

6 Lake Michigan so powerfully moderates the weather along the west coast of Michigan that this has given rise to what is known as the Fruit Belt, a warm strip of land about twenty-five to thirty miles wide that runs from Bridgeport in the south to Traverse City in the north, and produces hundreds of thousands of tons of peaches, pears, plums, grapes, apples, cherries, strawberries, blueberries, cantaloupe, and other small fruits as well as a large variety of vegetables, especially celery, green peppers, and tomatoes.

CHAPTER 10 ❧

By the time September arrived, grapes were ripe in everyone's vineyard and ready to be harvested. According to the old-timers who had been raising grapes forever, it was going to be one of the earliest harvests ever. In spite of the need for money, I did not return to teaching word processing or desktop publishing at the local business college. Instead, I re-opened my small learning center in the barn and resumed teaching classes in developing and using intuition. The class ran on Tuesday nights for six weeks from 7:00 P.M. until 10:00 P.M. In the second week, the class ran about ten minutes later than usual and as everyone prepared to leave I noticed a thunderstorm beginning to assemble itself off in the distant west. I wondered if I should try to contact the elves or the rain and wind to try to gain a bit of extra protection for our overripe grape crop hanging delicately from the trellis. But Jim had brought home my new laser printer and I was so excited I refused to close up the office and leave the barn until the printer was installed, powered up, and running smoothly.

It was after midnight by the time we left the offices in the barn, and just as we finally climbed into bed, the gathering storm broke. There were very high winds, heavy rains, thunder, and lightning. Fear rippled over me as I thought of what could happen to our ripened grapes in such a storm. I sat up in bed. It was time to talk to the wind and rain again.

With difficulty I focused on trying to clear my fears and, as the tempo of the storm increased, I called to the wind asking it to stop blowing so hard. There was immediate quiet, which startled me. It was the same response I'd had earlier in the summer, a response that had delighted and shocked me, but since then I frequently thought back on that experience as a fluke. Now, caught in silent shock, all my fears and disbelief took over. "What makes you think you can quiet the wind?" a cynical voice inside my head mocked. "That wind is never going to stay quiet just for you!"

My stomach contracted in fearful tension and with it, the wind began to blow with mounting force. I repeated my first request but the wind only whipped about the house more fiercely. Trying to calm myself, I called out again, this time my request sounding more like the pleading of a child. The wind only increased.

I went back to centering and calming myself, but it was as if the wind controlled me. As the gusts increased, I went from polite requests, to pleading, to panicky query, to demands that it slow down, and finally to outright orders to get off my property! At these last orders, the wind stopped momentarily outside my bedroom window and there was an ominous silence. Then it began releasing a long howl that started in with a low, rumbling hum, increasing in volume and strength until it ended so loudly and high-pitched that huge waves of gooseflesh rolled from my head to my toes. The whole house shook, and in that moment I knew that the wind was alive, that it could come in my room and get me, and I was terrified.

In a streak of stubbornness, I refused to give up or back down and found myself engaged in a mental and emotional battle that was more fierce than any fight I had ever had with any human being. I tried one line of defense after another; first I visualized trying to erect a line of force along the west side of our property as if I were a whole row of trees, catching and slowing the wind. When the wind just danced around me in circles, I changed tactics and rose above the property in the form of a huge golden light, trying to transform the gale winds into gentle breezes, but the wind scattered both the light and my efforts.

Gathering my wits, I called out to the elves, to the grasses, to the flowers, trees, grapes and devas, asking them to talk to the wind, tell it to quiet down, tell it to be gentle, but I could get no answer from anyone. Going on the offense with one strategy after the next, I tried to counter or curtail the strength and fury of the wind until finally, at nearly 3:00 A.M. I was exhausted and gave up. I had to get up early the next morning, and in meek exhaustion, I finally called out to the wind.

"Mr. Wind, I am tired of fighting with you. I have to get up early tomorrow morning. I ask only that you hear my request. Please blow gently on the grapes as they are quite ripe, even overripe, and will easily fall off the trellis if there is too much shaking and blowing going on. I trust that you can hear me and will do what is best."

With that I lay down. Before I had time to pull the sheet over me, the wind and the rain disappeared. In less than a minute, the stillness was so eerie that another wave of gooseflesh passed over me. The rain was gone and there wasn't even a breeze. I sat up for a fatigued moment and looked out the window right next to the bed. "Did you just want me to give up and trust you, or were you trying to teach me that I just can't control everything?" I wondered absentmindedly. Then, I lay back down, already drifting away into sleep.

The next morning, I overslept and was barely able to drag myself from the bed. I was still exhausted from struggling with the storm the night before. It was a beautiful day with clear blue skies and lots of sunshine. I rushed from one appointment to the next all morning, but my mind was back in the vineyard. I couldn't wait to get back home and go for a walk. I wanted to see if there were any grapes left on the trellis or if they'd all been blown off in the storm the night before.

At noon I drove home, changed my clothes and ate a quick lunch. I was just finishing the last of my sandwich when my friend, Wendy, called me for something and in the conversation asked how the grapes were doing. Several months earlier I had told her about my deal with the elves and had expressed great confidence that we were going to harvest one hundred tons of grapes. She was quite excited about both the elves and the deal and asked about the vineyards whenever we talked. That day I felt a twinge of apprehension but told her I thought they were doing fine even though we'd had a pretty bad storm the night before. After hanging up the phone I knew it was time to go out and see if there was any damage.

I headed out toward the back block of grapes. After reaching the south-west corner of the vineyard, I walked along the end posts for a bit then turned down one of the rows. Scanning the ground under the trellis I was relieved to see that there were no grapes on the ground.

The sun shone brightly and there was a light breeze. I went up and down several rows then stuck my head up under one of the vines to look closely at the ripe purple berries. All the grapes seemed to be hanging tightly in their clusters.

"How did you manage to hang on during such a violent storm?" I mur-mured to myself, picturing a trellis that had been shaken so violently I was half surprised to see it still upright.

"We had to get your attention and get you out here somehow!" came a booming voice. Startled, I jumped, and with my head up under the trellis, my long curly hair was quickly tangled among the tendrils that grew along the canes. As I struggled to free my hair, I realized it was the wind speaking. At the same moment I was overwhelmed by the perception that the grapes had grabbed me by the hair of my head and were forcing me to stand still to listen to their friend, the wind.

"What do you mean?" I asked, reaching awkwardly up and behind my head to sort out hair from grape canes.

"You haven't been out here much lately so we had to create an uproar to get your attention and a little of your time!" came the answer.

Busy trying to untangle my hair and its combs from the fingers of the vine, I thought perhaps I should have stopped the night before to ask the wind and rain what they were trying to say. Perhaps they had been trying to tell me that I had been away too long. Instead of listening, I had tried to shut them up, order them away, demand that they stop and be quiet.

"Sorry!" I replied with quick remorse, and after finally managing to free my hair, I went back to the house, got my gloves, trimmers, and a hat then went back to the vineyard where I worked until nearly 7:00 P.M. that evening.

At the beginning of the following week, I was away for most of the day and drove home long after dinner time, listening to the radio. A weather bul-letin came on announcing that a severe thunderstorm was coming across Lake Michigan. The storm, with damaging winds, heavy rains, hail, and lightning, was expected before 10:00 P.M.

Upon arriving home, I sat down to talk to the wind, the rain, the light-ning, and the earth. I decided to simply ask for what I wanted, then close my request with trust and love. One by one I called to them, asking them to be very gentle with our overripe grapes hanging patiently in their wait to be harvested.

I was determined not to start worrying or hanging on in fearful suspense. To my great surprise there was a moment of quiet peace and then a clear, firm voice said, "Your grapes will be just fine."

Toward 10:00 P.M. the lightning and thunder approached and became continuous. There was some rain, but no hail. The wind seemed to be restrained. It was as though the storm was all around us, but happening somewhere in some distant realm.

The next day I heard on the radio that there was a great deal of storm damage throughout Western Michigan. Golf-ball-sized hail had fallen, along with an inch and a half of rain. Many trees were down and more than 100,000 people were without electricity, but here at Lily Hill Farm we and our grapes were fine. I was very grateful, but growing more and more anxious for the harvest team to come and take our grapes. We were waiting our turn, and yet the wheel of time seemed to grind more slowly every day.

Finally, one week later, the harvest crew arrived in late afternoon, bringing the equipment and promising to start early the next morning. Jim and I were both excited and relieved. Harvest was the culmination of all our efforts earlier in the year. I was also a bit tense. For me, this year's harvest was important for reasons other than just bringing in a successful crop and collecting our money. The size of the crop would illustrate how important it was for the world to recognize the value of working with elves, devas, and nature spirits, or whatever group of intelligent beings Alvey, Kermots, and Mairlinna belonged to. That night I could hardly sleep.

The next day was Sunday, but the grape harvest, once begun, was a seven days a week, twenty-four hour a day operation for the Welch plant in town. The harvest crew of about six men arrived before we were out of bed and began getting machinery ready to run. Finally, they and the equipment headed toward the back vineyard. Harvest had begun!

The weather was warm, clear, and sunny. In the intervals between the arrival of grape-filled bulk boxes from the field, several of the old-timers who worked as part of the crew sat outside in lawn chairs and drank coffee. Regularly they got up and moved themselves and their chairs backward into the shade as the sun pursued them toward the west side of the building.

With keen interest I watched the bulk boxes arrive and counted them as they were loaded onto the trailer of the waiting semi-truck. Things seemed to be going smoothly and quickly. In fact, they were going almost too quickly. By the end of the day, the grapes had all been picked except for a few rows in the front vineyard. The crew left, promising to come back early the next morning to finish the rest.

I counted and recounted the number of grapes boxes that had yet to be delivered, added them to the number of boxes already delivered, and tried to stretch the amount of grapes that had yet to be harvested to make up for what was obviously going to be a harvest that fell far short of one hundred tons of grapes.

The next morning when the few remaining grapes were picked and delivered, the official receipts that came back from Welch tallied a total of fifty-six tons of grapes from our vineyards. I was so disappointed I could hardly speak. In fact, I felt sick.

As the day passed, I gradually shifted from sick disappointment to a frustration that was so intense I could no longer concentrate on my work or the preparations for my class that night. I closed up my office and went to see the elves. I was angry and felt cheated, but most of all I was embarrassed. I had told several people about my experiment and had said I was certain we would gather one hundred tons of grapes when the season came to harvest. Now I felt like a fool.

Only Alvey and Mairlinna responded when I walked out to the back of the property and called out to them, waiting impatiently and trying to act casual. When they finally appeared they seemed quiet and circumspect in spite of their usual greetings.

"We only got fifty-six tons of grapes," I announced.

"That so?" Alvey inquired politely. Mairlinna only nodded.

"I thought we had an agreement for one hundred tons?" I prodded without wanting to accuse.

"Yep, we had an agreement all right," Alvey and Mairlinna nodded at me and then at one another several times.

"Well? What happened?" I asked, my voice rising perilously. "How am I supposed to believe there's any value in working with you guys if the things you say you can do don't happen."

"How many tons of grapes did ye get last year?" Alvey asked politely.

"About thirty-four," I replied.

"And how many did ye get the year before that?" he said.

"About seventeen."

"And before that?" he inquired further.

"Thirty-six," I said.

"And ye're unhappy with fifty-six?" he asked, raising an eyebrow and tipping his head so that he appeared to be looking at me from under one eyebrow.

This caused something in me to snap and I replied bluntly, "I know it's over twenty tons more than last year and more than three times what we got the year before that, but we agreed on 100 tons and fifty-six tons doesn't even come close! If you promise and don't deliver, how do you expect people to believe that you exist and that it's worth their effort to try to communicate or work with you?"

There was a very brief moment of quiet in which Alvey and Mairlinna glanced at one another. "And did ye feel that ye kept yer end of the bargain?" he inquired. "Did ye walk yer land when we asked ye to? No! Almost the whole winter went by before ye found time to walk! And when ye did finally start, ye were so overcome with guilt that ye couldn't just walk. Ye had to get right in there and try to run the whole operation by doing the trimming, the tying, the shaping, the vine renewal, the tractor work and even running the weather! We asked ye not to spray without a notice, but at times ye went ahead and sprayed—and then asked if it was okay. We made it clear that so much spraying is harmful, but ye couldn't believe in not spraying, could ye? All we asked ye to do was walk yer land, not take over the whole operation! But ye made yerself a vague deal and never bothered to re-deal and make a clear decision as to how much walking was enough.

"Did ye trust in us? No! Instead ye tried to keep the balance of 'walking versus grapes' shifted in yer favor by working a little extra and hoping to manipulate us into feeling we owed ye more grapes! Did ye trust in the grapes to respond—or even in yerself to do what was right? No, instead ye worried about keeping a too tight tit-for-tat.

"Perhaps it's ye that doesn't understand. This was not a test fer us, it was a test fer ye! Are ye worth working with? First ye don't do what is specifically asked of ye! When ye did get out to walk or work, ye did it because ye had dreams of glory and being able to show off yer results!

"Then ye want yer crop to be better than everyone else's! Ye kept thinking that it just happened to be a good year for everyone—but that was not true. Other places around Lawton and Paw Paw suffered considerable damage, first from frost, then hail, then drought or too much rain. But here, on this ridge, ye and yer neighbors will all have an excellent crop. Why? Because we have watched over ye. We do produce what we agree to and it's only when ye get in yer own way that ye will backslide. In fact, yer neighbors are getting the crop ye could have had. They're all going to have a bumper crop of everything. But not ye. We put in only as much effort as ye did and we made sure ye didn't get one hundred tons because ye didn't do what ye said ye would, and then ye tried to cover it up by taking over everything! So, the question is: will ye give up after one try or be pleased there was an improvement and then improve on the improvement?"

I was stunned into a silence where nothing moved. It felt as though even my heart had stopped. Mairlinna stepped forward and patted my leg, then both of them disappeared. I walked home, tears falling as freely as they had the day we first made our agreement.

The next day was a very busy day but the sting of my conversation with Alvey burned in the forefront of my mind from one long hour to the next. At the end of the day I was getting ready to leave the office and go in the house to fix dinner when my neighbor from down the road called. She and I seldom talked more than once or twice a year, but I was always pleased to see or hear from her.

She wanted to know if our grapes had been harvested yet and I told her they had. She was surprised and said she usually saw or heard the harvesting crew in our vineyards but had somehow missed it this year. She asked how many tons we got and I told her we'd gotten a little over fifty-six tons. She had no knowledge of my agreement with the elves or the expected tonnage, but I still felt great embarrassment wash over me as I reported what I felt to be such a low figure.

"Gosh," she said, "We're harvesting now and it looks like we're going to get well over two hundred and twenty tons this year."

"Oh my god!" I exclaimed, "How many acres do you have altogether?"

"Almost thirty acres, and so far we're getting an average of close to eight tons per acre. I don't know what we did this year, but we must have done something right!" she said.

Alvey's words, "Yer neighbors are getting the crop ye could have had," cut across my mind and with an awkward pain I congratulated her on the bumper crop. We chatted for a moment then said good-bye and hung up. "Well, there's one neighbor who benefited from the agreement," I thought. I wondered what had prompted her to call me. She had never called to ask about our grape tonnage or to tell me about hers before, and then I knew. The elves wanted me to see that what I had set out to do was certainly possible. After all, it had been accomplished by someone who was just doing their ordinary vineyard practices and didn't even know they were being assisted by unseen helpers. I had the feeling the elves didn't want me to give up. Feeling like a failure, I went in the house to eat before teaching my Tuesday night class.

CHAPTER 11 ❧

Several weeks passed and I was still caught in the nets of embarrassment and anger over the grape crop outcome. Three days after the harvest I walked out to Alvey's corner of the farm and grudgingly apologized to him and his company of companions for feeling cheated and wanting to blame them entirely. He accepted my apology in a perfunctory manner; even so, a definite aura of estrangement remained between us.

Occasionally, my feelings of insult and defensive pouting over the grape harvest swamped me with a defensive righteousness and I felt they had deliberately embarrassed me in front of family and friends. I knew that there was more patching up that needed to be done and regularly intended to make a special trip out to see Alvey just to make a more honest apology, but all I had managed so far was to think about doing so. These thoughts fueled leftover shreds of anger, and I fretted frequently but was unable to bring myself to take a simple walk or visit any of our usual meeting places.

I kept wondering if we were really working together at all or if the whole effort was over. Some days I felt that our connection was lost forever. In the stiffness of my apologies immediately after harvest I had forgotten to tell them I wanted to work with them for one more year, or to ask if there was anything different they wanted me to do in the coming year besides walk my land.

Now I worried that they had decided that I was not worth working with. It seemed we had no clear agreement to do anything any more and gradually I found the original doubts about the reality of our relationship returning to haunt me. Maybe they were really just a figment of my imagination. Some days it was all a huge joke taking place in my mind. Other days, I felt we were just biding our time until we got back on speaking and working terms.

Finally, I sat down to meditate in my room, hoping for insight into what I needed to learn from the whole affair and wanting some peace of mind, an easing of the disappointment. It took me a long time to relax, and several times I sent a mental call to Alvey, intending to apologize for the whole mess, but there was no answer from him, Mairlinna, or anyone in the group. Mental distractions of all sorts kept popping up, but finally I dropped into the familiar peacefulness of deep meditation, forgetting the day-to-day concerns.

Some time later, I found myself walking among the grapes, simultaneously aware that my physical body was sitting on the bedroom floor back in the house, and wondering if this experience would count as an effort to walk my land. I went along slowly from row to row, ducking under the trellis here and there, trying to get up some kind of loving, caring spirit for the vines but felt dead inside. I kept moving mechanically toward the back row and had just started up Golden Mountain when Harvey surprised me! The shock of seeing him nearly brought me up out of the meditation but he greeted me with a smile and a nod, then asked how I was.

In a rush of emotion I told him we had not gotten the one hundred tons of grapes I'd expected; that I had been upset with Alvey; that Alvey had been overly blunt with me, accusing me of not being true to my end of our bargain; and now I couldn't seem to get any sort of good feeling for the grapes or working with Alvey, his group, the elementals, or anyone.

Harvey listened intently, with an inscrutable expression. Then, with great deliberateness, he slowly walked up to me and touched my arm. When he did, an enormous electric shock shot through me! It felt as if something wonderful and intimate, almost sexual had happened between us.

In sudden surprise, I stared at him. The first time we met he had been dressed in a flannel shirt and jeans with a hat on his head. Now I was embarrassed to realize he had no clothes on. He continued to look intently at me but I averted my eyes, could not speak, and felt a paralyzing shyness.

"Come with me!" he said.

Before my eyes he changed form and instead of the half-human creature with pointed ears and hooves where his feet should have been, he became a shimmering, iridescent dragonfly who lifted into the air. But even more shocking was the sudden realization that I seemed to be lifting into the air with him and my human form was gone—I was a dragonfly too! There was a loud humming or buzzing sound all around me, and I decided it must be the sound of the wings, but I didn't stop to check it out or ask myself what was happening. Instead, I followed Harvey through the air, over the vineyard, up over Golden Mountain and past the trees until we were hovering over the small lake that lay just inside the woods at the back of our property.

The logical impossibility of what was happening never occurred to me. Instead, I swooped and soared and glided in a playful dance with Harvey, mindful only of the exquisite joy and fun of the experience. Once or twice we flew together, Harvey alighting on my back for a ride, and I experienced the same powerful jolt of electricity as when he walked up and touched my arm, but for the most part we simply played, flitting about like children with wings dancing through air.

When it was over, I found myself standing in the same spot at the back of the vines where we had met earlier that evening. It seemed as though a lifetime had passed.

I thanked Harvey. He had broken the deep ache frozen inside of me since the grape harvest and my conversation with Alvey. He just stood there smiling and then with a nod he was gone.

With another jolt I was back in my bedroom, suddenly aware of stiff legs and feeling chilled. For a while, I couldn't move, mentally or physically. I tried to think coherently about what I'd just experienced, but found my mind seemed lopsided and that I could only think around the edges of what had happened. There was a distant sense of something shocking having happened to me, and I wondered if I'd fallen asleep and had a fantastic dream. It hadn't seemed like it because it had been so intensely real and clear—in spite of the seeming impossibility.

I leaned over to get my clipboard with paper and pen and scribbled down the whole experience, because I knew it would seem implausible in the morning. But even as I wrote, worried thoughts ran through my mind. "How can I write about such an experience?... what was this about... why did it happen... nobody will understand this... I don't understand it...!" But I wrote it anyway then climbed into bed and slept late into the morning. Over the rest of the day the unusual experience remained a dreamlike memory. The only thing that was truly different was that my depressed attitude toward Alvey, the grape crop, and life in general had begun to loosen. I could contemplate the whole series of events with a more distant sense of pain and with even a vague sense of curiosity in wondering what was being learned through it all.

One Sunday in late January, I returned home from my Spanish class at the local community college. The days were getting a wee bit longer, so I decided to go out for a walk. I moved briskly up the lane toward Golden Mountain, passing the back vineyard and going uphill until I stood at the top. Once there I called out to Alvey several times but no one answered.

Moving more slowly, I started downhill, heading alternately south and west, toward the place that Alvey had asked me to leave wild and untouched, but no one was there either.

Following the edge of the woods, I called out as I went along, but still no answer. I kept walking until I reached the pond in the far northwest corner of our property, where I stopped and stood, staring at the ice and lost in thought.

I'm not sure how much time went by before I noticed that Alvey was standing beside me, also staring at the ice. A little thrill of pleasure at seeing him went through me, and, for just a moment, I forgot my doubts and injured vanity. The rest of the group had gathered behind us, but not a word was spoken and there was a solemn air among them. Alvey continued to stare at the ice.

Finally, I said, "Hi, Alvey."

"Greetings," he replied, with the group behind us echoing the same.

"Alvey, I forgive you for everything that's happened and I still want to work with you."

"Forgive me for what?" he asked, turning to stare at me instead of the ice.

I had the distinct impression that I had insulted him. I felt terribly awkward. "Well... I mean... what I really mean is that I felt let down and... I'm sorry we haven't gotten on very well these last few months..." I was almost stammering.

Alvey shook his head and continued to stare at me. "My, my, how ye do persist in yer illusions!" he said.

The feeling of awkwardness increased to an acute level. A series of thoughts flashed through my mind. Maybe I was the only one still struggling with this whole thing... I should have gotten in contact with him earlier... Were we still working together...? Maybe we weren't...?

After sifting through a half dozen things to say that I thought might warm the atmosphere, I said, "I've decided to come back and see if you're interested in another try at working together. Um, are you?"

"Sure thing," he nodded. "Would've been disappointed if our first agreement to work together was the only one. Been disappointed before though, most folks decide they dreamed us or something!" There was a ripple of agreement through the group, and I could hear comments like "Yea, yea.... No faith.... They want magic rather than miracles!" and one odd comment, "Yep, so used to instant potatoes, they won't settle for real ones."

"Well... I'm sorry I haven't been out walking much this winter. In fact, I wasn't sure you were still interested in our deal. But I am. I don't want to give up yet."

"Does that mean ye intend to give up later?" Alvey asked quizzically.

"Oh no, I don't intend to give up at all! I'm just having a belief crisis and a career crisis and a personal crisis all at once and it's getting me down. I really want to continue to develop Lily Hill along the lines you have described. I just don't know quite how to go about it and still make a living."

Suddenly, the whole group came to attention and faced me directly. "Do ye trust us?" Alvey inquired from under that one eyebrow of his.

Without hesitation or doubt, I said "Yes!" and then stood there feeling entirely naked as everyone in the group seemed to examine me head to toe, inside and out.

Whispers and a funny kind of sideways chatter broke out among them but they continued to examine me curiously as if with great interest. This was followed by an abrupt quiet.

Mairlinna stepped forward and said, "How would ye like to work with us this year?"

I could hardly think. I was flooded with emotion and wished I had done better last year. When they had asked me to walk my land it had seemed simple, too easy, almost a non-role, an action without importance or relevance. But it had turned out to be far more difficult than I had supposed. Having failed to rise to the challenge, I did not want to assign myself a task that was associated with failure.

I loved working among the vines and considered agreeing to trim or tie, but they had criticized me for trying to run everything and then take all the credit for any success that resulted, so that seemed unacceptable too.

Several other possibilities passed through my mind and were discarded. I felt a rising pressure to come up with something or some way to work with them. I couldn't think of anything that would be reasonable and acceptable and wished I had given the matter some more thought before I went looking for them. I was stumped and the minutes were ticking past.

"Say," Alvey piped up excitedly, interrupting my inner search, "I have a great idea!"

"He's got an idea!... Is she ready?... What?... What is it?... Tell her yer idea!" the other elves clamored excitedly for a moment then abruptly became silent.

There was a suggestive pause, which was broken by Alvey who suddenly waved his arms about, looked at me innocently, and announced grandly, "Why don't ye walk yer land?"

The whole group of elves burst into laughter and loud agreement, grabbing one another and dancing in little circles, hopping up and down.

They were laughing at me and I knew it. I was caught somewhere between embarrassment and a desire to burst into laughter and dance with them. But all I could do was stand there, watching in a dumb sort of way. In my mind I thought, "I suppose I can walk my land again. I guess I don't have to avoid that option just because I did so poorly the first time. Maybe I should take the approach that I am going to do better and turn a failure into a success. I tell other people to be patient with themselves, to keep at it, try again, maybe I should take my own advice..."

Aloud I said, "Well, okay, I guess..."

"Uh-oh.... No trust.... She ain't a believer.... Never gonna get results that way.... Don't count on her...." the voices of the elves cut through the wintry evening.

"All right! All right! I'll walk my land!" I said in a loud, confident voice. "No problem, I'll do it!" But as soon as I said it, I was flooded with doubts about my ability to follow through. I started to change my mind, then still talking to myself, told myself there was no reason I couldn't make an enthusiastic commitment.

The elves had quieted down and stood immobile, still holding each other in pairs and threes as if their dance had been interrupted. They were looking at me intently and it seemed as if all of them were gazing from under raised eyebrows.

I could tell by their faces that they didn't think I could do it either. "They know what I'm like now... What if I don't follow through...?" For a moment I felt about as secure in my commitment as a spider web in a hurricane. It occurred to me to simply admit that I had some concerns about myself and my ability to hold up my end of the bargain but what I really wanted was something more interesting to do than just walk.

Gazing meekly at Alvey, I said, "You know, last year I kept thinking I should do something more important, or..." The look on his face caused my voice to trail off into nothingness. I took a deep breath and started again, "Um... well... I never really knew how often to walk or what was enough..." The whole group continued to stare blankly and I stopped again.

In my mind I was sure they were just being difficult to test my resiliency, so I started one more time. "Alvey, I'll be happy to walk my land, but could we talk about this a little?" I asked.

"Ye've got the circle!" he replied, sweeping off his hat and bowing nearly to the ground. The other elves promptly formed a half circle around me and sat down expectantly.

"Well..." I stammered a little, "I didn't do very well walking my land during the coldest part of the winter last year. It's just really hard for me to get out here in December, January, and February. These hills are usually covered with snow and ice..."

"Ride that chattering, fire-breathing, smoke-belching contraption of yours called the Pumpkin," someone shouted. "The snow will melt in fright!" But the group shushed him up immediately, amid a few chuckles and murmured agreements.

Silently wondering if the Pumpkin was really such a nuisance to them, I continued with my suggestion, "So, how about if I walk from March through November on a regular basis? Would that be good enough?"

Alvey performed the sweeping bow again with even more precision, placed the hat back on his head, adjusted it once or twice, and then replied dramatically, "It's yer illusion, ma'am, set it up any way ye want!" The rest of the group burst into laughter and applause, after which Alvey continued amiably, "Whatever ye decide is fine. Just tell us what ye're going to do, then do it! Just do it!"

Although somewhat distracted by his manner and his words, I nodded. "Okay. The other thing is that I've really come to enjoy working in the grapes. Would I be guilty of trying to run things if I came out and worked now and then?"

"Nope!" Alvey answered with a short shake of his head.

"Why was it bad for me to work in them last year and this year it's okay?" I questioned.

"It wasn't bad last year! It just isn't productive to come out here feeling guilty about not doing what ye agreed to do in the first place, trying to make up for it by doing something else, then top it all off with dreams of glory and the idea that ye're lending yer wonderful energy to the grapes and they're a-growing because of something ye did all by yerself. The grapes respond well to positive, loving energy. They get sluggish and retarded in the presence of selfishness, anger, or fear."

"Oh," I said, stinging at the suggestion I was in it for the glory.

The wind was picking up and a low moan went through the dense circle of evergreens that grew around the pond. No one said anything for what seemed like a long time.

Humbly, and with a huge lump in my throat, I turned away from the elves to look at the ice again. When I turned back to them, I said, "I can't tell you how much I want to keep working with you. I'll walk and I'll come out here and work now and then, but I really am not at all certain I can do my end of things well, or that I can do it without selfishness. Maybe the deal should be that I'll walk and do whatever work I can find the time to enjoy, and you guys show me what you can do on your own. I mean, I really want to be your partner, but I'll be one of those hidden or silent partners. I'll leave it to you and just trust absolutely that whatever happens, it's perfect. I'll practice doing what I say, and trusting, and improving my belief in a hundred tons of grapes. You'll have my complete trust, love, and support until I learn how to do things on my end a little better. Okay?"

"Okay," said Alvey, nodding briefly, and then with one motion, he and the entire group of elves ambled forward, crowding closely around me. They copied my pose and my gaze, staring intently at the ice. I wondered if their mimicry was some kind of private joke, but the feeling in the air was one of an almost grateful acceptance of my desire to work with them and of my statement of trust.

The wind continued to moan and purr through the fir trees above us. Then abruptly the small assembly broke up. Shaking hands with one another and nodding pleasantly, the elves formed themselves into two lines, and I knew they were preparing to leave. It was quite dark as I turned to watch, nodding quietly to Alvey and Mairlinna.

Alvey, who was usually at the head of the group, was at the back when they all began to march past me in unison, breaking into the song, "Hi ho, hi ho, it's off to work we go, we'll see you here again next year, hi ho, hi ho, hi ho. Hi ho, hi ho, it's off to work we go…!"

I was amazed. It was the song from the Walt Disney film *Snow White and the Seven Dwarves*. The majority of the elves had marched past and Alvey was drawing even with where I stood so I said to him in delighted surprise, "Alvey… that song… where did you get that song…?"

Without missing a step he looked at me sideways and said nonchalantly, "It's yer illusion, lady, we're just trying to fit into it!" And with that, they disappeared up the hill in the settling darkness. I walked home, cold and curiously unnerved at Alvey's elaborate references to my illusion.

CHAPTER 12 ❧

In mid-February, Juan began trimming vines, and in no time at all had the front vineyard nearly done. Each day I told myself I was going to get outside and see how things were going. I wanted to do better in my agreement with Alvey than I had the previous year and thought perhaps I could get out for a few walks before March arrived. But early in the year I had gotten myself involved in writing a proposal for an "America 2000" educational grant and spent a near-frantic month working on it in order to meet the deadline. This put me behind in everything else, and I was scrambling to catch up with teaching my classes, the bookkeeping, and a large group of teachers I was working with. There was no time for walking.

Finally, I realized I was falling into the same trap I had gotten into last year. I didn't have to do more than I had agreed, I just had to do what I said I'd do. When March came I would be out there walking. At that, I relaxed and began to trust my new agreement with Alvey. For the moment, I did not need to walk my land or worry about doing so. Instead, I continued to work at getting caught up in my office and occasionally went for imaginary walks, trying to send loving thoughts to the vines whenever I thought of them. I also sent frequent mental messages to Alvey, telling him how pleased I was to be able to work with him and the elves.

Ernie came by and offered to do a little bit of trimming for us, then went out to the vineyard to see how the vines had fared over the winter. He came back shaking his head in surprise and said, "You've got no winter-kill on your canes! This is the first vineyard I've seen that doesn't have any. Almost looks like you didn't have winter here!" When he left I sent more messages to Alvey thanking him for any part he may have played in the extraordinarily healthy condition of our vines that would have allowed them to resist damage from freezing.

The winter had been particularly dreary, and the sun had disappeared for weeks at a time. The weather alternated between short blasts of frigid cold and snow, then unexpectedly mild, but very gray and damp days. As I worked to catch up in the office and with other business, I waited for blue skies and sunshine to make an appearance and beckon me to the vineyards. But the skies remained gray and the sun slept on, far past the beginning of March.

Because of the alternating warm and cold spells, everyone complained and worried that the grape buds would open too early then freeze. But by the time spring officially arrived, the weather got colder and stayed cold. Between the heavy demands of my educational consulting and the comfortable trust in my agreement with Alvey, I did not worry much at all. I simply kept reaffirming the thought, "I trust you, Alvey!" while I sent warm and loving thoughts to the vines.

Around the third week of March, I went out for my first walk. I was determined to keep up my end of our agreement and for some reason everything seemed so much easier than it had seemed the year before. Maybe it was because I had a workable agreement. Perhaps it was the fact that I didn't feel responsible for all the physical work. Whatever the reason, I felt calm and at ease.

In fact, it seemed as if everyone was trying to help just to make sure I didn't try to do it all myself. When the heavier work in the grapes began, my daughter, Kelly Anne, agreed to play "wife" and keep all of us supplied with food and drink, answer phones, and run errands. This left Jim and me free to work long, uninterrupted hours in the vineyards. Kelly's husband, Mike, was home on leave from the Army and helped in the grapes as well. Ernie did some of the posting and trimming. Jim's dad, Ray, worked everywhere doing whatever was needed whether in the vineyards, the barn, or the house. I marveled at the wonderful sense of cooperation and the let's-get-it-done attitude maintained by everyone.

The rest of March passed, then all of April, and it was still incredibly cold and wet. The sun did not appear for weeks at a time and the local grape growers went from worrying about grape buds that might open too early to relentless warnings that they were opening too late. From the tone of their voices in the Vineyard Cafe, it was clear that they were somewhere between aggravated and philosophical.

Jim and I did not pay much attention to the weather. We were too grateful for the delayed spring. It allowed us to finish replacing old and rotten posts, get the grapes tied, get the fertilizer on and tilled in, and bury long-arms to replace missing vines, all before the buds began to appear. It was the first time since we had bought the farm that we were done before the spray season began.

As May arrived Jim and I began to discuss whether we needed to spray, not spray, talk to the vines, talk to the weeds, or get some concessions from the elves and their don't-spray attitude. The year before, we had agonized over what to do and ended up with a considerable amount of confusion, doubt, and disagreement. This year was not starting out much different as far as spraying was concerned.

I did not want to spray anything. In my mind, if Alvey said it was harmful, we should skip it. But Jim insisted we would have to spray if anything serious happened. Problems with insects, a serious case of some fungus disease, like black rot or powdery mildew, or weeds that seemed to grow out of all proportion to the grapes—in his mind these were serious enough to warrant abandonment of our no-chemical-sprays policy in an effort to rescue the crop. Back and forth we went. He insisted I was being naive and impractical. I insisted he was caught in rigid fears and just unwilling to believe that everything would be okay. So, I went for a walk to see if I could find Alvey and ask him what to do. I was sure he would be on my side.

I strolled along the lane toward the back block of grapes, thinking I would go up on Golden Mountain to look for them. But just as I reached the second hickory nut tree, a small, scruffy elf jumped out at me from behind the tree and proclaimed loudly, "Follow yer usual practices! Follow yer usual practices!"

Startled, my heart was pounding as he disappeared behind the tree and I didn't even get a chance to ask if he was answering my question about the vineyards. But assuming he was, I turned around and headed back to the house.

"He had to be referring to the vineyard spray practices because that was the question I had in my mind when I went out there," I thought. But I wondered if he was referring to the usual confusion of the past year, or the unquestioning spray practices we had followed when we first arrived at the farm.

As for usual practices, I went around and around again with Jim. It wasn't so much that we had permission to do it the way we had always done it. It was the issue of trust and my worry that there might be serious lessons to come, lessons born of our ignorance. We were trying to do things more in tune with nature. We wanted to respect the abilities of other forms of life to adapt. We wanted to tell others they could take up practices that were less dependent on chemicals and unnatural additives. We wanted to please the elves. We wanted to please Ernie who wanted to get our spray program started.

In the end, I came to the conclusion that for now, all we had to do was trust. We would spray, since that was our "usual practice," and then any change for the better would have to be attributed to Alvey, Mother Nature, and the energies and spirit of the vines in response to trust and loving care.

By the second week of May the long-awaited spring began to show signs of activity and grape buds began to swell and break open. I worked in my perennial garden, then my vegetable garden, then went for a walk. Everything was strangely quiet. I had the sense of being absolutely alone and cut off from all of the forms of intelligence and energy that had been so much a part of my life over the past year and a half. When I was working in my office, or at a meeting, I was often far too busy to think about my experiences with nature and her generally unseen creatures. Now, taking a walk, I had the strange impression that the elves, the devas, and other small forms of energy were "in a meeting" of their own, or just too busy to deal with me. I was aware of how drab everything seemed without the bright energy of their presence. For the first time I was deeply aware of how much they had brought to my life.

By the fourth week of May it was clear that spring had not yet made up her mind to stay. We were still having alternating periods of somewhat warmish and then very cold weather. Now the weatherman predicted that the thermometer was going to dip well below freezing. At first I found myself trying hard not to be concerned. Finally, I relaxed. I sent a mental message to Alvey and friends telling them, "I know it is supposed to be cold—but I trust you completely. This is your year!" Then, as if no threat to the grapes existed at all, I truly forgot about it.

That night, just before I went to bed, I noticed that the wind was picking up and the trees were swaying and bending dramatically. I knew that nothing would freeze with the wind blowing that hard and then I slept like a child.

The thermometer registered twenty-seven degrees when I got up the next morning, but I still had no concern about our grapes and the delicate condition of the buds and young leaves that had so recently appeared. The forecast for that day and the next night was just as cold, maybe colder. I just kept reaffirming, "I trust you, Alvey... I trust that the grapes are fine... I trust... because I know." That night, I waited up until midnight, expecting the wind to begin blowing. But there was no wind and soon I was too tired to hold the vigil.

The next morning I woke in the silence of a rosy dawn to find the temperature was twenty-six degrees. There was still no wind blowing at all yet I had the calm thought, "It's okay, I trust."

I turned on the radio and when the news and weather came on, the newsman talked of the serious freezes of the past two nights and the serious damage to grape crops in the Fruit Belt that stretched up the west coast of Michigan. I felt as if the reality he was referring to had no connection to me, our farm or our grapes. I thanked Alvey for whatever he had done to protect our grapes and then went about my day.

Toward evening I went outside to work in my perennial garden and before long Ernie drove up. He opened the window of his pickup truck and I walked over to talk to him, leaning on my hoe.

"Hi, been out to look at your frost damage?" he asked.

"No, not yet," I replied, then added an afterthought, "I don't think we have any."

"No?" he said, raising his eyebrows, then proceeding to rattle off a list of grape growers and the damage they had suffered. The damages seemed to range between 10 percent and 40 percent for the most part, but a few had suffered over 50 percent and even greater losses, and as he talked I wondered if I had been a little too optimistic.

We talked about other things and finally he said he was going to drive out to our vineyards and take a look but would come back around and let me know what he thought.

Ten minutes later he was back, literally bouncing in his seat. Through the open window of his truck he yelled out at me with excitement, "Not a leaf! Not a single leaf was touched!"

It occurred to me to ask him how much damage his vineyards had sustained. He grinned at me and said, "Nothing, not a bit of damage for me either. You and me are about the only ones in this area to come through okay though."

As he drove off I felt a mix of emotions. He had been as pleased as I was, and I was certain he had brought his own magic and love of grapes to our vineyards as a gift he was willing to share if we were willing to accept.

At the last of May, Ernie started our spray program. When he finished with both vineyards he came into the barn, stood in the doorway of my office, hat in hand, and said enthusiastically, "Lady, you have got a C-R-O-P out there in that vineyard! Looks to me like you're gonna have a good six tons per acre, maybe more if Mother Nature is willing!" He always gave full recognition to Mother Nature, even nodding his head when he mentioned her name and acknowledging that she had the final say in whatever humans tried to wrest from the face of the earth.

I was delighted and asked him how he estimated the tonnage so early. He explained that it was based on the number of clusters per vine. In a vineyard[7] approximately twenty clusters of grapes on each vine would result in a total crop of one ton of grapes per acre. Forty clusters per vine would get you two tons of grapes per acre, sixty clusters on each vine would bring three tons per acre, and so on. He said he had counted between 120 and 130 clusters on a few vines and that they all had shoulders—a tiny cluster that grew off to the side of the main cluster, up near the stem of each bunch. Shoulders on every cluster would add an average of one ton of grapes per acre, he told me.

I told him I would go out and take a look sometime in the next day or two and he left, smiling as if it was his vineyard. I smiled after him thinking that in some ways it really was his vineyard. If it weren't for Ernie prodding, reminding and supporting us, we would never have learned how to care for grapes at all!

True to my word, I went for a walk through the grapes a few days later. The number of clusters per vine was astounding. I counted 123 clusters, with shoulders, on the first vine. The second had 135, and I lost count after 150 on the third vine. Of course, the young vines here and there that were only two or

---

7   There are approximately 500 vines in one acre of grapes.

three years old had much less, but even some of these babies with only one or two skinny canes had forty and fifty clusters each!

"Imagine the grapes we could have if they all get pollinated!" I mused as I returned to the barn. And in what had become a nearly automatic response, I sent a flood of loving thoughts and trust to both the vines and Alvey and company.

When things began to slow down in the office a bit, I took the opportunity to work in the vineyard. I cut off suckers, buried long arms that had been missed in the first round, and trained new vines up to the trellis. There was no sign of the elves or Harvey, nor did any devas or other nature spirits come around. When no one answered my calls, I felt lonely but continued to work quietly. And before I left the vineyard each evening, I sat in silent meditation for just a few moments, sending love, trust, and what I hoped was a sense of joy to the vines and an affirmation of trust to Alvey.

It was approaching dusk one beautiful July evening as I came out of Spanish class so I went for a walk through the vineyards when I got home. It had been drab, cool, and quite overcast for summertime and even though today was one of the few episodes of warmth and sunshine so far, all of nature was unusually quiet. No wind, not even any animal sounds could be heard except for the startled flutter of several birds who had settled under the vines for the night and who took off in fright as I passed. One of them nearly ran into the side of my head as I went slowly down the row, my eyes moving appraisingly over each vine.

When I headed toward the back of the property, the sun was down, but it was still light. Near the second hickory tree I looked across the landscape in a strangely detached way, aware of the flat silence everywhere. I felt as if I were in another world, a silent place without life. Everything looked plain and weary, the air, the trees, the bean field, the hills that rose tiredly here and there.

I thought about that first time on Golden Mountain when the world had lit up with an incredible golden light and I had been overwhelmed with wishes for peace, beauty, love, and bounty. That had seemed like a magical time. Now, in sharp contrast, everything seemed dull, drab, and dead.

I shook myself. Why was there such a difference in my perception lately? It was like seeing two possible expressions of reality. One was drab and silent, the other filled with sparkling, golden, musical joy. Were there people who always saw the flat, dull world I was seeing now? People who saw only the hard, dark surfaces of physical reality? People who had never seen the world light up or had never experienced a single magical or mystical moment? What would they think if I came trotting along, talking about elves and discussing devas? Would they put me away if I insisted I had once been a dragonfly and played half the night with another dragonfly named Harvey—who was not really a dragonfly but some kind of half-man with hooves instead of feet and a set of horns tucked under his hat!

Thoughts of Harvey began to move around my mind, and I said aloud to no one in particular, "Hey Harvey, sure would be good to see you again, old pal. It's been too long!"

Less than ten seconds later I was startled out of my reverie when something loud and buzzing brushed against my hair and landed on my left shoulder. Arms flapping and with a small scream of fright I jumped crazily, slapping at whatever had landed on me and shaking my hair violently.

To my horror a large dragonfly slumped toward the ground then lifted with great effort. After flying in a crooked circle around my head, it disappeared in the deepening twilight.

"Oh my god!" I exclaimed, feeling another kind of horror. "Harvey, was that you? I'm sorry! I didn't mean it…. You scared me…. I didn't expect you to respond so quickly…. Was that really you…. I'm so sorry, please don't be upset with me."

I stood looking toward the back vineyard and agonized for a minute over whether I should go all the way to the top of Golden Mountain in the gathering dusk or give it up for the night. The high-pitched whine of what sounded like thousands of mosquitoes helped me decide. Either I had walked into a cloud of them, or by standing still, they had discovered me while looking for a meal. I turned and ran all the way back to the barn where I closed up for the night then walked to the house and went to bed, tired, discouraged, and disappointed with the flat conclusion of what had started out as a beautiful evening.

CHAPTER 13 &

Rain had been in the forecast all day yesterday and the day before. Now, the air was gray and humid and looked like it might turn into rain any minute. The weeds in my vegetable garden were getting tall. I knew they would quickly get out of control if I had to wait for several days of rain and several days of drying out before I could do the needed rototilling. I had intended to get out there and till for several days but had too many appointments, so I sent a plea to the wind and the rain to please hold off until my schedule was clear. I promised that if they'd wait, I'd get up early on Thursday morning and begin the tilling immediately, which I did.

By 7:00 A.M. I was in the garden behind the rototiller, making my way slowly down each row. I worked without stopping and by noon I was finished.

After putting the tiller away, I thanked both wind and rain, telling them it was okay to begin raining, if they wanted to. Quite promptly, before I even got to the house, it began to sprinkle. By the time I got into the shower it was raining, thundering, and lightning.

The rain continued for the rest of the afternoon while I worked in my office, appreciating the rain and the chance to get some paperwork done. The morning's experience made me feel cared for by all of nature. I kept feeling an odd oneness with everything—the grapes, the earth, the various elements of the weather—like a husband and wife who had grown accustomed to one another. I was acutely aware that it was because of the seeming response the rain, wind, and sun had made each time I needed them to cooperate. It was oddly comforting to think they cared.

The time in the office also gave me a chance to pursue something that had been on my mind. While looking for the book on Findhorn, and information on companion gardening a year earlier, I happened to come across something called the 1991 Moon Sign Book. It offered guidelines on planting certain vegetables and fruits during certain phases of the moon, so I sent for it. When I first got it, I went right to the charts I was looking for, ignoring the rest of the book. Months later I happened to be browsing through it and read about a fellow named Dan Carlson who was getting fantastic results in his gardens and fields with something he had developed called Sonic Bloom. It was a combination of special music frequencies played in the fields and organic nutrients sprayed on the plants.

The information stuck in my mind and had come up several times, but I was always too busy to look up the paragraph I had read and follow up on it. Now I took the time to find the book and call the number listed for information. To my surprise I got hold of Dan directly and talked with him about our grapes. He said he thought Sonic Bloom would do wonders for our grapes by increasing both the fruit set and the sugar level. After the conversation, I was even more curious. I sent for the video, a small spray kit, and whatever other information he had available. Once my order was in the mail, I couldn't wait to get it. For some reason I couldn't concentrate on anything else, and when the rain ended in the early evening, I went for a walk.

On my way through the back vineyard I met Alvey and the rest of the elves, all of whom seemed delighted to see me. I told Alvey about my conversation with Dan Carlson, then asked if he thought Sonic Bloom treatments might be a reasonable addition to our vineyard practices. It was spraying, but it was an organic nutrient spray. And the music seemed harmless.

"We never know what ye folks might come up with next," he drolled, "but occasionally it is a real gift."

"I sent for a video and a small spray kit to try it out," I told him. "If nothing happens we'll know… and… well, I'm going to try it in my vegetable garden and with my house plants. You can all come up and see for yourselves."

I left soon after and they seemed to have their heads together as if I had said something of great importance to them. They waved good-bye as if it were an afterthought and Mairlinna reminded me that I should be keeping notes of everything that happened.

I went back to the office and gathered my notes. Once I had them all in a pile I was surprised. Perhaps I had been upset with myself and my career for no reason. Perhaps I had been looking at the glass that was half-empty rather than half-full. More than a year ago I had quit writing to work in the vineyards. When three major educational consulting contracts were canceled, I panicked. I had no income from writing to look forward to, none coming in from educational consulting, and no guarantees of a grape crop big enough to make up for the losses of income. But staring at the pile of notes accumulated over a year and nine months it dawned on me that I had pages and pages of notes in dated diary form about my encounters with the elves and what I had learned from them. For the first time the thought crossed my mind that maybe I would end up with a book after all! I began organizing and compiling the notes with the suddenly serious intent to at least review what we had done and evaluate what we had learned from it. Anything else would be a welcome bonus.

July meandered onward with a lovely day once or twice, but for the most part the weather had been cold and gloomy. Everything, both in the grapes and my consulting work, seemed to be business as usual and had been that way for weeks. But there was a sweet humming sound around me wherever I went, and I alternated between two images that ran through my mind constantly. One was the golden world of the elves I had seen several times either on the hill or while in the vineyard. It was a world humming with a sort of lyrical joyousness and lighted by a different kind of light. The other was the flat, dull, gray-green world I had observed on the same hill and in that same vineyard.

This other world was relatively silent and lifeless. Each time I went for a walk, I was struck by the dull, ordinary appearance of the fields and the vineyards. It was such a sharp contrast to the pictures I carried in my mind whenever I thought about the grapes, the elves, or our farm.

Suddenly, I was keenly aware of something that seemed crucial—that what we bring to our reality is all-important! It was true for us both personally and as members of a group. The significance of Alvey's words, "It's your illusion!" now seemed overwhelming. What I had often said as an educational consultant was doubly true for creating a personal reality. It was not possible to teach someone something unless they already knew at least a little bit about what you were trying to teach! In other words, the learner had to bring something of his or her own knowing to the learning situation. Teaching important truths and facts to someone who had no awareness of the subject was a waste of time. The information would fall on deaf ears because there were no pegs, or areas of awareness, in the learner's mind on which to hang the new information.

It dawned anew, as it had many times in the past, that we were, individually and collectively, creating our own reality and that we could change it far more than we thought we could. This renewal of an old awareness was layered and dressed with an avalanche of new meanings that swept me into a state of exquisite clarity, a state that seemed to be in sharp contrast to much of what I observed in people everywhere. Why were so many stuck in flat, meaningless lives? "Being stuck" was an appropriate description of people whose perception always tuned in to the same view of reality, like a television set whose dial refused to turn and was stuck on only one channel. Why didn't we realize that this stuck perception created much strife and stress for ourselves? Blaming the other guy for what we, ourselves, perceived was useless and circular. Where was our human magic? Where was our power? What were we bringing to our perception? Was it the expectation of a dull, flat, already-programmed reality— or the bright, joyous view of an ever-evolving world? Why didn't more people realize that what we brought to our reality helped to confirm and create our actual experience of it?

At that moment the entire planet seemed full of terminally handicapped creators. The whole situation was tragic, and I ended up going for a walk, feeling really blue for the first time in months. For the second time in my life, my reality was changing at a quick pace, but others were still hanging on to their single-channel awareness with a fierceness that was bewildering. They appeared to live for their limitations, and any thoughts that I could teach them some of the things I was learning from the elves seemed like naive fantasies.

The summer was more than half over and it had been nothing but chilly, wet, and drab. The grapes were ripening slowly, and toward the end of the first week in August, the rain stopped long enough to let me work in the small orchard west of the house. It felt good to get outside.

We had received a letter from Welch stating that this year's crop would be substantially lower in tonnage and slightly later in maturing because of the weather. Ernie had dropped by, waving his copy of the letter and pointing out that we'd better get some sunshine soon or the grapes would never make sugar. I hadn't thought of that possibility, but did renew my vow of trust that everything would work out fine. Later that day, I took the Pumpkin out to go through the rows and look at the clusters. They were a long way from ripe. I simply sent a message to Alvey that I trusted him and his friends implicitly.

Toward the end of August, it was time to estimate our total grape tonnage and send it in to Welch. I went out in the vineyard on a warm, sunny afternoon, one of only a handful of such afternoons we'd had all summer. I was hoping to take a good look at both vines and grapes and make what I hoped was an educated guess.

But I ended up sitting on top of Golden Mountain looking over the hillsides of grapes when I heard Alvey and whole group of elves coming up the hill. I waved and they waved back. They gathered on the hilltop with me and sat down in a pile, nearly on top of one another, just as they had done in my office last year.

"And how might ye be these days?" Alvey inquired cheerily.

"Okay," I replied, then asked how they were.

"Splendid!" they chorused, then sat there looking at me with one of those attitudes that left me feeling I was being examined.

"We've got a lot of grapes this year," I mentioned to Alvey.

"Yep," he nodded, "it's a plentiful crop… and going be real sweet when ye bring them in."

I gave him a sidelong glance and wondered if he always knew what was on my mind. "Are they?" I asked.

"Are they what?" he countered.

"Are they going to be real sweet when it's time to harvest?" I looked at him directly. "This has been the coolest, darkest summer I can ever remember. We haven't had more than ten days of sunshine since last May. The old-timers are saying we're never gonna make it. The bigger the crop, the harder it is for the leaves to make enough sugar for the berries. We've got a big crop and no sun, and Welch is wanting to start sugar tests already."

Alvey lay back in the tall grass and was a study in nonchalance. He adjusted his hat to shade his eyes and breathed a long sigh of enjoyment. "It's going to be a long, warm autumn," he murmured, "with lots of good, warm sunshine. Yer grapes are going to be just fine."

In my mind I knew it was going to be a great crop but felt a sense of relief wash over me in hearing Alvey say it was going to be a long, warm fall.

"I trust you," I remarked, realizing that the trust was there but had needed a little shoring up.

A light buzz of conversation broke out among the group of elves. They exchanged views on where we might plant more trees and more grapes. Alvey continued to lie back in the grass, and I listened to the chatter but was caught up in the unusual pleasure of the sun on my face and the smell of the warm, wet earth rising around me. My eyes closed in a moment of relaxed joy and when I opened them I was alone on the hill.

I went back to the barn and when it was time to fill out the postcard from Welch, estimating our grape tonnage, I just didn't have the guts to write one hundred tons of grapes. Instead I wrote seventy-seven tons, which was what we had gotten the first year when I was sure we had been blessed with beginner's luck.

One by one the weeks ticked by until five of them had passed since I had talked to Alvey and the group of elves. In five days September would be over. I had been waiting every day for some version of a long, warm autumn to begin. The temperature had been generally a little bit warmer than we'd had all summer, but there were only a few days of sunshine here and there.

I was supposed to take a grape sample up to the Welch plant for sugar test-ing, but I couldn't. I knew I was avoiding bad news, but I told myself I just didn't have the time. The grapes were finally all purple, but not sweet enough at all.

Long ago, before widespread use of chemical fertilizers and insecticides, it had been common for grape-growers to produce grapes having 20 to 24 per-cent sugar content. For unknown reasons, sugar content began to slip lower and lower. Finally, Welch put their foot down and set the standard grape-sugar content at no less than 16 percent. Grapes less than the standard received less money per ton. Neither would they accept grapes with sugar lower than 14.7 percent, although there was no upper limit that I knew of. But they would be extremely lucky to get 15 percent sugar on the average this year.

I was waffling about taking a sample of our grapes up to the Welch plant for a sugar test when our neighbor to the west, Ira, stopped by unexpectedly to talk grapes and taxes. His wife was the one who had called and told me of their unexpected bumper crop last year. So I asked him how they were doing this year. He had another bumper crop this year, almost 300 tons of grapes on his thirty acres. Even though that was between nine and ten tons per acre, his sugar had just tested at only between 11 and 12 percent—a very low figure. He said he was sure he was going to lose the whole crop and would probably end up get-ting only what he could get from his crop disaster insurance.

When I told him we had a big crop too, he asked, "What're you hanging?"

"I think it's around seventy tons, at least," I told him.

"No way!" he blinked in surprise. "Your vineyards have never produced that kind of tonnage!"

"Sure they did—once! We had seventy-seven tons the first year we were here. Of course, we dropped way off after that, but last year we were up to fifty-six. This year we've got even more."

"No kidding?" he shook his head. "I've been here a long time and I've never heard of your vineyards producing more than thirty or forty tons of grapes." It was my turn to be surprised.

We talked a bit longer about taxes, government, how quickly land was being bought and sold around the Lawton area, and how many houses were going up. After he left, I pondered his comment about the history of our vine-yard's grape production. Maybe the elves and I had done better than we knew with fifty-six tons.

I also pondered the possibility that our grapes might not be accepted by Welch because of low sugar. If it took one week of sunshine to raise the sugar count one percentage point, also known commercially as one brix of sugar, it was my guess that we needed four to five weeks of nothing but sun to meet the Welch minimum of sixteen brix. Even if Welch put off harvest until the end of October, there was no guarantee that we'd have enough sun or that we wouldn't have a catastrophic freeze complete with sleet, snow, and ice.

The next day, Ernie came by in the early afternoon and said that farmers all over Lawton and Paw Paw were in a panic because their grapes were testing so low for sugar. According to him, Welch usually put together some kind of substitute program for accepting grapes with low sugar, but this year the only thing they had done was to schedule another sugar test. After he left, I looked at the calendar and realized that every year was a unique challenge. Last year our grapes were all harvested by this time. This year we would probably see most of October come and go before the grapes were in.

Five more days went by, and it was now October. The weatherman was not cooperating with Alvey's prediction of a warm, sunny autumn. I couldn't put off the sugar test any longer. I climbed in the Pumpkin and drove slowly through the vineyards, collecting what I hoped was a fair sampling of grapes from each. Then I drove to town and pulled up to the sugar shack at the Welch plant.

The results were a shock even though I thought I was prepared. The front block of grapes was only at 13 percent. The back block tested at 13.5 percent. What a let-down! All I could think was that we finally had a decent-sized crop and now we wouldn't be able to benefit from it because we wouldn't make enough sugar.

As soon as I returned from the Welch plant, I went out looking for the elves. They weren't in any of their usual locations so I wandered over toward the pond, calling out from time to time. When they weren't around the pond either, I walked back toward the house, detouring through the front block of grapes and thinking I would spread some encouragement to the vines to keep producing sugar. As I moved along Row Twelve, I discovered Alvey and the entire group sitting in a circle in an area that formed a natural opening because several vines were missing.

Alvey, Mairlinna, Kermots, and the whole group jumped up to greet me with their never-failing smiles and wishes for health and good luck. Without preamble I interrupted them and launched into the results of the sugar test and the stories floating around town that this year was a disaster for grapes—first the late start last spring, then the bad freezes at the end of May, then the lack of sun and warmth during the growing season resulting in the low sugar.

The entire group grew silent and after a minute or two I realized they were staring at me questioningly. I became aware that I sounded like I had lost my trust and at that point I stopped altogether.

In one motion the group turned and sat down in the circle they had been in when I got there. I knew they were ignoring me, and for a minute I didn't know what to do.

It came to me at some other-than-conscious level that I should start over so I pardoned myself for interrupting and, speaking as politely and cheerfully as I could, I greeted Alvey and the group as if for the first time. They jumped up and repeated their original greetings and when they were done I said to Alvey, "I took in two grape samples this morning and they tested at 13 percent and 13.5 percent sugar. The word is that Welch is starting up the harvest next Monday and will not accept anything less than 14.7 percent. We are right on the edge of success here. Our grapes need about two more weeks of sunshine and warm weather to be safely in the acceptable range. I just thought I'd let you guys know how we're doing and where we're at with the crop."

The entire group jumped up and down and gathered around me excitedly. "Now that's what I call working together.... It sure is thoughtful of ye to be working this way with us.... We don't get much response from yer world.... Now we know just what we need to do here.... Sunshine—that's what we need... a big dose of sun each day for the next week or so!...." They chattered on amiably.

Alvey bowed low as if he were acknowledging my report. When he straightened up there was such a gleam in his eyes that I was transfixed.

"Do ye think we're going to make it?" he inquired with an air of judicial circumspection.

"Certainly!" I nodded without hesitation. "I trust you guys with every bone in my body," I continued, even though my faith had been seriously scattered only ten minutes earlier.

They all nodded, then abruptly returned to their circle, everyone except Alvey, Kermots, and Mairlinna, who just stood there looking at me. After a very uncertain pause, I said I would be back to let them know how we were doing after taking in the next grape sample.

They thanked me quite graciously for the visit and I left, wondering if they were planning to test my belief and trust to the limit.

The next day was a Friday. Ernie drove up that evening and rushed in with the news that Welch was definitely going to start harvesting Concords on Monday. His son, Dave, did the harvesting in our vineyards as well as quite a few others. Since so few grape farmers had been able to meet the sugar standard, hardly anyone wanted Dave to start in their vineyard right away on Monday. Ernie was out scouting, looking for anyone who was ready, but everyone was buying time, hoping for a miracle.

Even though the weatherman was predicting record cold, snow, and freezing rain for the coming week, I decided that we were not going to panic and take our grapes off before they were ready. I sent Ernie, who was in quite a state of turmoil, out the door with the calm reassurance that everything was going to be just fine, and that we just weren't ready to harvest yet. But after he was gone I could feel the pressure mounting.

The harvest began as scheduled on Monday, and on Tuesday, Ernie came by again, hoping we had changed our minds about taking our grapes off. A quick conference between Jim and me resulted in a decision to hold the line, so I turned to Ernie and said, "No, not yet."

Ernie told us that Welch couldn't get any grapes that had enough sugar, and worse, they were rejecting load after load. He wanted to know what the results of our most recent sugar test had been and I told him I hadn't done another one since I last talked to him. When he left, Jim and I looked at each other silently, both of us thinking the same thing—what if we delayed too long and ended up with no crop at all? I renewed my pledge of trust but around the edges of my mind I wondered....

The snow and rain predicted by the weatherman did not appear and we ended up with a solid week of sunshine. However, we also had the first serious freezes. I finally took our second sample of grapes up to Welch for a sugar test and was thrilled to have them test out at 13.8 percent in the front block and 14.5 percent in the back block.

When the tests were over I hurried back home and immediately headed for the back of the farm, looking for Alvey and his friends. For once they were at home in the area they had asked us to leave wild and a number of them came out immediately when I called.

"I took another grape sample in for testing and we've moved up! The front vineyard is up to 13.8 percent and the back is up to 14.5 percent. We're almost there, Alvey, we just need about one more week of sun!" I was still out of breath from the quick walk and the excitement.

The elves caught my excitement and jumped up and down, clapping hands and congratulating one another.

Catching my breath at last, I repeated that if we could get one more week of sunshine our grapes could be harvested without losing a single berry. They nodded in agreement, someone said, "Of course, just a little more sun…!" and I left after a hurried good-bye, feeling more hopeful than I had in weeks and renewing my trust with enthusiasm.

CHAPTER 14 ❧

The next seven days dragged by. Most of them were damp, cool, and overcast with thin, meager sunshine. A few of those days were clear but sharply cold. Overall it seemed more wintry with each passing hour. I felt like a captive in an hourglass pushing slow-moving grains of sand through a too-small opening. Fussing about the lack of sun on the overcast days and the unseasonable cold on the clear days, the grapes hung in my mind from sunrise until sundown and beyond, until I was keyed to a near fever pitch.

Ernie came by again, urging us to get on Dave's harvesting schedule. The answer was still not yet. Over and over I renewed my trust in the elves but found myself wondering if I should prepare to lose the crop—just in case.

It was now the middle of October and early on a Thursday afternoon. It had been one of the longest weeks I could ever remember, worse than the week before Christmas for a five-year-old. Ernie was now coming by every day, sometimes twice, asking if we had another sugar test done and telling us it was important to get on Dave's harvest schedule. Jim kept deferring to me to give the word that it was time to harvest, but I was determined to hold out until it felt like the right time. Ernie left, but said he'd be back later that day and I felt that somehow his constant pressure to harvest the grapes was another part of some test we had to pass. After all, Ernie was so much wiser and had so much more experience with the grapes. It almost seemed like the elves had managed to put me in the middle between them and Ernie, just to see if I would listen to myself all while trusting them.

It was early evening and almost dark when Ernie did come back, telling us that cold and snow were forecast again. "Those grapes aren't going to get any riper in this kind of weather," he pointed out, and all of a sudden I agreed with him.

"Maybe you're right, let's go ahead and take them off," I told him.

"Are you sure?" Jim asked, looking at me in a most direct fashion.

"I don't know… I think so… I think Ernie's right," I spoke unenthusiastically at first. But then a rush of conviction filled me. "They're probably about as ripe as they're going to get. We might as well go for it!"

Ernie left shortly after, telling us Dave would stop by to do his own sugar test and see how things looked. After he left, I renewed my trust in the elves and decided I had to talk to them immediately. It was already dark and extremely cold when I went out looking for them. I came home disappointed, unable to find them anywhere.

The next day was Friday and Dave came by early in the day to do a sugar test with small samples from both vineyards. The news was good and bad. Grapes from the back were registering a whopping 15 percent sugar count and above, well over the 14.7 percent minimum. But grapes from the front vineyard were still just below minimum. I felt panicky and was sure half the crop would be rejected.

It was not until late afternoon that I had another chance to put on my winter coat and go looking for Alvey and his group. I had been all through the back vineyard, up, over, and down Golden Mountain, and around the pond before I found them. They were just coming out of the woods north of the pond where they trooped along cheerfully. I waited patiently for all the greetings and good wishes to be bestowed.

When it seemed appropriate I announced, "Alvey, we're going to harvest the grapes."

Before I could say any more the whole group erupted in shouts of joy.

"Whee-e-e and yessiree-e-e!... Hooray!... Harvest time!"

I wanted to join them, but couldn't quite muster the sense of excitement. I knew I had a lame smile on my face but it was the best I could do. When they continued to cheer and dance I had a fleeting moment of irritation and realized that I didn't know how to ask them if the grapes were really ready without admitting my doubt. I was afraid they would think I didn't trust that everything would turn out perfectly.

I stewed about how to ask what I wanted to know and in frustration interrupted their merriment.

"Alvey, not all the grapes are ready. There hasn't been much sun this week and it's really been cold. Almost everything from the front vineyard is below the minimum. Thousands of tons of grapes are still being rejected by Welch and dumped to rot in the fields. Should we go ahead?... I think we're next on Dave's schedule and... are we ready? Should we wait? Is there anything else you guys can do to help bring up the sugar? I don't know what to do and I'm sure we're right on the edge and..."

The entire group had quieted to dead silence but all were shaking their heads ever so slightly.

"There's nothing more we can do," Alvey said in the most forlorn of voices. "The rest is up to ye," he added and heaved a loud, melodramatic sigh.

Then without warning the entire group headed off in the same direction they had been going when I found them. Alvey was the last to leave and as he moved away he glanced up at me. "It's yer illusion!" he said with a grin and gave me a huge wink.

My mouth dropped open, and I stood there for several minutes after they left, pondering the meaning of his last remark and that dramatic wink.

All the way back to the barn I wrestled with that wink. I was certain that they knew something they weren't telling me.

As soon as I entered the barn, Jim asked if I had found them and what they had said.

"They said there was nothing more they can do. And they didn't say whether we should go ahead or wait. But Alvey gave me this huge wink and I just keep having the feeling that I'm supposed to know what to do... but I don't know..." I paused, still seeing that wink clearly in my mind's eye. "I don't know what it would be...."

I walked toward my office in some combination of frustration and resignation. "Maybe I'll call up to the Welch plant. Maybe they're going to offer some kind of payment program for low sugar grapes and we just haven't heard about it yet."

"Why call them?" Jim asked in a tone that said clearly he thought it was a bad idea. "They aren't the ones who'd be making the decision! That decision comes from New York."

"I don't know, it just seems like a good idea. Maybe they can tell us something." I was already at the phone, dialing the number of the National Grape Co-operative office in Lawton.

Jim followed me, objecting more strenuously. "Who are you going to talk to and what are you going to ask? Are you going to complain and say it's not fair, that you want them to take your grapes no matter what the sugar is? They're probably closed anyway, it's after five o'clock already...."

A voice on the other end of the phone said hello, and I was immediately uncertain of what to say. I felt pressured from all sides. Jim was walking away in great irritation, and I wondered if he was right and I would end up sounding like a whining fool. There was pressure from the voice on the other end of the phone that said "Hello?" a second time. But the biggest pressure of all was the memory of that huge wink.

"Um, hello," I began uncertainly, "My name is Penny Kelly and my husband and I are grape growers. We're about to have Dave Moore harvest our grapes and not all of them are ripe enough to meet minimum sugar so, um, I was wondering if anyone over there knew whether Welch was going to put out a last-minute offer for low-sugar grapes?"

"I don't rightly know," the voice said. "Welch has already accepted all the low sugar grapes they can take. And the wineries in the area are not taking any more either."

"Do you have any idea who might know if something like that was in the works?" I pushed, unwilling to give up.

"Well," he said, "best person to talk to might be Morley Matheson, but he's not here right now."

Jim had returned to the door of my office and stood silent and disapproving, but listening.

"Do you know where Mr. Matheson is or how I could reach him?" I pressed on.

"Well, he might still be over in the sugar shack," he offered, "would you like me to transfer you over there?"

"Would you, please?" I answered gratefully.

There was a click, a short silence, and I was certain I would either be disconnected or that no one would answer. Then another voice boomed, "Hello?"

"Hi," I responded, "this is Penny Kelly and I was looking for Morley Matheson, is he there?"

"Well, hi, Penny Kelly, this is Tim Taylor and Morley Matheson is gone already!"

I was surprised and delighted. Tim was the man we bought our sprays and chemicals from. It was a relief to be talking to someone we knew.

Jim, still standing quietly in the doorway of my office, was now interested rather than disapproving. He walked back in and said, "Why don't you put the speaker phone on?"

When I did, Jim let Tim know he was there and we had another round of greetings. Immediately, I began to ask Tim if he knew where Morley Matheson was because I wanted to know if Welch was going to come up with any more low-sugar programs.

He didn't even bother to answer the question. Instead he said, "Why? What did your grapes test out at?"

The back block is around 15.1 percent, but the front is below minimum, around 14.5 percent, and we don't want to lose any of the crop."

"Well hell!" he said, "those grapes are ready! If you don't want to lose any of them, I'll tell you what you're gonna do. You're gonna pick a few boxes from the back vineyard and you mark those boxes or keep track of them. Then you pick a few boxes from the front vineyard, and you put half 'n half on the semi-truck, then you send them up here. We take a small sample from each box and mix it all together to get an average sugar level. You should be able to let the back grapes bring up your average and get those grapes accepted in here!"

Jim, now listening intently, asked Tim a few more specific questions and shortly, we hung up. The relief I had been reaching for all day washed over me.

"Very good, my dear," Jim said warmly with a look of appreciation.

"You know, it just might work!" I said hopefully.

The phone rang later that evening, and Ernie announced that the harvest crew would be here in the morning. I went to bed still renewing my trust in the elves, sending loving thoughts and waves of energy to the grapes, and daring to be a little excited.

The next morning was Saturday. I wanted in the worst way to stay home and be part of the harvest operation, but I had a prior commitment in the town of Richland nearly an hour's drive away. I left the house at 10:00 A.M. and as I drove down 88th Avenue toward M-40, I passed the harvest crew and their equipment headed toward our farm. As I tooted and waved, my stomach rolled over. Today was the day we had worked toward all year. In a matter of hours it would be done and over.

The rest of the day was packed with appointments. Normally, I never noticed time or the clock when I worked with people yet today I checked off each passing hour with barely bridled impatience. When the last of the clients went out the door, I was right behind them.

On the drive home I found myself speeding twice in tense anxiousness and finally put the car into cruise. I didn't want a ticket, but more than that I didn't want to be stopped by some dutiful policeman who might pull me over, delaying my arrival home and some resolution to the crushing anxiety I had suffered for the past weeks. A little crude reckoning based on past experience told me that the crew would probably be just finishing up by the time I got there, and I would know the score. The closer I got to home, the more tense I became. What if our strategy of mixing grapes from back and front vineyards hadn't worked? How many loads had been rejected?

At last I turned down 88th Avenue. There was Dave, the harvest crew and their equipment—heading for M-40 while I was heading for home! It was the exact reverse of the morning's passing. It struck me as utterly hilarious that we should meet in reverse positions at the end of the day, and I began to laugh a ridiculously uncontrolled laughter. At the same time, I was aware that if Dave had finished in one day, there couldn't be very many grapes. It was also his practice to leave his equipment in one place until the entire crop was harvested—

and there was the whole circus—harvester, wagons, and crew—leaving our farm behind. A feeling of apprehension washed over me. We all waved back and forth as their caravan went by and a minute later I pulled into our yard.

Ernie was still there, sitting quietly in his truck. Boxes of grapes that should have been up at the Welch plant were sitting in the driveway and my heart sank. I got out of the car, then turned and reached into the back seat to get my briefcase, purse and jacket. When I stood up and turned around, there was Jim, grinning at me from ear to ear.

"Well?" I inquired with forced hopefulness. "How did it go?"

"We don't know yet," he beamed at me. "They aren't finished! And with our mixing, they haven't rejected a single load either!"

His words sat there without meaning for a brief eon of time while I stared at him blankly. Then the two pieces of news began to sink in. My insides, completely geared for disappointment, felt scrambled and chaotic as I struggled to adjust to news that was twice as good as I had expected.

"What do you mean, they aren't finished yet? I passed Dave, his equipment and the whole crew leaving as I came down 88th Avenue..."

Jim hugged me in a fit of glee. "He had some other vineyard near here that he just had a little bit to finish up with, so they went to get that done while it's still light. They'll be back here in the morning."

My mind shifted automatically into immediate calculation. The lower the grape tonnage, the quicker the harvest went. If they weren't done yet, that could only mean that either the back-and-forth action of picking from both front and back vineyards alternately was taking an awful lot of time, or we had an awful lot of grapes being harvested and none of them had been rejected— the mixing technique had worked. Gradually, it all hit home and seemed too good to be true.

Jim hauled a scrap of raggedy paper out of his pocket. "The last load for today just left. So far, we've got about sixty-five tons accepted. If they take the load we just sent off, that will raise us to about seventy-three tons. Tomorrow we'll get the last of them which will probably bring us to somewhere around eighty-one, maybe eighty-two tons!"

I could hardly believe it. I wanted to cry, but was too choked up. They had done it! In a year plagued by a late spring, severe freezes during the bud stage, cold and wet weather, a huge crop, almost no sun and an early fall complete with snow and freezes, Alvey and his group had managed to produce the biggest grape crop we ever had—and gotten them ripe enough to harvest! It was a miracle. And all I had needed to do was trust. It seemed like everyone had experienced a bad year except us. Even Ernie had suffered a couple of rejected loads from his vineyards.

I couldn't talk. Jim went off to finish dealing with Ernie, but not before telling me I had to find the elves and give them our thanks.

I went in the barn, put my things down and decided I needed a cup of tea. Tears rolled over the brim of my eyes and dripped off my chin onto the stove as I stood there waiting for the water to heat up. Mountainous waves of feeling rolled over me. I was overjoyed, thrilled, then humbled, excited, thankful. I started to giggle, then stopped, overtaken by a moment of awe. Laughter gushed up from deep inside of me and I rolled along the kitchen counter-top in rollicking gales of mirth, then dropped abruptly into solitary silence, sending a profound thank-you to Alvey and his group. It was a lifetime of feeling in the space of five minutes.

I reflected on the trust I had continued to reaffirm all year. I had to admit it had wavered a bit at the end, but I had doggedly set the wavering aside. It had been there, but somehow I had ignored it. Feeling triumphant in some new way, I poured the water over the teabag and announced to an absent Alvey and an empty room, "I knew I could trust you!"

CHAPTER 15 ❧

The most wonderful sense of success and satisfaction surrounded me. On Sunday the rest of our grapes were harvested and shipped off to the Welch plant with total tonnage tallied at 82.17 tons. When all the receipts were in I felt as if we had accomplished something immensely important.

On Monday morning, as soon as I had cleared away breakfast, I went walking through the vineyards. Over and over I thanked the vines for their efforts to produce the huge crop of grapes and their stamina in holding on in spite of weather conditions that had been abominable from the start. Here and there a leftover grape bunch hung quietly at the end of a row. I picked a few, ate them, and thought they were the most delicious grapes I'd ever tasted.

When I had thanked the vines in every way I could think of, I walked to the top of Golden Mountain and sat down. I intended to go looking for Alvey, but first I wanted to thank the earth itself for her bounty. I had barely sat down though when I heard the whole group of elves coming up the back side of the hill. I stood up, waved them in my direction, and when they gathered in front of me, all I could do was grin and gush.

"Alvey, you did it! It was the biggest crop we've ever had. And the vines made enough sugar to meet the Welch requirements! I don't know how to thank you! I can hardly believe it still—and yet I know it's real... and it never would have happened without you... and you, Mairlinna... all of you... I knew you could do it... I never doubted you for a minute..."

"Wait... wait... wa-aitt a wee minute!" Alvey waved his arms up and down like a large bird.

I stopped gushing and smiled at him, but he simply gazed at me long and quietly.

"What's the matter?" I asked.

"Ye mean ye're not upset that ye didn't get one hundred tons of grapes?" he raised that one eyebrow of his.

I hadn't even thought about one hundred tons of grapes! "Um, well... I forgot about the one hundred tons... actually, I was pleased to get them harvested and accepted at all. I thought eighty-two tons was darn pretty good. It was a lot more than last year. And it's even more than we got in our beginner's luck year. I thought you guys were just going to show me what you could do on your own... and it was such a crummy year for growing anything... it's a miracle we got any grapes at all... your miracle!"

Alvey's eyebrow lowered and he gazed at me with wide eyes. Without preamble he said, "First thing is, we didn't do it all! Ye did yer part, the grapes did theirs, and a few other nature spirits did theirs. We would've liked a wee bit more walking and feedback from ye, but we had to be satisfied with getting your complete trust. We did get something of a report that day in Row Twelve when ye were getting a bit panicky, but it was better than nothing.

"Second thing is, it bothered us to have to help produce the kind of year that would play havoc with everyone else's crop just so yers could experience success in the face of everyone else's loss. It was clear to us last year that ye were well-meaning, and ye might be worth working with, but, like most people, ye were looking for some kind of proof we don't like to have to give. Still, we are mindful of the things we have been learning from ye, and we hope ye appreciate what has been sacrificed by others so that ye can have yer taste of proof.

"Third thing is, we made sure we didn't produce one hundred tons of grapes because we wanted ye to understand that, while trust is important, if ye want to reach one hundred tons of grapes, ye have to put yer heart and soul into this farm. Ye have knowledge and techniques from the human realm that can be combined with trust and the energies of love quite profitably.

"What ye bring to our agreement is very important, both to us and to yerself. Therefore, we hope that ye will work with us much more deeply. If we do our part, and ye do yers, one hundred tons of grapes will be but a small part of what ye can produce. If ye continue to develop Lily Hill Farm, ye will be able to bring a better understanding of balance and health to the world. Of course, ye are free to work with us at any level you wish, but we want ye to know that we want ye to work in much more involved ways, not just by trusting us to do all the work. We have our magic, but ye have yers too… and we quite enjoyed working with ye this past year. Would ye be interested in working with us next year?"

I could not respond immediately. My mind felt like it had been blown up like a balloon as big as the sky. I was aware of the sunshine, the breeze, the cold, damp ground underneath me, and the group of elves in front of me—but I could not gather myself to speak. The realizations that swept through me as Alvey spoke were knife-sharp and strong.

I felt that whatever increase in grapes we had achieved was the result of their magic touch. They felt I had contributed something. They wanted to work with me again. They were still telling me that one hundred tons of grapes was possible, and yet I had stopped believing it was necessary to reach that goal before I would credit them as being real and being worth working with.

But the most overwhelming of all was the awful thought that the miserable growing season we had just suffered through and the loss of crops for other farmers had been arranged so I could have some proof that they were real. It was the proof I had expected the previous year and that Alvey had scolded me about.

Gradually, I found my voice, but it sounded very small. "Why did you do it?" I croaked.

"Because there is a universe of intelligent, creative living forms that ye humans are ignoring. Because we can only compensate for human ignorance and destruction to a certain degree. Because ye are willing to plant more trees and trust in the earth. Because the world is seriously out of balance. Because ye are interested in the nature of balance and because we hope ye will teach what ye learn about balance to the rest of the world." Alvey took off his hat and bowed slightly, but for a long time. When he set it back on his head, he and the rest of the elves marched quietly away. For the third time in as many days, I cried.

It was an early evening in December, and I was hurrying over icy roads to my Russian language class with my daughter Kelly Anne. In the middle of an animated conversation about the class, she suddenly mentioned that her husband, Mike, had cut down a tree. For some reason her comment didn't fit the context of the conversation, and I ended up ignoring her words, thinking I must have misunderstood her. We continued to talk and laugh all the way to class.

But somewhere in the middle of the class her statement took a central place in my attention and I became more and more upset. As soon as we got in the car to go home I questioned her.

"What did you mean when you said Mike cut down a tree? What tree?"

"You know... that tree standing all by itself along the last row of the front vineyard. He said Jim told him there was a tree that was half-dead at the west end of the back vineyard. But he couldn't find it and decided Jim must have meant the tree at the back of the front vineyard. So he cut down the one that was all by itself back by where those old furnace parts were piled."

I felt sick. I knew which tree he had cut. It was a beautifully shaped young tree and I loved it. I had rested under it a number of times because it was the only shade near the front vineyard. I did not want to believe that it was gone. I asked when he had cut it down and she said "just before we left for school."

With that I was outraged. I knew that Mike had been having a bad day, in fact it had been a bad autumn for him. Recently out of the military after six or seven years of service, he was still without a job, and struggling to adjust. When we left for school, he had been sitting casually in front of the TV. I had the distinct impression that he had gotten so frustrated he'd just run out and cut down the tree to release his anger and frustration, then gone back in the house to watch television.

I said nothing, but when we got home I went straight to my room to get ready for bed. Once in bed I sat up, cross-legged, and went into deep meditation in an effort to contact the spirit of the tree or some kind of deva that was part of the tree's energy.

No devas or spirits of any kind came to me or even answered my calls, but at one point I had a clear vision of the tree just lying there, still alive, still aware, with the life slowly oozing out of it.

Soft moans began to echo all around me, and I had the perception that the tree was crying. It did not understand why it had been cut down. Great sorrow filled me. I apologized several times to the tree and to whomever or whatever might be listening or caring about the dying tree. Then I ended the meditation and cried myself to sleep.

The next day was full of appointments, but at lunch time I hurried out to the front vineyard where the tree had been cut down. To my discomfort, the elves were standing around it when I got there. Alvey nodded and so did Mairlinna when I reached them. We all stood silently, staring at the tree. It was just as I had seen it the night before, at the same angle, its life energy slowly dissipating.

"Why did this one have to go?" Alvey startled me with his question. He was looking at me sideways with both eyebrows up.

"It didn't," I told him. "Mike cut it down by mistake."

Several of the elves heaved long, loud sighs as Alvey shook his head. I felt so bad. It had been a favorite tree of mine. It was perfectly shaped, and right there on the edge of the vineyard, it had provided a shady place to rest on hot days.

"What should I do?" The question was more to myself than anyone in particular. In my mind I was wondering what to do or say to Mike.

"Plant ten new trees to make up for this one," Alvey replied crisply, breaking into my thoughts.

The entire group of elves was acting as if they were attending the funeral of a loved friend. One by one they filed past the tree, hat in hand, patted the trunk gently, then moved in a slow line down the hill toward the pond.

I was left standing there alone. They hadn't needed to tell me again of their love for trees. They hadn't needed to say how disappointed they were. It had shown all over their faces.

For the rest of the day and all of the next, I churned inside, furious with Mike for cutting down the tree. It seemed to be just one more incident in a string of "mistakes" designed especially to provoke Jim and me, or produce some trouble, a few headaches, or do some damage. It was as if he wanted to get even for the disappointments life was handing him, and he was taking it out on us. It seemed like everything he touched ended up broken or destroyed. I wanted to help him experience success, but more than that I wanted to teach him ten thousand lessons. I wanted him to understand the concept of energy exchange between people and plants, between people and animals, and between people and other people.

I wanted him to be aware of trees as magnificent living beings whose fate it was to be trapped in one spot all their life and never be able to run away from danger or retreat from harm or unpleasantness. I wanted him to see all the ways he tried to be macho and how destructive to the world of nature those macho attitudes were.

I wanted him to stop trampling, driving, and plowing his way through soft grasses and wet fields as if he were some roughish brute and learn instead to tread lightly upon the earth as if he were walking on some gentle lover's hair. I wanted him to stop trying to prove whatever vague thing he was trying to prove to everyone and learn to accept himself as he was. But, in the end, I wanted to make sure that he would not cut down any more trees.

As evening approached I called the house and asked Mike to come out to the barn. When he arrived I told him quietly that I wanted to talk to him and asked him to have a seat in the kitchen.

He sat down at the table. I walked over to the cupboard and picked up a cutting board and a large meat cleaver. Then I walked over to the table, picked up his arm, put it on the chopping block and put the blade of the cleaver in position on his bare forearm, applying a bit of pressure as if I were going to carve a piece of meat. His eyes grew large as he stared at the cleaver on his arm. His breathing became uneven and he began to shake but didn't move.

Looking directly at him and with a very soft but no-nonsense voice I asked him, "What's the difference between you and the tree you cut down the other day, and you and me right now?"

In a shaky voice he said something about himself being alive and the tree being just a tree.

"Wrong!" I said fiercely. "That tree was a living being too. Now, what's the difference?"

With eyes still glued to the cleaver on his arm he mumbled something else that made no sense and I said even more fiercely, "Wrong again! What's the difference?"

When he started to give a third meaningless answer I interrupted him and said, "Wrong a third time, and three strikes you're out! So I'll tell you what the difference is. The difference is I care about you, and you didn't give a damn about the tree you cut down. The difference is I'm communicating with you, and you never even tried to communicate with that tree. The difference is I'm listening to you, I care what your purpose in life is, and I'm wondering if I can help you with it. I'm wondering if you care whether I cut your arm off, because you certainly didn't listen to that tree or care about what you were doing to it at all. It never occurred to you that the tree had a purpose, that it was alive and well and wanted to stay that way."

He began to babble in self-defense. "But I did. I was using my intuition. I went up to the tree and talked to it and I thought it was the right one…"

"That's right," I interrupted again, "you thought—and that's the problem, because your thinking is all screwed up with anger. And thinking is not intuition! You've been having a bad time since you got out of the Army and you just wanted to take out your frustration on somebody or something. You didn't listen to what Jim told you to do, and you sure as hell didn't try to communicate with that tree. If you were really thinking, then how did you happen to cut down a tree on the north side of the front vineyard when Jim said you were to cut down a tree at the west end of the back vineyard?

He struggled to come up with an answer, babbling something about not being able to find a tree at the west end of the back vineyard, but I cut him off bluntly, "Never mind! It's too late! From now on you don't cut so much as a blade of grass without checking with me first. Nothing! Not a twig or even a flower. If Jim says to cut something down, you come and get me to make sure the tree or bush is either dead or understands what we're trying to do and agrees with that. Do you understand?"

"Yeah," he nodded, his eyes still wide, staring at the cleaver on his arm.

"Good!" I said. "And to replace the tree you cut down, I want you to plant ten new trees this spring. Do you understand?"

"Yeah, sure. Where do you want them?" he said without hesitation and in true military style.

"I don't know yet," I replied as I removed the cleaver from his arm. A long, white dent remained, and he rubbed the spot gingerly. We had a few minutes of pointed conversation in which I tried to reinforce the lesson that he was to check with me before any future cutting or mowing. I told him about an incident in which Jim and his dad had mistakenly cut down a tree to the west of the house and how the tree had screamed as it went down—a scream that made my hair stand on end, and which I never forgot.

I asked him again if he understood that trees were living beings and no one living here was to cut or trim anything until they had made sure that all parties agreed—including me and the tree, the bush, or the grasses themselves. He tried to make appropriate responses, but seemed to be too shaken to say anything coherent. Finally, I sent him back to the house.

When he was gone, I found myself shaking, wondering if I had gotten my point across. I didn't think he would go chopping down any more trees for a long while.

It was mid-December. My classes had all been brought to a close, and I had made plans to go across the state with Jim for a short vacation while he was on business. But at the last minute I ended up staying home because of too many obstacles in both our schedules. The cancellation of the trip left me with two relatively quiet days so I went for a walk through the vineyards in the afternoon.

I called to Alvey and Mairlinna, but there was no response, so I spent a little time thanking the grapevines again for the wonderful job they did and their heroic efforts to produce sweet, sugar-filled grapes in spite of the cold, wet weather conditions that had plagued them for almost the entire growing season.

I was still getting over the loss of the tree and suspected Alvey and his friends did not show up because they were still getting over it too. I knew they were disappointed in us, and part of me wanted to see them just to reassure myself that we were still okay with the whole group of elves.

But a bigger part of me wanted something else. For two months, ever since the grape harvest, I'd had an on-again, off-again chest cold and continuous, severe laryngitis. Many times it had been difficult to teach my classes. Several times I joked that my body was protesting a much heavier teaching schedule and the implementation of several new contracts. But the fatigue and feverishness, the constant ache in my throat and sinuses, and the difficult, raspy breathing were a real problem.

More than once I wondered if it was because of the deep conflict Alvey's words had kindled. What, exactly, did he mean when he said they were hoping I would teach balance to the rest of the world? Obviously I hadn't figured out what balance was for myself! I also had the impression that they were leading me to something, but I had no clear idea what it might be. The whole thing was too big and too vague for me to get my hands around. And most of the time I was too tired to deal with it anyway.

I had worked very hard for over a year to bring my teaching and educational consulting back to where it had been that fateful March day I decided to go work in the grapes. My office routines and communications were finally going fairly well, and yet I had a persistent feeling of unease that I couldn't quite put my finger on. I didn't know if some change was coming, or if I was on the wrong track, or what. All I knew was that something wasn't quite right.

I had made a sort of commitment to the idea of developing Lily Hill Farm, but had no realistic sense of what to do, where or how to begin. I had been following my nose and developing it as a teaching-learning center. This hadn't left much time for working in the grapes, or my garden, or my flowers, or any of the other things I loved to do outside. It hadn't left any time for planning just how to set up the greenhouse I had been dreaming of ever since the elves had mentioned it. And even though I loved the thought of living my life doing all those things, I just didn't know how I would make a decent living doing them. I reasoned that if we ever got one hundred tons of grapes, that might allow me to do things a little differently. But the idea that my career crisis might return in a new form was enough to drive me crazy. I felt I needed to talk to Alvey and try to clarify in much greater detail just exactly what he meant by "develop Lily Hill Farm." I needed him to expand on the reasons for his request and to tell me how to get started. I wanted an outline that would guarantee the financial end of things, and I wanted to know exactly how one went about teaching the nature of balance, but I came home from my walk dissatisfied. No one had answered any of my calls.

Looking for some way to avoid the nagging feeling that something in my life was out of kilter, I dragged out the Christmas decorations and soon forgot the whole issue.

CHAPTER 16 &

The holidays came and went and already it was the new year. I got out for a walk around the farm and enjoyed it immensely, snow and all. Even though I didn't see Alvey or any of the elves, I came back so invigorated I was ready to get out the rototiller and go to work in the garden immediately. I wanted winter to be over and the 1993 growing season to begin!

A few weeks later, I went out again, hoping to find the elves. It had been such a long time since I'd talked with Alvey and his group. I walked along the lane toward the back of the farm and when I got to the back vineyard, I turned into one of the rows and wandered toward the east end of the farm. At the end of the row I turned left, which took me north toward Golden Mountain. Several times along the way I called out to Alvey, then Mairlinna, but no one answered. Rather than go to the top of Golden Mountain, I followed a path behind and around the big hill following the edge of the woods. The trees waved gently in the winter wind but all else was silent. When no sign of the elves appeared, I eventually turned and started down the gentle slope, still following the line of the trees. But as I turned the corner to walk through the area the elves had asked us to leave wild, I stopped in horror. One of the trees in their area had been partially chopped down. Huge branches were lying on the ground or swinging up high in the wind, half-cut like some grotesque body with arms dangling.

"Oh no!" I cried out. "Oh no, not another one."

I burst into tears. Without even thinking about it I knew Mike had been back here looking for firewood for their woodstove. At the same instant I recalled Jim's earlier instructions to him, "A tree at the west end of the back vineyard...."

Why hadn't we realized before that the west end of the back vineyard was the wild area we had agreed to leave alone? I was furious with them and frustrated with myself. It was another violation of our agreement with the elves. What made me even angrier was that Mike hadn't come to check with me, nor had he even bothered to take what he had cut. He just chopped and hacked here and there, leaving the remains looking like the grisly evidence of an interrupted murder.

Feeling frozen and helpless, I cursed both Jim and Mike and took a few steps closer to the tree. Then I saw them. Alvey and the entire group of elves were standing in a tight knot, watching me with arms crossed.

"I'm so sorry," I said through my tears. "We made a mistake... I think they forgot this was your area. Please, forgive us."

No one said a word. They continued to stare at me. I started to apologize again, taking a step closer but when I did, Alvey put his hands up with such a fierce attitude that I stopped on the spot. He seemed to be refusing to allow me into his area. The silence lengthened.

"What can we do?" I asked, feeling so rejected I thought I might crack.

"Ye can do what ye say ye're going to do," Alvey offered. Silence fell again.

I truly did not know what I could say or do to convince them that we would not go chopping down any more trees, especially in their area. As I stood there, dumb, they turned and walked away.

I cut off a sob and began to run back toward the barn, nearly choking with frustration at our collective stupidity. Once back in my office I paced about in fury at what I considered to be Jim's thoughtlessness and Mike's thick-headedness. I had specifically told Mike after the last tree-cutting incident that he was not to cut a single thing without coming to me and getting some kind of clearance. As for Jim, he should have known better. I ranted to an empty barn for the next hour.

Gradually, I calmed down. "Why did this happen again?" I asked myself over and over.

It was dusk and growing dark when I decided I had to see Alvey again and I couldn't wait. I put on my coat and boots and walked back out to the wild area. I called out to him again and again, determined to wait patiently until he and the rest of the group appeared. Finally, Alvey and Kermots came to the edge of the lane.

When there were no greetings and wishes for my good health I said to them, "I don't know why this happened, but I'm really sorry that it did. There's always a gift in every tragedy, and I promise you we'll plant ten new trees for each of the ones that have been mistakenly cut. But is there anything else we can do to repair the damage?"

They stood there quietly for a few more minutes and finally Alvey spoke. "It would be kind of ye to pile up the smaller branches making a brush pile... the rabbits and the little creatures would be pleased."

After a short pause he continued, "If ye really need the biggest logs for firewood ye might as well take them. But we would be pleased if ye'd leave some of the smaller logs in a pile shaped like one of yer tents, but not so fancy that other people would notice and be curious. We wouldn't want to have somebody coming around to investigate.

"We also wouldn't mind if ye would clean up around the rest of the trees ye've cluttered up. Not only have ye been slowly chopping down some of our favorites, ye've piled old vehicles, furnace parts, and oil tanks around the rest of them. Beyond that, it would be kind if ye'd leave the wild area as it is." His voice had a crisp, but not unkind tone to it and I began to feel better.

He and Kermots left abruptly. I called a heartfelt thank-you after them and walked quickly back to the barn.

That weekend was my birthday, and Jim was home. He asked me to go out to the wild area with him to look at the tree Mike had cut.

"Well..." he hesitated after we arrived, "that's the tree. He did cut the one I told him."

"Did you forget that we promised them not to mess around in this little corner?" I inquired.

"No, not really... Well, yes, I did... I just... I mean, what are we supposed to do when a tree gets old and rotten?"

"If it's to be a wild area, why can't we just let it fall? It can't hit anything, and the elves seem to have as much use for rotten and fallen trees as for young, healthy ones."

"I suppose," he sighed, but I knew that this kind of approach was foreign to him. For him, it was natural to be moving small mountains of earth around, landscaping, cutting down trees, and shaping the environment the way he wanted it to be. For him, leaving trees to die a natural death was an unnatural idea.

On the last day of January, I went out for a short walk and again found myself wishing it were spring so I could get out in the garden and the vineyards. As I walked, bits and pieces of the vision of the farm that Alvey and his friends had painted in my mind almost two years ago recurred over and over.

There was something fascinating about the pictures of how the farm either could, or would, look. I wanted to make it be what they showed me it could be, but I had no idea how I could make a reasonable living that way. It seemed too complex, or maybe it was too simple, too obvious, too uncertain, or whatever! I just knew that I wanted winter to be over, and quickly.

Jim and I were already planning the coming grape-growing season and had recently made a tentative decision to use the organic foliar feeding system called Sonic Bloom on our grapes this year. I had been experimenting with it since last August, and it had done wonders for my office plants, the vegetables in my summer garden that had lingered on until December, and a small winter garden I had planted indoors.

At first I played the cassette tape with the special musical frequencies for twenty minutes each day and then began spraying the leaves of the plants with the organic nutrient made from a seaweed base and loaded with trace minerals. They loved it! Within several weeks the plants and trees growing here and there around the barn had taken off in an unparalleled growth spurt. They grew so much and with such vigor that I had cut back the music and sprays to every week, then every other week, and finally to once a month. And after four years of dismal failure in trying to grow a few vegetables indoors in the winter, with Sonic Bloom I had actually been able to harvest things like peas, beans, cucumbers, and tomatoes growing inside in January.

Sonic Bloom was expensive, but Alvey had said that we should bring all that we could muster to the grape-growing process, and we had decided that a full trial of the music and the nutrient in both vineyards would be our contribution this year.

Over the Valentine's Day weekend we drove to Wisconsin to meet Dan Carlson and visit Hazel Hills Experimental Nut Farm. We came home bringing lots of new ideas and information, a dozen experimental strawberry plants that were supposed to produce exceptionally large berries, a lot of excitement, and a very firm decision to use Sonic Bloom.

Ernie came over to visit the week after we returned, and still high on the excitement from our trip, we told him about Sonic Bloom. We played the video for him, showing how the music and nutrient were used, as well as the results with different crops. Then we sent him off with some of the literature, and let him borrow the video to show others what the possibilities were.

When he left he was really enthusiastic, but when he came back a few days later he seemed subdued, as if he wanted to be very careful, almost skeptical. Since most growers were members of the National Grape Co-op, he had taken the Sonic Bloom information to the Co-op consultant, Charles Reiskoff. Then he showed it to some of the committee people at Welch Foods to make sure they didn't mind if we sprayed our grapes with it. Like most big food processing corporations who contracted with vegetable and fruit farmers for their products, Welch had a number of policies regarding the use of pesticides, herbicides, and fungicides used. Those of us who raised grapes had to keep thorough records of what we sprayed on the products Welch ended up buying. A few poisons could not be used at all. Some of them had to be used before the bud turned into a blossom, others could not be used less than thirty, or perhaps sixty, days before harvest. Others had no limitations on either use or timing of the spray. After looking at the information on Sonic Bloom, the official response was, "Go ahead, this is not a federally registered chemical, this is just another foliar fertilizer—and a pretty expensive one at that."

Ernie also told us that he had taken the information and the video around to several other farmers he thought might be interested. Evidently, they pooh-poohed the whole idea. Their consensus was "That's just another form of foliar feeding! We already tried foliar feeding, and it didn't do any more than plain old root-style fertilizer!" And I guess they just laughed at the idea of playing music in their vineyards.

Either they did not quite believe or they hadn't understood that the music frequency, which sounded a lot like a strange, repetitive birdsong, caused the stomata on the underside of the leaves to open wide and drink in lots of water and the organic nutrients that were being sprayed on them, thus making the plants grow in a quick and healthy way. The fact that Sonic Bloom was a certified organic nutrient was overlooked or ignored.

The live video footage of incredibly productive orange trees with 100 per-cent more Vitamin C, huge tomato plants with tomatoes as sweet as sugar, five-foot-tall alfalfa with 30 percent higher proteins, bean fields with 800 soy-bean pods per plant, and seventeen-foot-tall corn with three or four ears per plant—all this see-for-yourself evidence was ignored.

The dramatically increased shelf-life of produce that did not rot even when it was not refrigerated was of no concern to any of them, and the belief that we thought we could reduce or eliminate pesticides, fungicides, and her-bicides was viewed as downright dangerous! In the end, Ernie seemed to side with everyone else. Although he did not try to discourage us, he made it clear that he thought we were just getting our vineyards in good shape and should not be taking any risks with it at this point. When I asked if he wanted to try it, he shook his head and backed way off.

After he left, Jim and I decided to meet with Charles at the National Grape Co-operative office and hear with our own ears that there were no restrictions on using Sonic Bloom. We didn't want to have our crop rejected because of some technicality that was never reported to us, but we heard the same thing from him that Ernie had said, "Go ahead, this is just a fertilizer, there are no restrictions on this kind of stuff."

It was the middle of March. Juan was almost done trimming in the front vine-yard, and for a while it looked like we were ahead of the spring rush to get everything done in the vineyards. Usually, we were behind. Usually, we were struggling to get things trimmed and tied before bud break started. But we were so anxious for spring and for the grape season to begin that we started extra early.

It didn't last though. Juan surprised us by leaving for Texas right after he finished the front block of grapes. His grandmother or someone was quite sick. So there we were at the end of March with the back vineyard not even started. If Juan did not finish trimming, we could not begin tightening wires, replacing old fenceposts, or burying long arms. "Why did these things happen?" Jim and I asked each other in frustration. "Why can't we get ahead and stay ahead of the springtime work? Why do we have these setbacks all the time? The universe is supposed to be on our side!" But there was no answer.

With the work in the vineyard almost at a standstill, I was incredibly impatient to do something. I was so anxious to get outside and start my garden that after weeks of planning, choosing seeds, setting up records, and careful organizing, I decided to start the garden indoors.

Gathering all the cups and bowls I could find, I put between sixty and 180 seeds in each cup, poured a little Sonic Bloom over the seeds, played the music for an hour, then went to bed letting them soak overnight.

The next day I planted everything in planters, peat pots, old flower pots and whatever I could find. The wet seeds were a real pain to work with, but I got the job done and took them downstairs to the shop where they would be out of the way. I also planted the experimental strawberry plants we brought home from our visit with Dan Carlson. Jim built two beautiful yellow indoor planting boxes for them, along with a special lighting system. They were finally in the planters and my gardening had begun, even if spring had not!

Three days later in the cool, damp darkness of Jim's woodshop, I was quite shocked to discover that the peas and radishes were coming up. The next day everything was up, and I was horrified. It had been less than four days since they had gone into the pots. I knew it had to be the Sonic Bloom.

Within one week everything was growing like crazy—pumpkins, beans, cucumbers, squash, cauliflower, cabbage, cantaloupe, watermelon, tomatoes, onions, peas, radishes, peppers, and several herbs. Worse yet, in order to get them some light I had hung the peas under the fluorescent lights of the shop ceiling, and already they were winding delicately around the fixtures suspended six inches above them. I hadn't expected things to germinate so quickly, especially indoors. In my winter gardens of previous years, it had taken from ten days to three weeks for the seeds to begin coming up—if they came up at all! And I certainly hadn't expected the plants to grow so much in such a short time.

By Easter Sunday, there was good news and bad. The good news was that Juan had returned, and trimming in the back vineyard was under way again. The weather was still extraordinarily cold, and this kept some of the pressure off us as nothing was going to begin growing at such low temperatures. The bad news was that my in-house garden plants were growing fast and the weather was still extraordinarily cold! I felt caught. I wanted the weather to stay cold until work in the vineyard had been completed, and I wanted it to get warm so I could transplant my seedlings into the garden. Twelve days after I had planted them, the peas were ten inches tall. They needed to go in the ground immediately, they needed access to a fence, and I needed to cut back on my Sonic Bloom treatments.

Eventually, the trimming in the back vineyard was finished and the tying began immediately. Everyone was keeping one eye on the thermometer. If the temperature got warm, the buds would swell and break open. After that, tying would have to be painfully slow and cautious or the delicate buds would be knocked right off the canes in trying to get them fastened to the wires. If we didn't tie—deciding to wait until the buds opened and got a little tougher— the risk was that a good stiff wind could begin blowing and whip the canes around, destroying the buds just as quickly as tying at the wrong stage of development.

My dance between wanting it to stay cold for the grapes and wanting it to warm up for my garden was exhausting me. Finally, the tying was finished about the same time that April was coming to a close. Where was spring? Every day was cold and gray with heavy frost every morning. There was absolutely no sign that the vines were waking up from their long winter's sleep, and a reluctant sun refused to coax the thermometer into even a slow upward crawl.

I needed something to do besides watch my garden grow and watch over the reluctant weather. I went for a walk, hoping to find Alvey and just make sure we still had an agreement to work together after all the trouble with the trees. It had been a long time since I'd seen him or any of the elves so I went around the entire farm and was on my way back to the barn when there they were, under the hickory tree.

"Well hello!" I said, feeling delighted and relieved that my thoughts of abandonment were unfounded. "It's so good to see you again. How are you all?"

By the enthusiastic greetings I could tell they were pleased to see me. In response to my question as to how they were, they began to clown around and ask one another, "How am I? Am I this way? No, yer that way. I am? Which way? How can ye tell?"

I was chuckling at their antics when Alvey, leaning casually on the trunk of the hickory, spoke up through the noise and laughter, "Nice tree ye got here. 'Bout time ye planted those replacements, eh?"

I knew he was referring to the trees we had mistakenly cut down, and I had the odd feeling he and the group had watched me walk around the entire farm, avoiding me deliberately so they could suddenly appear under the hickory tree, one of their favorite places.

I told Alvey I had called our area conservation group earlier in the spring and ordered 150 trees, from maples, oaks, and walnuts, to pines, firs, and spruce. All we needed to do was pick them up and plant them. I didn't say that since then I had forgotten all about them. Instead I made a mental note to follow through.

Changing the subject to my original purpose for seeking them out I went on, "Alvey, are we still working together this year?"

"Have ye changed yer mind?" he asked.

"Oh no, but it's been such a long time since we talked, I thought it might be good to renew our agreement, you know, make sure we're together."

"We haven't changed ours, have we?" he turned to the small group of elves, and they began to question one another with great seriousness, everyone talking at once. "Are ye finished with her? Have ye given up? Can we do it? No, can she do it? Are we together on this? Is she together?"

Finally, with one motion, they turned to Alvey and nodded their heads affirmatively in a solemn manner.

"And we're each going to bring all that we know to this year's crop, right?" I inquired in my best business manners.

"Yep!" Alvey and the group nodded vigorously.

"Okay, that's good," I said. "One of the things we're definitely going to contribute is the Sonic Bloom. If you guys bring your magic touch, and Mother Nature is willing, we'll have another great year. I'll trust, like I did last year, and if you guys could make it a good year for everyone around us, that would be really perfect."

With one of his dramatic sweeps, Alvey suddenly removed his hat and bowed deeply, all the elves following suit.

I thought they were never going to stand up again. When they did, I realized they were honoring my wish to make it a great crop year for everyone on the ridge and around Lawton. There was a lump in my throat as I realized again that proof didn't matter much any more. It was enough just to be able to work with them, learn from them, and trust myself in the bargain.

CHAPTER 17 ❧

I stood outside in the pink morning watching my breath turn to clouds of frost and drift slowly through the frigid air. It was the first day of May, far too late in the season for such cold weather, and my wish for the new growing season to begin was becoming more intense each day. Jim had tilled the garden, but it was much too chilly to set out tender vegetables.

Partly due to the habit of discipline and partly just to keep myself occupied, I went back in the barn, resigned to another day in the office. Irritated with the delayed spring, I looked around at the desks, chairs, table, cabinets, and shelves. Everything was littered with piles of unfiled papers, unanswered correspondence, bills to pay, all kinds of educational projects turned in by the teachers I had worked with, books I was reading, manuscripts I worked on intermittently, junk mail that I wanted to look through before tossing, catalogs I loved to escape to when I had too much to do, empty teacups, and a fair amount of dust. On the spot, I decided in a fuzzy, unplanned way that I was through with educational consulting and determined to reorganize my life so I could grow grapes and garden in the summer and be free to write all winter.

If I was going to become a gardener and writer I didn't need all that paperwork and clutter. It was time to clean up my office to reflect my decision about career direction. With gusto I began sweeping away the remains of the last year, certain that spring would begin the moment I was finished. Whenever it did, I wanted to be ready so I could spend my time outside. My decision to get out of educational consulting might have been fuzzy, but the determination to spend my summer in the garden and the grapes was clear and strong. It was one of my typical reversals, one that was totally oblivious to the energy and effort I had put in to rebuilding my consulting business after the elves had managed to get a whole summer's worth of contracts cancelled!

It was two o'clock in the afternoon before the cleaning marathon began to taper off. Four large wastebaskets stood overflowing with debris. I looked at them and was only momentarily aware of how uncertain the "grape, garden, and writing" path looked. If cleaning was the first step, I had no idea what the second step was. It was too much to contemplate, so I gathered the wastebaskets, went downstairs, and out through the east door of Jim's shop to burn the evidence of what I had been for over a decade. On the way through Jim's office, I admired the strawberry plants in their bright yellow planters. They were large, bright green, growing beautifully, and in blossom.

When I finished burning the papers, I did not come back in the same door I had gone out. Instead, I walked around the barn and came in through the west entrance, never suspecting the door to Jim's shop might not have closed all the way.

Later in the afternoon, I made a trip down to Jim's office to deliver his mail and several faxes. To my horror, a couple of the beautiful strawberry plants had been uprooted and were gone. A few others had been nibbled on, and there was a trail of dirt and leaves across the room leading under the sofa.

Crying out in dismay, I ran across the room and looked under the sofa. There was nothing there but the remains of a destroyed strawberry root. I ran around looking under everything and when I went into Jim's shop, I discovered the open door. Very upset, I closed it, then went back upstairs. Our experiment with the strawberries had definitely suffered a setback.

When Jim called about an hour later to say he was on his way home for the weekend, I told him that something had gotten into the barn and eaten several of the fresh green plants. He was just as upset as I was.

When he arrived, I went downstairs to meet him. We stood in his office, staring at the mutilated strawberry patch and mourning the loss of the plants. As I stared at the planter, it looked like the damage was worse than I remembered it, which didn't help.

We went back upstairs to eat dinner in a silent mood, while he occasionally asked, "If we are on the right track, why do we have these kinds of setbacks?" Even though it was only a few strawberry plants, we felt as if we had suffered some large, incalculable loss. I had no answers and was reviewing my patient and tolerant attitude toward all animals, wondering if I was being too simple-minded about the whole subject.

After dinner we went downstairs to survey the remaining strawberry plants. With a shock I realized that over half the plants were now gone. Whatever was eating them was still in Jim's office!

With a vengeance we set about looking for the culprit, intending to end his thieving existence immediately with one good whack of a shovel. An hour later we found a very small, shaking woodchuck hiding in an open drawer of bolts in the supply room. Coaxing it into a box, we put it in the van and drove a mile away, letting it go near Cedar Lake on the other side of the highway.

I found four of the half-eaten plants under the sofa, replanted them gently, encouraged them to rest and then grow—and all but one of them did.

After that, we decided to get a dog. Maybe small critters wouldn't be so comfortable just walking in with a dog living here.

At the end of the first week in May, we finally had a few warm days. The seeds I had planted a month ago were in very sad shape, and I knew it was time to get them in the garden or give up and start over. The peas were already thirty inches tall and quite tangled; the pumpkins were root-bound. The rest looked wan and stringy.

I had planned a much larger garden than we'd had before, so we had converted a portion of last year's cornfield into a new garden on the east side of the lane. With great expectations and high energy, we brought home about thirty-five cubic yards of wood chips, spread them over the new garden, then tilled them in. I thought the wood chips would make some great soil, and I was quite excited about the renewal of our decision to grow everything without the use of chemical fertilizers or sprays.

Several days later I started transplanting and was frustrated to the point of tears! It was the most miserable dirt I had ever tried to work in. The dirt in my original garden just across the lane was like black silk, smooth and rich and moist. It felt alive in my hands and almost talked to me when I worked in it. The dirt in the new garden was yellow and heavy and full of rough clumps that hurt my hands and feet and knees. The recently applied woodchips made it even worse. When I got out my rototiller and tried to till the whole garden in order to get a finer soil, the tiller jerked and bounced around so badly I could hardly hang onto the darn thing. I felt like a ragdoll tied to the end of the handlebars on some wild ride.

I didn't know much about dirt. Some of it was black, some was brown, and I knew the difference between sand and clay, but beyond that I never thought about dirt much or got upset about how it acted and felt. Now, I found myself hating that dirt. I abandoned trying to put in my tender transplants and decided to try planting potatoes. By the end of the day only a few rows were planted. I ached from the effort to dig in such heavy soil and was in serious doubt as to whether anything would grow. That night, as I drifted off into an exhausted sleep, I was certain I should not have tried to put a garden in an old cornfield.

A week later I was still planting the garden and had calmed down a bit on the subject of garden soil. I was sure that whatever was wrong with the soil, Sonic Bloom would help the plants make it. At least the weather was still warm, and I was beginning to think that spring might finally be here to stay.

The grapes were growing quickly now, and we were trying to get the first application of Sonic Bloom on the vines with their new canes. Ernie, who usually handled our entire spray program, was unwilling to participate in the use of Sonic Bloom. He didn't want the stuff in his new sprayer, and thus the job fell to Jim.

Jim ended up borrowing an old sprayer, one that was really too small for the job, from Dean. After a week's worth of trouble in setting up speakers, having to get the pump on the sprayer rebuilt, replacing spray nozzles, and a number of tries to calibrate nozzles and ground speed to get the correct amount sprayed, we managed to get the first application on both vineyards. There was already eight to ten inches of new growth on the vines, and we were well past the recommended growth of two to three inches, but it was such a relief to take the first step.

We also had found a dog. She was a five-month-old Sheltie thoroughbred, the last pup from an unplanned litter born in January's sub-zero weather to a horse and dog breeder who had not expected the litter to survive. Now at four months, she was free for the taking so we adopted her and named her "Linden January."

Several days after bringing her home, I went for a walk, taking Lindy with me and looking for the elves. We went all the way to the west end of the farm, around the pond, and up the hills into the wild area before we finally found Alvey and about half the usual number of elves in the group.

They greeted me with a subdued respect, keeping their eyes on Lindy and the rope that kept her at my side. I had the distinct impression that they were a bit wary of the dog so I said, "How do you like our new dog?"

"She's a beauty!" Alvey replied crisply.

"Yes, she is," I returned, "I hope you don't mind her being here."

"Not at all," he said, but there was no reassurance or conviction in his voice and the rest of the elves still stood very quietly, watching the dog.

"I'm going to train her to be my garden dog," I offered what I hoped was an explanation. "I want her to bark at the deer, the raccoons, and the wood-chucks."

"Ye could have put up a fence," one of the elves murmured from the back of the little group, and Alvey made a quick motion with his hand for silence.

I didn't know what to say, and we all just stood there for a moment. A feeling of defensiveness moved through me. I thought it was not fair that they should hesitate in accepting Lindy. After all, she was just another creature like the rest of us.

"She'll be a great help with yer sheep, if ye get them soon and train her early enough," Alvey noted in a matter-of-fact voice.

I just stared at him. Alvey and I had never talked about sheep. I had dis-cussed it with Jim for over a year, but eventually I'd given up on getting any. Now Alvey was talking as if it were an old subject that was being reconsidered.

"Do you think it's a good idea to get some sheep here?" I asked.

"Do ye want to heal yer soil?" he looked at me in a pointed fashion.

"Well, yes... I do," the words jerked out of me, squeezing themselves from between the alternating thoughts on sheep and soil that raced through my head. For nearly a year, I had wanted some sheep and maybe a couple of angora goats. I had wanted them mostly because I really liked the idea of a few small animals here on the farm. I thought perhaps I could do something with the sheep's wool and the angora from the goats, maybe learning to weave on a small loom, but in the end, I had decided I would be too tied down because of the time needed to take care of them, and I figured I didn't need any more to do. I was also worried that we would use up too much valuable land in trying to support them.

"I'm not sure we have enough space for animals to graze," I told Alvey, still not thinking in a very organized way. "Where would we put them?"

"Down in that hollow at the northeast corner of the front vineyard. Take out those vines that never produce anything, put in some kind of shelter, raise the level of the ground just a wee bit, and run some fencing around and down toward the pond. They'll be quite happy there," he said with a nod.

I thanked him for the thoughts and walked home, uncertain that we could handle sheep or anything that needed routine care and feeding. How had Alvey known that I was upset with our soil, and was he using that knowledge unfairly to pressure me to become more deeply involved with the farm than I already was? I was running in more directions than I felt I could sustain. I had already abandoned my position of no more educational consulting and agreed to take on more responsibility in a project with a group of Head Start mothers. Now I was committed weekly through the summer and until at least mid-October—and it just wasn't in my nature to put in less than full effort at anything.

In addition, this year's garden was a very big garden, I had made arrangements to sell our extra vegetables at a small roadside farm market just up on M-40, and I wanted to do a good job at this, too. Taking on animals seemed out of the question, regardless of what it would do for the soil.

As the days passed, I continued to work in my garden every chance I got, my mind often traveling back in time to when I was a child. Back then I belonged to a large family that grew a large garden every year. I hated that garden and the constant work it meant, rain or shine, hot or cold. And I resented the fact that we had to eat our own canned and frozen garden vegetables instead of buying all those exciting cans and boxes at the grocery store like everyone else.

How had I changed so much? Now the vineyards and the garden were a central feature in my life. I loved the physical labor, the absence of telephones, the wondrous variety of living, growing plants, and the miracle of food that came right out of the soil.

In this year's garden, my transplants were slow in adjusting to outdoor life, and the vegetables I had direct-seeded were uncommonly slow in coming up. I kept anxious watch over them daily, grateful when the small green shoots began poking through the rough soil. Things came up quite unevenly, with some areas up long before others, turning green and getting tall. Others came up slowly, turning an ugly reddish color and not growing at all. A deep frustration, coupled with a sense of helplessness, began to form somewhere inside of me. What was wrong? Between the hard, yellow soil and the stunted plants it did not look like the start of a banner year for gardening.

In a search for answers, I began reading books I never would have looked at before. Instead of my usual assortment of books on the brain, intelligence, perception, and the cognitive sciences, I spent hours browsing through the garden section at the bookstore. Among those I brought home was a small, thin book called *Rainforest in Your Kitchen*—because it was small and thin. It also sounded interesting. When I finished reading it, my entire sense of the relationship between food, agriculture, the grocery store, and me had changed in the space of a few pages. The idea of a direct, causal relationship between the rainforest, seed companies, my kitchen, and the nature of balance—which had never occurred to me before—was firmly planted and painfully obvious. We were all in a massive food rut, eating the same few things week after week, for years. Our demands—for the same kinds of food every week, for cheap food, for foods that looked pretty, for foods that shipped well instead of nourished well, and for foods that were out of season and therefore neither ripe nor containing any nutrients—were major factors in the serious loss of biodiversity across the planet. For a long time I had been vaguely aware that biodiversity was an issue for a few concerned people here and there, but I lumped them into a group loosely labeled "fringe fanatic."

Certainly, I had never thought of the loss of biodiversity as the extinction of a plant with unique properties that might have saved my life some day.

I hadn't thought of biodiversity as a wide margin of safety containing plants so diverse and unusual that they might have genes or characteristics allowing them to survive nuclear winter, or chemical warfare, or unexpected geological changes in the earth or the climate—foods that might be there for us when our habitual favorites had long since given up the ghost of survival. I had never given a thought to chickens and the fact that 90 percent of the chicken business was made up of white Leghorns. One nasty, uncontrollable virus and eggs could become a rare item for a long time!

Where our ancestors used to eat a huge variety of some three hundred food items as part of their annual diet, the average American diet now included only a handful of foods which we ate over and over again. No wonder overwhelming allergies were among the fastest-growing health complaints! Not only was the body subjected to the same foods every week, we weren't getting the benefit of the nutrients contained in the foods we weren't eating. For most of us it came down to hamburger, potatoes, peas, corn, iceberg lettuce, cardboard tomatoes, white Leghorn eggs, coffee, tea, or soda pop, and white bread with peanut butter and jelly.

Old varieties of vegetables and fruits were being lost because no one was growing them any more. The old varieties were no longer acceptable because they were either funny-shaped or ripened gradually instead of all at once—thus making them incompatible with huge corporate farming practices. Other varieties were ignored because they didn't stand up to transportation and processing.

Many long-established and family-owned seed companies were being taken over by giant corporations that did so much cross-breeding and genetic hybridizing that the seeds they produced just could not survive in a normal environment. These new seeds had to have pesticides, herbicides, and fungicides to keep them alive long enough to pick the crop! And since hybrids didn't produce healthy seeds that would grow, produce, and reproduce year after year like open-pollinated seeds, the big corporations had built-in return customers—you had to come back and buy new seeds every year!

All of a sudden, it was clear why so many farmers had gone belly-up in the seventies and eighties. Farming was not a high-profit venture to begin with, but it did reproduce its own seed and fertilizers along with the crop to be sold. Lured by the promise of huge crops via petrochemicals and hybrids, farmers had put out large amounts of cash for these new supplies—cash and supplies they had never needed before. But any increase in crop was offset by government-controlled prices that were kept painfully low. And the increase in crop was temporary. Somehow, the use of chemical sprays damaged the soil, which began to produce less and less.

After all my dealings with the elves, I still wasn't sure just how the sprays managed to damage soil, but it was clear that farmers ended up buying more and more seeds, and more and more chemicals to force those seeds to produce. What was once a self-sustaining way of life became a pool of quick-sand that sucked generations of farms and their families into oblivion.

Instead of seed-gathering and planting based on factors such as genetic adaptability, resistance to disease, excellent taste, good texture, high nutrition, and dependable reproductive ability, farming had degenerated into seed sales campaigns, chemical advertisements, bigger equipment, and a serious lack of attention to anything other than a crop's looks, its ability to survive transportation, and economic survival.

For the first time, I understood the few news reports I had heard more than a decade ago. I knew what those rock music concerts named something like "Farm-aid" had been about. They were trying to save those farmers who had gambled with agri-business and lost.

Suddenly, I saw my garden with new eyes. I had purchased the best and latest in seeds. I had spent over a hundred dollars on them. They were all hybrids and next year I would probably have to spend more to get that same amount of seeds. I had also bought exactly the kinds of foods that were described in the book as available in any grocery store. Why hadn't I tried something new and different? I had planned a bigger garden, but it was just more of the same old thing—more potatoes, peas, corn, tomatoes, and melons. I had no idea what kale tasted like, or black-eyed peas. And why hadn't I thought about buying varieties that would produce viable seeds? I knew how to collect flower seeds from my favorite blooms. Why not from vegetables?

Overwhelmed at how one thin book could change my awareness, I went back to working in my garden. This year's vegetables weren't even up and I was already planning next year. I didn't know it but I had been bitten by the farmer bug in a terminal way—there was always next year!

CHAPTER 18 ✍

Toward the end of May we were extremely busy in the grapes. We sprayed our second application of Sonic Bloom spray, did the tilling, and then spidered throughout both vineyards. I didn't want to spread any chemical fertilizers in the vines, but Jim thought it was best to apply potash and urea. After a serious back-and-forth discussion, his persistence won out, and we applied about half our annual dose of each, hoping that Sonic Bloom would supply the rest over the growing season.

The vines looked quite healthy and it was a pleasure to work among them. Jim and I were burying long arms in the back vineyard and chatting as we worked. As usual, our most common discussion was how to get more time to do the necessary things in the vineyard each spring, in spite of full-time jobs that kept us so unreasonably busy. But no solutions for expanding time occurred to us that we hadn't thought of a dozen times before.

Gradually, we lapsed into a comfortable silence, enjoying the work and each other's company under the springtime sun. Occasionally, I'd talk to a vine here and there, asking what it needed or if it liked the shape I was trying to coax it into. Often they'd light up and give off the most beautiful smell.

On Memorial Day weekend I left for Alaska and a small vacation at my sister's house. She had been in Anchorage for years, and I had promised her long ago that when and if one of her children got married I would come to visit. Now there was a wedding, my niece was getting married, and I did not want to back out of my promise. Not everything in the vineyard was done, the weatherman was predicting a heat wave for next week, and I knew it would probably be quite hot by the time I got another chance to work among the vines, but I packed up and flew north to celebrate one of the more important rituals of life and love.

When I returned, temperatures were skyrocketing; the sun burned hotter and the air grew steadily more humid every day. It was too hot to work outside except in the very early morning, but I wanted to be among the vines so one sunny afternoon, in spite of the heat, I went looking for Alvey. I wanted to get his observations on the response of the vines to the Sonic Bloom sprays and the absence of pesticides, weed sprays, and fungicides. I also wanted to hear some kind of atta-boy and pick up a little encouragement. But once I got in the vineyard I forgot all about Alvey and his friends.

There were some kind of blue-green beetles munching on the grape leaves. The leaves looked smaller and were pale in color compared to the leaves I'd seen in other vineyards on the way to town. Some of them had dried brown areas on them. Other leaves looked positively yellowish around the edges and up the center, along the main vein. Still others looked torn and ravaged.

I came back to the office with a handful of leaves as hard evidence of the trouble and started looking through our book on grape diseases, but according to the pictures there, the yellowish leaves could have been the result of at least five different problems. When Jim called I told him of my distressing discoveries. On the road and far from being able to do anything, he suggested I call Tim Taylor and ask what he thought. So I did.

After questioning me carefully, Tim said he thought there probably weren't enough blue-green bugs to bother doing anything about. He said the yellowish leaves were either a sign of low nitrogen, a potassium problem, or the serious lack of sunshine and warm temperatures that we had experienced so much of throughout the spring. As for the torn leaves, they were probably caused by the ferocious storms that had moved through our area for the past week.

Even though Tim sounded reassuring, I felt an edge of uneasiness. Jim and I had agreed we were going to avoid chemical spraying and fertilizing at all costs this year. For the first time since we bought the place, we were also going to try our hand at taking care of the vineyards ourselves. Instead of leaning heavily on Ernie to let us know what we needed to do and when, we announced to him that we intended to supervise everything ourselves, suffer our own mistakes, and learn to correct them. But neither of us was all that confident in our abilities to manage the whole thing.

I was not sure I would recognize any of the more common diseases, let alone some unusual problem that might come along. We didn't have the years of experience that Ernie, Tim, or Charles had, and there was a real consciousness in us that maybe we were fools to think we could stop spraying chemicals cold turkey. Grape cultivation had been going on here long before we came along. Without warning I was overwhelmed with doubt about our "no-chemicals" decision. What made us think we knew better than the grape farmers who had been doing it all their lives? I looked dubiously at the pile of pale yellow leaves on my desk. Maybe it was just the cold weather after all. Perhaps in the sudden and recent warmth the plants were growing faster than they could take up needed nutrients. I put the leaves into the compost pail and closed the lid with an unsettled feeling.

When Jim came home a day or so later, we went through the vineyards examining leaves, vines, and young grape clusters. It was time for the next Sonic Bloom spray, and we tried to soothe our worries about the vineyard by applying our third dose of the organic nutrient. But two days later it was still extremely warm and humid, the perfect conditions for mildew or black rot and we caved in on our resolve not to spray chemical fungicides. We applied a very small dose of Nova, much less than the recommended minimum. It had preventive as well as curative properties, and we hoped it would be enough to prevent problems. I felt we were betraying the vines, the earth, and ourselves, but we didn't have any other options and we didn't want to lose the crop.

Later that same day, I went out looking for Alvey. I was miserable and depressed and intending to apologize to them for the spray. But to my surprise they were quite positive and tried to cheer me up. They left me with what seemed like a far more difficult challenge than going organic and avoiding a few chemical sprays.

According to Alvey, it was absolutely essential that we stay out of the vineyard when we were feeling worried or upset. He said the vines didn't actually read our minds and then worry about the specific problems we were feeling so badly about. Instead, they quickly sensed the negative energy and tended to respond by shutting down into a sort of sleepwalking mode. This left them unable to metabolize the things they needed to stay healthy. He pointed out that it also resulted in a slower growth process, slower maturation of the crop, and a slower response of the vines to problems like bugs and diseases.

He also comforted me and said that if spraying a little Nova would relieve our worry for now, go ahead and use it. Evidently, the spray was no more damaging than projecting fear and worry into the vineyard. He also said that our belief system was strong enough to push us in the right direction, but not strong enough to carry us all the way yet. Given the elves' usual attitude against chemicals and sprays, I suspected they were up to something. It was abundantly clear that they didn't like pesticides and such, but they seemed to have embarked on a different approach to working with us than the one they started with. Perhaps they were just being patient, but it crossed my mind in a vague fashion that they were trying to lead us deeper into a whole new mindset with the grapes, rather than just insisting we give up sprays and chemicals. Whatever it was, Jim and I found ourselves trying to reassure one another that it was okay, but I began to secretly wonder if it was simply unrealistic to try to grow anything without chemicals.

Jim and I went across the state for a long Father's Day weekend and arrived home long after midnight, in the early hours of a Monday morning. We planned to sleep in, but the phone rang shortly after eight o'clock. The call was from Dave Moore who wanted to know if Charles Reiskoff had been in touch with us yet.

Dave had taken a little walk through our vineyards while we were gone and found trouble. He called Charles, at the National Grape Co-op office, and Charles came out to look, confirming Dave's diagnosis. Dave advised us to talk to Charles as soon as possible. Jim made the call, I got on the extension, and when Charles answered we were horrified to hear him say he had found symptoms of phomopsis, evidence of black rot, a problem with chemical burn, and signs of nutritional deficiency in both front and back vineyards.

After a lengthy discussion, we were advised to immediately spray a full application of the fungicide Nova to stop the black rot. It was too late to do anything about the phomopsis for this year. We were already past bud break stage of growth.

Charles asked us what we had sprayed on the vines because they showed evidence of chemical burn. He knew that Sonic Bloom was the only thing we had sprayed, and I felt a moment of resentment at the implication that the organic nutrient was harming the leaves. But after a few moments, the idea of chemical burn was dropped and the nutritional problem was picked up. Now, instead of being burned, he said the leaves looked slow-growing and "hungry." Jim told him that we had put on less fertilizer than we usually applied and Charles said if they were his grapes, he would immediately put a dose of fast-acting nitrogen on them. It would help the grapes to catch up in their efforts to produce a crop.

This disturbed both of us. In order to get any real or immediate effect on the vines at this late date, we would either have to buy an expensive, highly soluble formula, or get a cheaper mix and put it on in large amounts, then hope the grapes would absorb enough of it. The problem with chemical fertilizers was that you had to put a lot on in order to get an effect and when it rained, much of it would run off into ponds and ditches or sink into the water table, creating high nitrate levels. Federal standards for nitrate in water were 10 ppm (parts per million) and our water here on the farm was already at 9 ppm.

We hung up the phone, silent and depressed. There was no arguing with such an array of experienced grape growers. Jim drove off in one direction to get fertilizer and I went in the other direction to pick up some Nova for the black rot. We worked all afternoon to get the fertilizer on and in the evening Jim sprayed the full dose of Nova.

Throughout the day we kept trying to look at the situation with positive eyes. The possible loss of our crop was too overwhelming to consider, but neither could we come up with any long-term good in the need to buy and use the powerful chemicals we had tried so hard to avoid.

I kept thinking about a comment that Dean had made over coffee the previous week, "Thirty years ago we didn't have phomopsis." If they didn't have it back then, why did we have it now? Was it the agricultural practices? A fungus usually appears on something that is beginning to deteriorate. The natural purpose of fungus was to help finish up the process of deterioration in a quick and complete manner. Was that what was happening to our fields? I had recently heard about a large area in Florida that simply refused to grow anything except fungus any more! Were we killing our soil and soon ourselves? How could we get off the chemical-spray merry-go-round?

Alvey warned us not to go in the vineyards when we were depressed and blue. I was thoroughly dejected, and Jim was so frustrated that we finally stopped talking about the grapes and even tried not to think about them. But neutral was a hard attitude to maintain—especially when we had started with such high hopes and aspirations.

At the end of that same week, we were forced to put another combination of sprays on the vineyard. The weeds were taking more than their share of nutrients from the soil. So we used Gramoxone to burn them off, and a mixture of Karmex plus a simazine compound to prevent them from germinating again.

We consoled ourselves by taking an experimental approach and applied the chemicals using what Dan Carlson called the Sonic Doom method. Even though the weeds were already eighteen inches tall, very thick and healthy looking, we used a light-to-medium dosage of herbicides with less than half the amount of recommended water. We put the music frequency on so the weeds would open and drink their fill, sprayed lightly with nozzles that created a super-fine mist, then prayed mightily that such a weak solution would at least knock down the weeds with what we hoped would be minimum damage to the soil, the water table, and the many small creatures who lived in the vineyards.

With the weeds as tall and thick as they were, Ernie would have sprayed the maximum amount of herbicide recommended at three times the pressure and twice the amount of water that we used. Normally, by this time of year, we would have been on our second weed spray, not just completing the first.

Usually after using Gramoxone, the weeds were quite yellow and 90 percent down in a day or two. Four days later, our weeds were still standing tall and quite green. Their color had paled a bit, but only a bit. Ernie came by and looked at our results.

"You didn't use enough weed killer!" he told us. "You didn't use nearly enough water either, and your spray was too fine and misty. A heavier spray will saturate the weeds so the herbicide runs all over the plant and drips all the way to the ground. That way it knocks down everything green from the ground up. You might as well put another spray on. This one didn't do the job."

There was nothing we could say at this point. We had hoped that the music frequency of Sonic Doom would make the weeds drink in enough herbicide to at least set them back, keep them from getting any taller and healthier. We didn't think it was necessary to burn them off right to the ground because we didn't want herbicide running all over the soil. Stopping growth was a reasonable compromise, or had seemed like one.

After Ernie left, I wondered if we really knew what we were doing. Perhaps we wasted the herbicides we had by not using enough. After all, the Sonic Bloom process was supposed to nourish everything that grew, making plants super-healthy and resistant to all sorts of diseases and problems. What if that was true and our weeds—which had already received three Sonic Bloom treatments—were strong and healthy enough to resist the Sonic Doom treatment? Perhaps we had only done more damage to the soil and wasted both money and effort. What if we ended up with gigantic weeds that turned their noses up at all but the strongest doses of herbicide? Oh lord, what if we had created a vineyard full of weeds impervious to weed killers? I supposed that we could get a stronger poison, but that would just defeat everything and would certainly worsen the imbalance between the earth and us.

Ernie was back again the next day to see how the weeds were responding. When he left, shaking his head, he said we would definitely have to spray again if we wanted to stop the weed problem before it got completely out of control. He told us he thought that if Sonic Doom was going to have an effect it would have knocked those weeds down already.

Later the same day, Dean was over here razzing us about the music we were playing in the vineyard. He was actually quite interested in what we were doing, but he said other folks were getting quite a laugh out of our efforts.

At the end of the day, I sat on the edge of the bed like a lump. There were times when I wondered if the entire grape-growing community was laughing about our fumbling attempts to do things differently. I knew there was quite a grapevine of gossip winding through our area, and I didn't really care if we were the gossip of the day. But it did bother me that everyone seemed to have a closed mind about almost everything. We didn't really know better than the old-timers, and we weren't trying to show anybody up. We were just experimenting. We had a policy in all of our business dealings which was simply, "If it's a good deal for me and a bad deal for you, then it's a bad deal for both of us." We felt that chemical sprays and poisons might appear to be a good deal for us, but it was a bad deal for the earth itself, and therefore it was a bad deal for all concerned. We weren't trying to convince anyone that they were wrong or bad, we weren't preaching that everyone had to do things our way, and it wasn't some kind of political contest or game where we were trying to win so we could make others lose. We just felt that growing grapes and gardens without chemical poisons was not only the sensible thing to do, it was the right thing to do. We were willing to put in the time to learn new ways, we were willing to make mistakes, we were willing to risk our crop. It didn't have anything to do with what anyone else thought.

Two days later it was time to put the fourth Sonic Bloom treatment on the grapes. We sprayed the front vineyard early on a Friday morning and the back vineyard early on Saturday morning. The weather remained hot and humid, and we were forced to spray some more Nova to keep the black rot at bay. I was terribly disappointed in us. I wanted so badly to stop the chemical bath.

The first week of July was over, the dog days of summer had arrived, and it was hot, humid, and much too uncomfortable to work outside for any length of time. With a combination of frustration and relief I worked in my air-conditioned office all day. That night found me melting in the center of the bed while the ceiling fan whirled the heat around the room in slow circles of sticky, humid warmth. I wanted to sleep but I was too hot, too tired, and too concerned about my father and his health.

A phone call from my mother early in the day had informed me that Dad was going to have more surgery at the end of August. I had promised to be there if they needed me, now the date was set, and she had called to let me know I was needed. A major artery that ran down the center of Dad's body, and then split to go on down each leg, had an eight-inch blockage in it. The result was a left leg that drooped uncontrollably making it extremely difficult to walk, and it had no sense of feeling in it other than being ice cold. They were going to cut out the block and replace it with a section of vein from his leg. The surgery was risky because he only had one kidney left, and they had to work around his colostomy. The last time he'd had surgery his lungs had collapsed again and again, making the recovery long and harrowing. My father was young, only twenty years older than me. Over the past two years he had suffered his way through a variety of serious health troubles. How had he gotten in such bad shape? Worse, the stress of it all had brought my mother's blood pressure to a dangerous level.

I fidgeted in the dark, damp heat for hours thinking, That could be me in twenty years! I don't want to end up like that... what am I going to do? Isn't there anything I can do?

There were no comforting answers, and making my restlessness even more intense, my father's words, spoken in a moment of despair, kept coming back to me, "Don't wait, Pen... don't wait for your golden years to do the things you want to do. The golden years aren't so golden, mine have been a nightmare, and now all the things I wanted to do all my life will never be done. Don't wait!" And as drowsiness finally arrived, his words followed me into my dreams and echoed after me through the night into a morning that was hazy and listless.

A week later my mornings were still hot, tired, and listless. I was uncertain whether it was his words, the heat, or the mid-point of summer that brought on my annual career crisis, but suddenly there it was sweeping me into corners that offered no way out. Every year I went through the valley of new possibilities followed by a trough of anxiety. I didn't want to be an educational consultant any more. Now, for the first time, I saw my own pattern. It started in early July as I worked up a good case against the large chunks of time needed to prepare for late summer seminars, chunks of time I wanted to spend in the garden. By early August, I had my I-don't-have-to-answer-that-damn-phone defense in high gear, and I was sure the hours I'd spent researching the potential of selling vegetables, herbs, and homemade breads were beginning to form a clear picture. By mid-August, I felt I had developed some worthwhile ideas. I was going to make a serious and drastic change.

The whole thing usually came to a positively frothing conclusion in late August or early September when it was time to go back to teaching. Ready or not, willing or not, off I would go, sadly leaving behind my dreams of being able to write in the winter and garden and raise grapes in the summer. My unwillingness to continue teaching classes and working as an educational consultant had been overpowered by my unwillingness to go without food, clothing, cars, and some sort of roof to keep the rain off my computer. Once I was back in the consultant's yoke, shorter, less intense versions of the career crisis would recur at unexpected times throughout the year.

Fortunately, this year the crisis had been relatively short. There were only a couple weeks of vague agonizing, of wanting to do something different, new and more exciting, if not more financially rewarding. This year the fever had waned and my argument was swallowed in an invitation to sign a rather large, luscious contract. My cowardice had cowed me into yet another year of consulting. "If I can make enough money to pay off the farm and finish building our barn, then maybe I could write and raise grapes and garden," I told myself. But once the contract had been signed, I was a mass of seething frustration, unable to eat or sleep. The seething and the heat continued on into the month.

I worked outside only when I could work in the shade, so my perennial garden had a lot of attention. Finally, the evenings began to cool off and I went for a walk through the vineyards. It was the first time in weeks that I had been able to get myself together enough to go walking among the grapes without feeling worried, scared, or generally upset about one thing or another.

This walk, I told myself, was going to be different. This walk was going to be an open-minded learning experience. I was going to examine the vines and the berries and teach myself to quickly recognize anything that looked unhealthy, distressed, or diseased. At Jim's insistence, I took the attitude that it was much better to diagnose and deal with problems than to get upset over their presence.

As Lindy and I walked along the lane past the front vineyard, I saw for the first time the long, yellow strips of dead weeds directly under the trellis. The Sonic Doom method had worked! It was the same in the back vineyard. When I bent over and looked closely, I was amazed to find that the weeds were not just set back, and they weren't just down—they appeared to be completely dead. There was no sign of the typical reemergence of green foliage coming up from persistent roots that had remained undamaged. Slowly, but in an incredibly effective way, the Sonic Doom had given ordinary knock-down weed spray the power to kill the whole weed with a minimal dose and without saturating the soil.

It was encouraging, even energizing, to think we could at least reduce the strength and amount of weed killers while we looked around for some less damaging ways to raise our crop and manage our land!

Reaching the back vineyard I began to zigzag slowly through the vines, stopping frequently to stick my head right up under the trellis. I looked closely at everything—both sides of the leaf canopy, the canes, the grape berries, their color, size, and shape—whatever was there for me to see.

Halfway through the vineyard I was a bit discouraged, thinking to myself that I still hadn't learned how to recognize a single condition other than a few symptoms of phomopsis here and there. I was deep in thought about the specifics of what to look for when a voice startled me.

"What's the matter? Don't you know a healthy vine when you see one?"

I thought maybe it was Alvey and turned to look but there was no one there.

A moment or two passed and then the voice came again, "The reason you don't recognize any serious diseases is because we're quite healthy!" It was the grapevines themselves!

"Oh!" was all I could say, but my perception began to change slowly at that moment, and I was sharply aware of the slow-moving change. It was like watching a movie screen change from black-and-white to color, a sparkling, brilliant change. Suddenly, the vines appeared to be green and vibrant, the growth was lush and healthy, and I noticed for the first time that there were an incredible number of grape clusters on them. It struck me that I had gone out looking for disease and problem vines. Even though I hadn't been able to find any serious trouble to back up the state of mind I was in, the mindset I started out with had prevented me from recognizing what was there—healthy vines in good shape with lots and lots of grapes on them. It was a perfect illustration of how important it was for us to be aware of what we were bringing to our reality. And it was a perfect case of the adage "You have to believe it before you see it."

I began walking again, this time looking at the clusters of grapes hanging before my eyes. The more I walked, the more awed I became at the size of the crop. An earlier comment from Ernie came floating back to me. He had been out to look at our weed spraying job and came back in to announce that it was a bad spray job, but a great crop. "You've got 150 clusters and more on some of those vines," he said. That was quite an increase even over last year's bud count, and a phenomenal increase over the usual ninety or so. But at the time, I was so discouraged about the diseases and the weed spray, I paid no attention to the numbers he reported.

I left the back vineyard and walked quickly to the front vineyard. It was the same. Young grape clusters hung from the trellis like socks hung side by side all down a clothesline. I started to cry. "Oh my god, oh my god..." was all I could say.

Then excitement filled me. "We can't lose this crop! What can we do to get around the phomopsis...?" I was thinking when the voices of the grapes came to me again.

"Keep feeding us... play the music... please..." they chorused.

"I will!" I answered.

I had gone from a tight lump of fear that we would lose the crop, to a determination to learn more about diseases and pests, to a tight bundle of excitement. "What if that crop matures and is harvested?" I thought as I walked back to the house. I had the feeling that our life here would never be the same again.

CHAPTER 19 🔊

I was away doing a seminar for the last week of July, which felt like a lifetime. Jim was out of town when I returned, so I ate a solitary supper, then, even though it was still hot and humid, I went for a walk toward the back of the farm. I walked slowly, wondering how the grapes were doing and if the elves thought I had been away too long. I was vividly aware that it was August. It felt like August. The summer was flying by, and I kept thinking I should begin planning my September classes, which triggered another wave of anxiety over the whole educational consulting career crisis.

I pushed the anxiety aside and kept walking. The sun hung just above the tree line, and I was only halfway to the back vineyard when Alvey and his group strolled out of the cornfield on my right.

"Alvey! Hi! I was just thinking about you guys. It's good to see you again," I said warmly.

"May yer greeting serve us both. Indeed, it's been too long!" he responded in a happy tone, removing his hat and bowing slightly.

"It has been a while, hasn't it!" I replied, feeling I needed to explain. "I was committed to a seminar that took the last part of July to prepare and teach. Then I needed a couple of days for re-entry! Have you guys been taking care of the grapes while I was gone?"

"We have," he nodded. "And it is a good crop," he continued in a matter-of-fact voice.

"Good! I missed both you and the grapes. It seems like I've been away a lot this summer. I've had a hard time getting out here because there are too many places to put my time and attention. It seems like there are always too many priorities to juggle. I keep waiting for a break in the pace of the demands but, in fact, it's been like this for almost two years now."

I wasn't complaining, I was just making an observation, but I wondered if Alvey thought I was making excuses for not walking my land.

He simply nodded and after a thoughtful moment asked, "How is it ye choose among the activities that come before ye?"

Uncertain about what he was asking, I took a deep breath and then stalled momentarily before launching into a long, detailed explanation about just trying to do as many things as I could, things that all seemed important for one reason or another.

Alvey's hands were clasped behind his back. He stared off into the distance and seemed to be listening intently. The rest of the elves stood quietly. When I finished speaking there was no response to what I said, and I thought maybe I had confused them with too much babbling that sounded like a string of half-excuses. I tried to explain again, this time with rising passion and a touch of defensiveness.

"You know, Alvey, I didn't want to do that seminar this summer, but I contracted to do it more than a year ago and I wasn't going to let them down at the last minute. The grapes are very important to me and I love working in them so much that most of the time I wish that was all I had to do. But I love my children, and I have grandchildren now. I just have to take some time for them. My garden is important too, so that takes a little piece of me as well. Working in my flowers, baking my own bread, and finding time to write in my journal—somehow I make time for all these things. Then there are all the other things that demand a little piece of me, things like teaching my classes, answering the telephone, grocery shopping, bookkeeping for our business and the farm, meetings, contracts and reports…" My voice trailed off into silence. Still Alvey said nothing.

Almost as an afterthought I spoke, mostly to myself, "You know, I would really be quite content to just work outside in my garden and my grapes. I would love to come out here and visit with you guys more often, but just like everything else in my life, I only have so much time and I can only put my attention on one form of reality at a time."

"Aa-a-ahhh!" said Alvey and the entire group of elves in singular chorus, startling me. "So… now ye are beginning to understand the nature of balance!" And with that, they turned and disappeared back into the cornfield.

I stood there for the longest time, staring at the corn, trying to understand what they meant by that last comment. I knew it had something to do with the conversation we had been having, but suddenly my mind was a blank. I could not remember what we had been talking about! After a few minutes, I remembered that I had been babbling about not having enough time or something related to attention. Oh! That was it! Choosing where to put time and attention. Did that have something to do with balance? But what balance? How was I choosing? What was I choosing? Was I choosing at all or just reacting to things? And what was it we were trying to balance?

In the end, I never did make it out to the grapes. I felt that Alvey had given me some kind of clue or important key to something, but I remained caught in some immense mystery that was either too simple or too deep for me to comprehend. I could not put any ideas together to produce any sort of "Aha!" of my own. I turned and walked slowly back to the barn in the gathering dusk.

The end of a very damp, humid August approached. One Saturday morning Ernie drove up the driveway and strode into the barn. Waving his arms and speaking with gusto he reported that grape farmers everywhere in our area were suffering serious losses from out-of-control mildews. "Everybody has it!" he announced and wanted to know how much mildew we had. I didn't think we had any, but I really didn't know one way or the other, so he and I climbed into one of the golf carts and went through the vineyards to have a look.

There was no trace of the telltale mildew spots anywhere. The vines and the grapes were beautiful and healthy. He seemed pleased and surprised and said ours was the first vineyard besides his own that didn't have a mildew problem. He told me that a lot of people were reaching the point where the sprays weren't doing the job because the humidity was just too high. Some people had passed the point where continuing to spray would eliminate any profit completely. He left smiling and congratulated us on the good health of our vines, the size of the crop, and the absence of mildew.

After he left, I was grateful in a wry sort of way. For some reason our vines were healthy even though the growing season had not seemed like a smooth one. Momentarily, I was relieved, but then worried that the healthy look was only skin deep. Why didn't we have the mildew problems that everyone did? Was it the effect of love, or perhaps Alvey's benevolence? Or was there something we didn't know or were overlooking? Whatever, I decided it was time to renew my trust in the elves and the vines and believe that all would work out just fine. Then I went back to work in my office.

Labor Day came and overnight any remains of summer disappeared. By the middle of September the grapes were ripening, but very slowly. There was a lot of talk floating around that the grape harvest was going to begin on September 25. That was only two weeks away, and I found it hard to believe that anyone would be ready.

The weather had turned unusually cold and there had been a lot of rain—days and days of cold, wet, discouraging rain. I wondered if it had really been as bad as I thought or if it just seemed that way.

Our first sugar test was due in a couple of days, and I was half afraid to find out where we stood. We had such a big crop and the bigger the crop, the slower the rise to acceptable sugar levels. The cold would also slow the ripening process, but now we had the problem of so much rain. Rain would dilute the sugar readings tremendously. After a rough growing season and with a very large crop, I was experiencing déjà vu. It felt like a repeat of last year and I had a vague feeling of uneasiness in my middle. There was no such thing as a sure thing, and I had learned long ago that you couldn't count your tonnage until the check was in the bank.

I struggled to find the sense of peace and trust that had carried me along the previous year, but even when I did find it, I couldn't hang on to it.

To keep ourselves busy and away from worry, the whole family, all four generations, had worked from morning until night, finishing up a number of projects both indoors and out. Some of the projects had been in progress for weeks or even months. On wet days, things such as kitchen countertops and cupboard doors went on in the barn kitchen. On dry days, flower gardens were weeded and herbs transplanted. The vineyards were mowed and the vegetable gardens tilled. Porch steps were painted, windows washed, fences and hillside steps were repaired, and bushes trimmed.

The entire farm looked quite neat, and in a brief visit with Alvey he congratulated us on the improvements in our "image." He also suggested we give some serious thought to a relatively self-maintaining arrangement of plants and animals. I kept turning the suggestion around in my mind, but I was not at all sure what such an arrangement might be let alone how such a thing might be accomplished.

On Thursday of that week, it was time to take a sampling of our grapes in for their sugar test. Ernie came over to visit as I was looking for a couple of buckets, so he climbed in the cart with me to ride through the vineyards, holding the buckets as I collected the bright purple clusters. On our way through the front vineyard he exclaimed over and over at the number of grapes hanging on the trellis. "Look at them all," he shouted over the roar of the Pumpkin, "the clusters are sticking out everywhere!" I couldn't help giggling at his amazement, but secretly I was proud of how well we had done in this first year on our own.

When I had a representative sample from both front and back vineyards, I dropped Ernie off at his truck and headed up to the sugar shack at the Welch plant. Both vineyards registered the same at only 12.7 percent sugar. I thought I had prepared myself, and staring at the test results I tried to be philosophical, but I was stunned at the poor readings! They were dangerously low for a harvest that was rumored to begin in less than two weeks.

I calculated that with one week of sunshine needed to raise the sugar brix one percentage point, we needed a whole month of sun and warm, dry winds to meet the Welch goal of 16 percent sugar. It seemed like last year happening all over again, but worse. And just like the year before, I told myself all I needed to do was trust. If we made it last year, we could certainly do it again this year, couldn't we?

I drove home asking myself if we should do another Sonic Bloom spray. It might help feed the vines and keep their energy up so they could continue making sugar. Still, how much magic could it possibly create? I needed to talk to Alvey soon. I kept reminding myself that, of course, I trusted everything would turn out tops, but I could not rid myself of an uneasy feeling. Our next sugar test was due in only a week, and I knew we were going to need all the help we could muster.

A couple days later word came down that it was the Niagara grape harvest that was scheduled to begin on September 25—not the Concord harvest. What a relief! We had a magnificent crop. It needed time and sunshine. I needed to stop worrying.

But the sunshine did not arrive. It remained cold and dreary for days. I tried not to be afraid, but I was, and I didn't seem to be able to help myself. I kept thinking I should go out in the vineyard and take some video footage of the fantastic numbers of grapes on our vines because something might go wrong and if, for some ungodly reason, they didn't get harvested, I was sure no one would believe how good the crop had been. But it stayed cold, rainy, and overcast—and I didn't want to take a bunch of dreary pictures. Our grapes deserved a blue-sky background and bright sunshine with full light so the excellent crop could be seen and appreciated. I put off any videotaping.

When the weatherman began to predict killing frosts, I worked in my garden, harvesting as much as I could as fast as I could, and worrying because there was no way to protect the grapes other than a continuous blanket of trust—something I still couldn't dredge up no matter how deep inside me I reached.

It didn't help that by the end of September we were having serious frosts almost every night. Up here on the ridge, our grapes seemed to be doing very well in spite of the cold, but some of the farmers down in the valley did not fare so well. They had already lost their top canopy and without leaves the vines would have difficulty making sugar.

Our second sugar sample went in on the last day of the month. I didn't think we'd had enough sunshine to raise the sugar more than one-half a percentage point, but to my great surprise, the results were dramatically improved over the last sample, having moved up to over 14 percent. I came home on a cloud of excitement and went out to find Alvey to share the good news. On my way I tried to shower the vines with love and energy.

I spotted the entire group of elves at the far east end of the back vineyard, moving in a line toward the wild area so I called out a hello and began to run toward them. The closer I got, the more they began to pop up and down in excitement, calling out their own hellos.

By the time I reached them I was out of breath but broke into a delighted report. "Alvey, guess what! Our grapes have made great progress even without much sun or warm weather. We're averaging 14.2 percent and will be above the minimum of 14.7 percent with only another half-percent increase! If we could get just a little warm weather, we might break all our previous records. I think I've been worrying for nothing. The harvest hasn't even started yet and our sugar is almost there!"

Alvey nodded vigorously, obviously pleased, and the rest of the group buzzed excitedly among themselves at the news.

"What would ye like us to do to help the situation?" Alvey inquired in a most solicitous manner.

He was suddenly so serious that the bubbling feeling drained away and a flash of the familiar anxiety returned. I pushed it firmly away and said, "If you could speak to the wind for us, ask it to keep moving, that would help prevent any serious damage from freezing. And we need a week of warm weather to make that last percentage point of sugar. The closer we get to 16 percent, the less chance they'll freeze and the better the price we'll get from Welch."

Alvey nodded and turned formally toward the rest of the elves. In one motion they huddled in a circle from which came a flurry of conversation in low tones that I could not understand. Moments later the circle broke. Alvey and Mairlinna turned and approached me with great deliberation.

They stopped directly in front of me and Mairlinna spoke gently. "We would ask a favor as well, if ye kindly could? We appreciate yer efforts to trust, we particularly have enjoyed yer visits while walking yer land, and we feel yer attempts to reduce the killing sprays are wonderful. But our agreement this year was built on the understanding that we would bring our magic by doing all that we know and ye would bring yer magic by doing all that ye know. We do not mean to make little of what ye have contributed, but the entire group feels that ye could bring much more than ye have. So while there is still time, we would like ye to review the magic ye have offered and to bring what ye know to the grapes, the vines, and the harvest."

I nodded, confused and uncertain, and when no one said anything else, I spoke aloud, trying to sound confident and enthusiastic, "Sure, I'll do everything I can, without reservation, okay?"

Mairlinna nodded as the entire group of elves began to march away. I stood very still, not sure what to do other than watch them go.

Alvey was the last to turn and as he did he looked at me pointedly and said, "Ye promised to put yer heart and soul into it this year. It's what ye know that we need in this situation!" Then he was gone.

I walked thoughtfully back to the barn, not seeing the lane, the fields, or any of the physical reality that surrounded me. I was deep in my mind, reconstructing the exact agreement we had made earlier in the year. I was certain that I had told Alvey we were going to bring our knowledge and use of Sonic Bloom to our working agreement around the grapes. It seemed obvious to me that the secret to a successful harvest had to be in what I knew about Sonic Bloom. As soon as I reached my office, I called Dan Carlson and told him what was happening with our grapes. He suggested we leave the music frequency on all night if it was going to freeze. He said the music would give us a couple degrees of frost protection, and that we should give the grapes one more Sonic Bloom spray, putting it on as close to 6:30 in the morning as possible. I hung up the phone feeling that I was making a good effort to bring as many resources and as much of my own "magic" to this year's grape crop as I possibly could. I wasn't really worried any more. I knew we were going to make plenty of sugar in plenty of time.

CHAPTER 20

That weekend we gave the vineyards one last taste of Sonic Bloom. I felt sorry for Jim who had to get up at 5:30 A.M. on a Saturday morning to get it mixed, then ride through frosty fields to spray it. Other than that I maintained a strange sense of detachment from everything, which allowed me to keep from worrying. In fact, it seemed like nothing really mattered. At that moment, things could have gone very well or could have ended up a disaster, and I felt I would hardly have been moved, either way.

On Monday, October 4, the sun came out, the daytime temperature went up, and the Concord grape harvest began. So did the pressure. Ernie called once and came over once to let us know Dave was looking for ripe vineyards to harvest.

I told him that ours were not ready, and he left in a flurry to find someone else who was. When he was gone, I kept having this nagging feeling that our grapes were ready and that I should take another grape sample up to Welch for a sugar test, but I was too busy that week. My classes were starting, and I had dozens of details to pull together to get the Learning Center and myself ready.

The thought also crossed my mind over and over that right now no one was ready to harvest, but just as soon as our grapes were ready, everyone else's would be too. Then everyone would be after Dave, his crew and equipment. I kept thinking that I should gamble and call him, telling him we were ready because by the time he got to our place, which usually took a day or two, we probably would be ready.

Thoughts like these were always followed by logical arguments and practical considerations. What if we weren't ready? What if he got here, called my bluff, and the sugar was just too low for acceptance? He might leave and be disgusted at the false notice, putting us at the bottom of his list.

I didn't want to lose any grapes, I didn't want to make him wait, I didn't want to play guessing games to get him here and not be ready. I knew it was a real hassle to move all that equipment and the harvest team from place to place and that once he was here, that was it—those grapes were coming off, ready or not.

All day I kept wishing I had time to go collect another sampling of grapes and take them up to the sugar shack for a test. That would tell me whether to gamble and call Dave or not, but collecting a grape sample and going for a test would take at least a couple of hours out of an already jam-packed day. I would never be ready to greet students by 6:30 that evening if I stopped to deal with grapes and sugar. I had to teach Tuesday night, too, and I was scheduled to be with my Head Start mothers all day Wednesday, so I knew I would not really have time to get sugar tests until Thursday.

By the time Thursday arrived, I was more than impatient to get out in the vineyard to collect my samples and get them up to the sugar shack for analysis. The results were phenomenal. The back vineyard registered at 16.3 percent and the front was at 15.8 percent I could hardly believe it! A lot of people were still below the minimum of 14.7 percent

I didn't even bother coming home to call. Instead, I drove straight to Dave's house and told his mom to tell him we were ready to harvest.

Then I drove home, got out my video camera and went out to make a movie of our wonderful crop. The sky was blue, the sun was shining, the breeze was gentle—it was just the kind of day I had wanted for video taping. I took footage in both the front and back, then went to get my 35mm camera to take some slides.

When I was finished taking pictures, I put the camera away and went back out to the vineyards for the third time, looking for Alvey, but neither he nor the elves were anywhere to be found. I had no one to share my good news or excitement with.

Two days went by, then two nights of seriously hard frosts, and there was no word from Dave and the harvest team. "Where was he?" I wondered constantly. The thermometer was at 24 degrees when I got up Saturday morning, and I was having difficulty maintaining my sense of detachment and peaceful trust.

The frosts continued, becoming killer freezes night after night. We put the Sonic Bloom music on and played it all night every night, but by October 12 we had lost all of our leaf canopy. When I looked across the fields, the vineyards had a deep blue cast to them instead of the wavy green I was accustomed to seeing. Without leaves and loaded with grapes, they reminded me of six thousand pregnant women standing cold and naked on their due dates, ready to let go of what they had produced.

Jim and I kept asking one another, "Should we call Dave again? Is he coming this way? Have you heard where he's going to harvest next? Is he still harvesting the 'double curtains?'[8] Should we leave another message for him?" But we had no answers and the constant flow of questions served only to keep us from concentrating too heavily on our worries.

Still, nothing helped to unroll the knot of fear that seemed to have permanently settled in my middle. If the grapes didn't come off soon we wouldn't have anything to show for our efforts. When I went for a quick walk along the edge of the front vineyard and tasted a handful of grapes, they tasted dry and were lightweight in my hand. I realized they were freeze-drying right on the vine. I was on the edge of a barely controlled panic. I couldn't seem to get hold of myself. Whenever I thought of the grapes I had a vague feeling that just felt bad, and I couldn't get rid of the feeling. Something was not going to go right.

On Friday of that week, three more hard freezes later, Dave and his team finally arrived and started the harvest. By noon the first full load was

---

8 "Double curtain" is a term used to denote a trellising system that uses two upper wires and one lower, instead of one upper and one lower wire.

delivered to the Welch plant and tested at 15.9 percent sugar. It was only one-tenth of a point off the perfect mark of 16 percent, but was obviously down from the high of 16.3 percent of two weeks earlier.

Shortly after the semi-truck returned to our farm, I was horrified to discover that one half of the entire back vineyard had been picked to produce that one load. A load was equal to eight tons, more or less. If we kept that same rate for the rest of the harvest, we'd have only around thirty-two tons of grapes. I was sure something was wrong. There were a few bulk boxes filled and sitting in the driveway, waiting to be delivered, but unless the harvest team had missed a number of rows, we were a long way from realizing the benefits and financial profit of the huge crop that hung on the vines.

I was terribly upset but pushed the feelings aside for the moment. I wanted to get some footage of Dave and the actual harvesting process for my grape video, so I took the camera out to the vineyard to do some taping. After getting some shots of both the equipment and the men at work, I walked into the vineyard to take shots of the vines and the trellis immediately after the harvester had passed over them. I happened to scan the ground under the trellis and the number of grapes on the ground was truly distressing!

Usually the harvester didn't drop any grapes. After Dave and his team had come and gone we were hard pressed to find a single grape except the few that hung on at the very ends of the rows, protected by the heavy endposts from the vigorous shaking delivered by the harvesting machine. Now the ground was blue in a continuous trail of grapes lying under the trellis in each row. I was sick.

In spite of a virtual downpour, the rest of the grapes were picked the next day and delivered to Welch. Even with the rain the sugar was good, ranging from 15.9 percent down to 15.2 percent, well above the rejection level. But it was a very depressing forty tons total grapes picked and delivered.

As it turned out, the repeated freezes over the previous two weeks had reduced the grape berries to lightweight shells, hollow ghosts of what they had been in their prime. In addition, the effects of the phomopsis had made the grapes so loose they could not hang on to their clusters. Instead, they fell off too easily and too many feet in front of the harvester's conveyors. Those that made it into the bulk boxes were so dry and lightweight that their tonnage amounted to almost nothing. Between the freezing and the phomopsis, we had suffered a tremendous loss.

I felt so bad. It was supposed to have been our best year so far, a year to demonstrate the wonders of Sonic Bloom, a year to gather one hundred tons of grapes. Now we had no bumper harvest to show as our results. We didn't even have an especially great crop. Forty tons was right where our average was three years ago, before we started working with Alvey and the elves.

That night I sat alone with a cup of tea and my thoughts. This was the third year we had tried to get a hundred tons of grapes out of the vineyard. For the third time we had tried and failed to stop spraying chemical poisons. And after three years we still did not understand why the elves wanted us to develop Lily Hill Farm and use it to teach the nature of balance. For some reason I thought this third year would be the most successful and most rewarding year of all. But it had been just the opposite—our most disappointing and least successful from the standpoint of grape tonnage as well as stress.

I thought back to that first year of meeting and working with the elves. I was sure the whole year that with our very next harvest we were going to announce to the world that we had produced well over one hundred tons of grapes from a little vineyard that usually produced thirty-some tons— and that we had done so with the help of some elves who had indicated their willingness to work with anyone that was interested in working with them. I was so excited about the possibility of a miracle, so sure that we had an answer to the food crisis our world seemed to be heading toward, that it never occurred to me that anyone would even question the reality of elves.

All that first year I could already see the announcement on television. It had to be television, of course, because I had grown up with TV, I was the TV generation. Those of us raised in the presence of the tube were judged constantly from the point of view of a huge national audience that lived somewhere inside of us. Both audience and screen were built-in to a corner of our minds, with a half million people watching everything we thought and did, rating us, deciding our fate. Television was really a lesson in global consciousness and in the fashion of a good global citizen it was easy to imagine the excitement of finding myself on national TV, announcing the discovery of a solution to world hunger or at least the elimination of poisonous chemicals.

But with a blast of bitter clarity I realized how childish this mental picture had been. Even if the big crop had happened and the announcement had been made, the reality was that half of those who heard it would not believe what they heard, the other half would not care enough to act, and those who were really in a position to do something useful with the information would probably not hear it at all. In five minutes the glorious announcement would be over and the audience left waiting for the next story to entertain or aggravate them. In the depths of painful awareness I realized how pitiful it would be to live out the TV mentality and discover you had been famous for five minutes once. Then what? Would it have made any difference? Would it have generated the change that was needed? Probably not. Worse, how frustrating it would have been to make such a public announcement then be hounded by people who had contradictory beliefs or a totally different perception of reality—one that had no room for elves!

Like a punctured balloon my mind spluttered about in the discovery that there really was no audience—other than myself, perhaps my family and a few friends. For weeks, I was undeniably grateful to have suffered the embarrassing lessons around dreams of glory in the comfort and privacy of my own back yard.

Still, the lessons continued. The next year when the elves managed to produce a truly magnificent harvest of more than eighty-two tons of grapes—a record for our vineyard in spite of a very poor growing year—I thought I had the proof that I was looking for, proof that the elves existed and could indeed produce a tremendous crop. But the need for proof had not only been costly to other growers in the area, it had revealed how selfish and fearful I was.

In our celebration of the big crop, we were unexpectedly visited by a couple of people from the National Grape Co-op who wanted to know what in the world we were doing here that we had pulled off such a big crop for such a small vineyard in such a bad year. If there was ever a time to give credit to Alvey and his group of small miracle workers, that was it. But we didn't—because we couldn't. Physical reality was self-evident and needed no proof, and it was immediately clear that a big grape harvest was not proof to anyone that elves existed.

Of course, this year I fully expected the fulfillment of the original goal—one hundred tons of grapes. But the fact that now had to be faced was that in two out of three years we had not had anywhere near the crop the elves said the land was capable of producing. We had not been able to stop the chemical sprays, and even though we had reduced the herbicide and pesticide amounts a tiny bit, we had certainly not reduced the fertilizers or even come close to eliminating them.

Perhaps what we were trying to do was impossible. We had always been possibility thinkers, but now I felt cynical and wondered if possibility thinking was something for the naive to hang onto while they continued to struggle. Were we wasting time, money, and energy insisting it can be done this way only to discover too late we had been completely distracted from the truth or common sense? Was it really possible to get one hundred tons of grapes out of 13.8 acres of vines? Especially when there were still a lot of holes in the vineyard where vines were missing? Especially when we had such minimal experience?

We needed a miracle, but miracles were mysterious events that happened to saints and holy men back before the Industrial Revolution started. Maybe we were just plain fools, beating a path down the wrong road in the wrong direction and hoping for a miracle that would save face.

Maybe we were doing something that simply didn't make sense. Something was incongruent about the whole situation. Was it the elves? Obviously other people would suggest that we might be off our rockers making deals and taking advice from elves. Were we? It didn't feel like we were. It felt right and good, even though it sounded a little crazy. As for making sense, I began to question why we were raising grapes at all. They were just there when we bought the farm, they hadn't been part of our plans until then. But once we took them on, it seemed that the only nonsense we'd run into was the idea of spraying poisons all over the place and pretending it didn't make any difference.

What were we doing wrong? And were we doing what we thought we were doing? Somehow our original goal had undergone a continuous metamorphosis into something new and different. Maybe we were lost. First we were chasing the Big Grape—one hundred tons of big grapes. Then it seemed to change to an effort to stop pouring on the chemicals. Later it had become an effort to communicate with all the forms of intelligence that seemed to be involved in the world of nature. We became ever more conscious of the other creatures that lived here on the farm with us and the natural systems that supported their existence. Gradually, our focus had somehow become a drive to heal the soil, returning it and the vines and ourselves to good health. Through it all, we began trying to do things in such a way that we would all—humans, plants, and animals—live in secure wholesomeness, feel safe and nurtured.

I thought as soon as we started the communication and stopped the poisons and chemicals, the land and the vines would bounce right back to a healthy balance. But they hadn't—and this year we almost lost, big time.

No one else we knew really seemed to care about nature, about what they ate or what they were doing to the soil. They weren't trying to change their lives to avoid chemical fertilizers and poisonous sprays. Why were we trying so hard to change ours? Did it really matter? Exactly what were we trying to do here—get one hundred tons of grapes, prove some elves exist, or change agriculture and fix the world? Were we being realistic at all? I didn't know, and I didn't know what to do about it. I went to bed and tossed half the night. For the rest of the week I floated on the seas of doubt. Did we know what we were doing? Or were we two children pretending to be on some grand adventure?

It was Friday afternoon. The long week was over and I wanted to talk to Alvey. I had been struggling to keep a philosophical attitude ever since the harvest, and several times I wondered if Alvey and his friends were sad or upset about the way it turned out. All year they were really excited about the size of the crop and had expectations as high as ours had been. I wanted to comfort them if they were disappointed.

I walked to the back of the farm and was down by the pond when over the hill they came, stopping under the wild apple tree just outside the pines that encircled the water.

"Hi," I said, turning away from the water and moving toward the apple tree. "I was looking for you guys."

"And here we are! Greetings and the peak of health to ye!" Alvey smiled and bowed energetically while the entire group bowed and nodded as if to back him up.

"Thank you, and the same to you," I answered, then blurted out, "How are you guys feeling about the grape harvest? I keep trying not to feel down about it, but I'm really disappointed. I'm glad we at least got some crop harvested. It wasn't a total loss. But I've been concerned about you guys and wondering if you felt let down at the poor showing after such a great start. I don't want you to think I have given up on you just because we haven't gotten our one hundred tons of grapes yet. That hardly matters any more."

THE ELVES

I drew these sketches of Mairlinna, Alvey, and Kermots to show my family how they looked to me. When I showed Alvey these sketches, he said I had made him "too handsome" and that he was "more earthy than that." They appear quite solid, like ordinary flesh and blood. Each is unique in appearance. They have an excellent sense of humor that borders on the outrageous and are very patient teachers.

Mairlinna

Alvey

Kermots

THE LAND

◀ The flower garden at Lily Hill Farm where I first struggled to communicate with weeds and earthworms, half-asking and half-telling them to "get out of the way."

▶ The small fish pond, surrounded by rocks and flowers, which Alvey was so pleased about. It was one of our first attempts to make a more friendly habitat for birds and small animals.

▼ This is the wild area that Alvey asked us to leave untouched and in its natural state. I often meet him and the other elves here.

▲ The vegetable garden produces quite a bit of food in a relatively small space.

▶ An example of an untrimmed vine. Dozens of canes sprout in every direction; some grow to fifteen feet and have thirty to forty buds.

▶ An example of a trimmed vine, trimmed using the Kniffen method. All but about six canes have been removed. The best canes for Concord production are one year old, pencil-thin in diameter, chocolate brown, and have buds about five inches apart.

▲ A view of the front vineyard from the upper deck of the barn. At the far right of the photo is the circle of huge evergreens that surround the pond, another favorite meeting place with Alvey.

VINEYARD MACHINERY

▲ The grape harvester, a large machine, easily ten feet high. It straddles the trellis and moves along, vigorously shaking the vines, causing grapes to fall into moving conveyors. The conveyors dump them into one-ton grape boxes being carried by tractor and wagon in an adjoining row.

▼ When new wires were needed in the vineyard, lots of people pitched in to help. Here, my father takes a break beside the tractor and rig used to pull wires from post to post, while others pound the staples that hold the wires in place.

▲ The grape harvester, seen from the front. The driver stands up top on a platform. The large metal fingers that shake the trellis and vines are easily visible, and the chute through which the grapes move on their way to the grape boxes hangs on the left.

▲ The Pumpkin, an old Harley-Davidson golf cart modified for vineyard use with a toolbox on the front and a dump box on the back.

STAGES OF THE BARN

▲ The barn as it was when we first bought the farm in the spring of 1987. This view shows the south and west sides.

▶ The barn after the first stage of remodeling (May 1989). The floor-to-ceiling windows on the middle level were in my office and classroom.

◀ The barn in late 1992, during one of its intermediate stages of development.

▼ The barn, showing the south and southeast sides (July 1996). Still under construction, it has grown to five times the original size. When completed, it will house a teaching kitchen, an exercise/meditation room, a large classroom, several offices, various repair and wood shop areas, a garage, and space to park large pieces of farm equipment during the winter.

▼ The north and west sides of the barn (October 1996). The long row of windows look out from the summer kitchen and the sliding glass door opens into the "Evergreen Suite."

These sketches do not do justice to the shimmering, etheric beauty of the devas, but they give some idea of how they appear. In reality, the devas seem transparent.

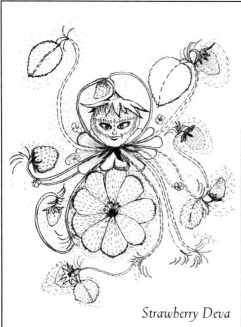

Strawberry Deva

THE DEVAS

Lily Deva

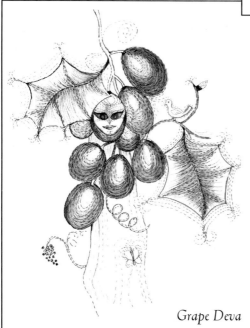

Grape Deva

The dotted lines in these sketches represent the lines of what seem to be light flowing in, around, and through each deva. They are regal, exquisite, gentle, and seem to pulse with life. When they appeared to me in my bedroom, they were about two by three feet. When they appear outside in the gardens, they can be about two-thirds as tall as I am, or smaller, seeming to emanate from the structure of the plant or bush itself.

As I said it, though, I was aware that it did matter. That one hundred tons of grapes was still a big carrot hanging in front of me and denying it left me feeling uncomfortable.

Alvey and the whole group stood quietly with heads bowed. "Yes, 'tis a pity…" Alvey mumbled.

The rest of the elves were clucking in sympathy, shaking their heads and asking one another in low voices, "Alas… Pity, pity… What are we going to do…?" when Alvey began to amble closer to me. The entire group began edging down the slight incline between the apple tree and the pines until they formed a complete circle around me. They had never done that before in that way and I was ever so slightly alarmed. Then Alvey spoke, directly and with a velvet softness.

"'Tis a pity that ye would be feeling bad over getting forty tons of grapes. 'Tis a pity that ye still haven't grasped the real concept behind a hundred tons of grapes. 'Tis a pity ye didn't use the very skill of highly developed intuition ye teach to others to bring this crop in at a better time. 'Tis a pity ye would spend even a minute worrying that we would feel bad. 'Tis a pity that ye still don't understand the nature of balance…" His voice trailed away.

There was an immense quiet. I guessed it had been pointless to worry that Alvey was feeling bad. It seemed that the possibility I might lose faith in him and the elves had not even crossed his mind. It occurred to me that Alvey probably never felt bad about anything. I wondered how he maintained his equanimity.

Mairlinna spoke, interrupting my thoughts that seemed to have a distant, fuzzy quality. "Ye agreed to bring everything ye know to this work of raising grapes and finding the nature of balance. And ye did know when it was time to call Dave. Yer intuition was telling ye what to do and what the risk was. Ye knew ye wanted to call him, and the risk was that the grapes would come off, ready or not.

"Ye knew a sugar sample would help make the decision, but ye delayed the sugar sample because ye thought other things were more important. Instead, ye did things that ye didn't even want to be doing—things that didn't have yer heart or yer soul in them. And the delay cost ye half yer crop. Ye would have had close to seventy-six tons if ye had acted on what ye knew." When she stopped speaking there was silence again.

"Ye still took in a fair crop," Alvey spoke up, matter-of-factly. "Forty tons is more than ye were bringing in on yer own before ye started working with us, the vines, and the soil! The idea to keep in mind at this point is that ye don't have to suffer heavy losses or a complete absence of crop while discovering the nature of balance.

"The other thing to remember is that ye depended too much on Sonic Bloom to correct any mistake ye might make. Sonic Bloom is good stuff, but ye transferred your magic to something outside yerself and this left ye filled with uncertainty, fear and gloom. Ye can't give away yer power and expect to get anything done. And the reason ye were worried about us had more to do with a sense of not having done what ye agreed to do—which was to bring the magic of what ye know along with yer heart and soul to the raisin' o' the grapes."

I stood surrounded, feeling as if I was watching the events from above. Their words had not upset me as they had at previous harvests. Instead I felt curiously calm and thoughtful. Mairlinna was right. I had not gone to get the grape sugar tests when I needed them. I had not called Dave when something in my gut kept telling me that the grapes were ripe and ready. Instead, preparing to teach my classes in Intuition had been more important—even though I had not wanted to teach this year. And yes, I was sure all year that Sonic Bloom could outperform any disadvantage of Mother Nature or stupidity of humanity.

After a moment, I nodded a calm and thoughtful thank-you to Alvey and the whole circle. I wanted to go somewhere quiet and think about what they had said. I didn't feel like I had to make excuses or anything like that. I just felt I wanted to remain in the curiously thoughtful mode until all of what they said or I could settle within had been absorbed and settled.

As if reading my mind the circle parted and the elves moved back up over the hill and out of sight. I took a shortcut back to the barn and sat in a darkened office for hours, thinking about the meeting and the words of the afternoon.

It had been cold and blustery all week. Winter was showing her face early even though it was only the end of October. I went for a walk late in the day and found Alvey back near the wild area we had set aside for him and the elves. As soon as the usual greetings were over, I told him I had been thinking about his and Mairlinna's words at our last meeting. I told him I agreed with their observation that I had not used all that I knew and he was correct in pointing out that I had relied far too much on the Sonic Bloom as my part of our agreement and to guarantee a good crop.

I assured him I would not do that again, but I was still not at all clear about his comments on discovering the nature of balance, and his statement that it was a pity I still hadn't grasped the real concept behind a hundred tons of grapes.

I went on, "I've been thinking about your comments on this harvest and feel I've learned a major lesson about how to play the whole game called 'harvest.' Knowing how to grow grapes, what to spray and what not to spray, how to keep them healthy and well-tilled, all are important—but so is knowing how to play the harvest game, knowing when to make a move! Not only did I concentrate on something other than grapes right at the most critical decision-making time, I was greedy in waiting for just a couple more percentage points of sugar. All we really needed was to get the grapes into the range where they would be easily accepted by Welch. They didn't have to be at 16 percent or above. I was focused on the wrong challenge. It wasn't making sugar this year, it was the timing of our harvest."

Alvey nodded politely and I continued in a rush. "But the thing that is still not clear has something to do with the subject of balance. Do we have to find some kind of perfect balance before we can grow one hundred tons of grapes? If so, what kind of balance are we looking for? Is it something physical, like perfectly restored soil, or something in the way we think? Is it something as simple as not doing what we used to do? I think I know what it would mean to find the balance in nature, but I'm not sure where to begin looking for the whole picture of the nature of balance. Do we need to rethink the whole farm and plant another vineyard in order to get the one hundred tons?

Alvey's eyes rolled in a wide circle and he cut off the gush of my words. "Planting more grapes will certainly put ye further out of balance at this point!" he exclaimed. "Where did ye get the idea of one lonely crop needing all the space and having to make all the money? And how are ye going to keep the rest of yer life in balance if ye plant the rest of the land to more grapes? One bad year and yer whole life is upside down because ye put too much dependence on one thing.

"Discovering the nature of balance requires ye to think of the whole farm in combination with yer whole life. There is no difference between ye and yer soil, ye and yer water, ye and yer air. What ye do to them turns 'round and becomes what ye do to yerself for these are the very sources through which ye nourish yer body."

"Yes, yes… I understand all that," I told him, "but there's something else I can't put my finger on. If you want me to somehow share this idea of balance with the rest of the world, I have to understand all that it is, how one achieves it, and how it is maintained. I have this awful feeling that it's all quite simple, that it's right in front of my nose, and yet I can't see it or seem to get a good grasp of where to start."

"It's yer illusion ye're caught in!" he countered crisply, using a familiar phrase. "Ye're right in the middle of it, yet ye still tell yerself ye can't understand it. Start with yer life… balance that!"

The rest of the group muttered agreements and I heard a cascade of phrases encouraging me to "recognize the obvious" or "get my life in hand."

"But I don't know what to balance in my life or if I even know what that balance would look like!" I cried in frustration.

"Develop yer farm!" they all cried in unison, and then quite unexpectedly, they gathered into a tight group and off they went. Alvey was the last to leave, parting with a long quizzical look that seemed to imply so much without saying a word.

I walked back to the barn feeling as blue as I had the weekend of the harvest. There was something they wanted me to do that I somehow did not understand yet. We were trying to raise grapes without using poisonous sprays, we were trying to fix our soil, we were trying to develop the farm but something wasn't right. They couldn't possibly expect me to become a full-time farmer and think I could make a living at it in this day and age. Yet that was the blank wall I kept running into.

The next day was Saturday, and I was restless and miserable all day. I reviewed the notes chronicling my entire experience with the elves over the three years of our acquaintance. It all seemed to be leading somewhere—but where? We only had fifty-seven acres of land. That wasn't enough to grow either single or multiple crops in a quantity that we could base our income on, and we didn't know how to get into those kinds of markets anyway. I felt like I needed to do something different or reorganize myself—but how? I knew it had something to do with developing the farm, but I did not see how we could survive economically.

CHAPTER 21 ✦

I had been very sick since the beginning of November. A bacterial infection in one ear soon spread to the other, then to my sinuses and my throat, finally into my chest. Ignoring the symptoms had given the infection a good head start, and when I finally paid attention, I tried to doctor myself. It was too late and I ended up at the hospital in the middle of the night, certain that my eardrums had exploded and my skull and face were soon to follow. After that, I was in bed for three solid weeks. My two classes in intuition were interrupted and put on hold, a trip I had planned to Guatemala had to be canceled, and most of the three weeks I was too sick to do anything except sleep. During that time, I had many intense dreams, dreams in which someone told me my ears were infected because I wasn't listening to myself, or that my head felt like it was splitting open because I was split—I didn't want to teach or be an educational consultant any more but I was doing it anyway.

When I finally began to stay awake for periods of time, I thought deeply about the dreams. Gradually I faced the truth that I was sick because I was not paying attention to the signals and symptoms that life was flashing in my face. I had ignored the symptoms of the bacterial infection in the same way that I had ignored the very real need to sort out the conflict between the necessity of making money in order to survive, and my desire to be a writer who gardened and raised grapes during the summer.

Alvey's words. "Start with yer life," kept coming back to me. For years I thought my life was nicely balanced—except for the ever-mushrooming pressure to make more money and the annual drive to get out of educational consulting. I knew that the nature of balance was not limited to growing grapes, fixing the soil, or deciding what to spray or not spray. But each time I stopped to consider all that it might include, I was overwhelmed and suffered an immediate relapse into my old career with its familiar patterns of thought and habit.

Now, lying in bed and face to face with my life, I no longer had the energy to run from the truth. Healing was a comprehensive subject. I couldn't heal physically if I couldn't heal my thinking. My thinking dictated my physical choices. The choices resulted in both my physical experiences and my feelings. These experiences and feelings were heavily impacted by the meanings that had somehow been assigned to them by family and culture. Family and culture seemed to be determined by intangibles such as money, career, status, education, possessions, and other symbols of importance assumed by the culture to be the determining factors of life, but were they? What was life without health? Could I claim that I was healthy if I was unhappy? I couldn't avoid it anymore; it was plain that physical health was only a fraction of the equation of health, and my whole life would have to be overhauled as the balancing of one issue would simply trigger the need to deal with another whole layer. It would be like peeling an onion and weeping, one tearful layer of upset at a time.

It was the middle of December before I felt good enough to get up, get dressed, and begin some semblance of living again. An obscure need to make some sort of reconnection with the farm and the land pulled at me. Gingerly, I put on hat and coat and went out for a walk around the farm. The winter-like weather we had suffered in October was gone, and now that it was almost

Christmas, the weather confounded us by presenting herself in a cloak that was more like early autumn. I did not really think about looking for the elves, but they found me and seemed delighted to see me.

After lively greetings and well-wishes, Alvey inquired about my health. I told him I was feeling much better and was finally off the medication after more than a month on it. As I spoke, I wondered how he knew that I had been quite sick, or if his question just happened to bring up the subject of health.

He looked at me innocently and remarked, "Tsk, tsk, ye best get yer life in balance soon!" while the rest of the elves chortled with great amusement. It was evidently not by chance that he had asked about my health.

While I pondered what to say, he continued with a chuckle of his own, "And would ye be interested in working with us one more year?"

"I honestly can't imagine not working with you, Alvey!" I told him with a smile. "Raising grapes just wouldn't be the same!"

"Good!" he said, "and what would ye like to bring to the effort this time 'round?"

I had given some thought to this during the long weeks in bed and I was truly anxious to try again. "How about several things," I suggested. "First, some walking, and my trust, then some physical work in the vineyards, then my intuition. That ought to cover it and allow me to use everything I have learned so far."

When they all just stood there looking at one another and shifting from one foot to the other, I wondered if I had made a cheap offer. Even Alvey was looking at his feet and poking at the ground with his stick. It was clear there was something else they wanted.

"Well?" I asked, half-impatient, half-humorously, "What else do you want me to do? Go ahead and ask! And don't worry, I can take it! You guys have certainly taught me how to evaluate whether I can do what I'm being asked."

"We want yer heart and soul, yer body and mind to go into it this year," Alvey said slowly. "We asked ye to put yer heart into it last year, but somehow it got translated into 'ye bring what ye know, and we'll bring what we know.' Then yer effort got translated into using Sonic Bloom… and… this year we want it all."

"All what?" I said after a minute, trying to digest the implications of what he'd said.

"All yer time, all yer energy, all that ye know, all that ye can bring to it, all that ye can dream," he hesitated, then suddenly went on as if explaining something. "It's obvious yer never going understand the nature of balance unless ye live it."

"Talk to yer friend," Mairlinna spoke up with an air of urgency, "the one who would like to be able to understand the power of focused consciousness. A clear commitment to develop the farm combined with the power of focused consciousness would allow ye to discover the nature of the balance that must be regained here on this earth if we are all to enjoy life, health and the joys of existence."

"We could work so well together!" Alvey commented positively. "I mean all of us… if more people could just understand that they are not the only form of intelligence living here. We have so much more we can give if only we had someone willing to receive…." The entire group of elves was murmuring agreement along with offers of good health, long life, and a peaceful world.

For a moment, I flashed back to that first experience with the elves. I had been extremely upset that our country was heading toward a war with Iraq over the invasion of Kuwait. The elves had commented in that first meeting that our world was seriously out of balance and so close to a nightmare they were sure we were all asleep.

Suddenly I understood fully that the nature of balance was far more comprehensive than I had first grasped. It went far beyond my small life, our ideas of developing Lily Hill, our attempts to reduce the use of chemicals or to rebuild the soil. It was more than just being personally healthy. It included things like a balanced population, raising and educating children while connecting them much more firmly to nature and the soil, finding lifestyles and expressions of work that nourished the soul and developed human potential while replacing whatever was taken from the earth. It meant a full reevaluation of how we spent our time, our energy, our money, and perhaps even a restructuring of our institutions and culture.

I was engulfed in a sea of emotion at the mountain of changes that appeared necessary to even begin thinking about the nature of balance in our present world.

"It has to start somewhere," Alvey said brightly, interrupting my avalanche of awareness.

"Sure..." I squeaked, "um, yeah... I suppose it does... and, um, sure, I can put my heart and soul, all my time and energy into the grapes this year..."

"Into the farm!" Alvey corrected me with exasperation sounding in his voice. "To grow a hundred tons of grapes ye need to put yer heart and soul into the whole farm!"

"Yeah, okay...." Somehow I managed to say good-bye and make it back to the barn. I spent the rest of the day planting tulips, moving lilies and hyacinths, and tilling my flower gardens while dozens of ideas on the nature of life in a balanced world swirled through my mind like hurricane-force winds.

What would it mean to put all my time and energy into the farm? Would that make me a farmer? I had often wanted a change, but was seriously uncomfortable with the idea of being a farmer. It went against all my old prejudices. I would have to deal with my pride.

Neither did I have any clear idea of how to make a real living from the land. I was two generations removed from making a living on the soil. When I had brought the subject up a year earlier among people I knew or those who were already farmers, without exception they had commented that we could never make it on just fifty-seven acres of land. "You need at least 160 acres," one farmer said. "Gotta have 500 acres and the right crop at the right time," another had advised. "Forget it!" was the most common answer. "People are getting out of farming, not into it. Let the big boys do it!"

Surely, Alvey and his group could not be serious about developing Lily Hill Farm as a means of making a living?

Several days and ten thousand thoughts later, I knew I was groping in the dark and didn't know where it would lead, but I decided it was time to seriously consider developing the farm. I was going to act as if I knew what I was doing and make an effort to develop a more organized approach. We had not taken a positive and pro-active approach to what we'd been doing. Rather, we had been more caught up in worrying about what we needed to stop doing and what we needed to stop thinking or believing. And the shotgun approach we used to target new goals had certainly been less than successful.

Since our mediocre harvest, we had made several trips to the bookstore, spent many dollars and myriad hours seriously reading and discussing subjects such as soil science, composting, integrated pest management, foliar feeding systems, vegetable trellising, super nutrition, the basics of healthy living, food combining, self-healing, the benefits of organic food and raw foods, as well as many other topics that had never gotten a minute's attention before. Among those topics were people who talked about life without pesticides as if it were really possible. Neither Jim nor I was quite sure how to go about making a change—a successful change—to what we now realized was clearly a more natural and organic method of raising grapes and taking care of ourselves. But we were determined to learn.

Perhaps Alvey was right and the key to understanding what we were doing here on this farm was to begin developing it, to start living it. We didn't know what it would develop into, or how we could make a living, but we were sure that it was somehow tied to all the things we had been reading about.

The weather was still warm a few days later so I went for another walk, looking for Alvey and Mairlinna, my mind still fumbling through the hurricane of ideas and awareness that stemmed from our last meeting.

I walked all over the farm, but didn't find them so I ended up on Golden Mountain sitting among the dried grasses, staring across the landscape. I was just about to leave when I heard them coming through the thicket at the bottom of the hill to the east. Skipping and running I headed down the hill toward them.

"Hi, Alvey, hello, Mairlinna!" I called out as they came into view and we neared each other.

"Greetings! It makes the day a bit more fair to meet with ye," Alvey replied in a gallant manner while removing his hat and bowing low. The rest of the elves bowed as well, bobbing down and then straight up, again and again, in a comical pattern. They reminded me of a toy piano I had once bought for my children with doors that popped open and closed as you pushed on the keys.

Alvey cleared his throat loudly and they all came to attention immediately, huddling together with too-serious faces.

"And what would ye be needing today, ma'am?" he asked, eyebrows on the rise.

"Actually, I just wanted to let you know that I was kind of overwhelmed at your request the other day. I wasn't feeling very confident when we parted. So, I just wanted to firm up my commitment to work with you."

Alvey nodded, so I continued. "I'm still trying to figure out how I can give my heart and soul, body and mind, time and energy completely to the farm and still make a living. After all, I do like to eat!"

"Yep! And that's exactly where most of ye first get out of balance!" he chirped.

"What do you mean? That we get out of balance because we need to eat?" I asked with surprise.

"Oh no," he replied, "of course ye need to eat. It's just that when ye give up the right to produce yer own food ye've moved away from the central balance point of life here on earth. Next thing ye know ye're eating whatever ye can find, proper or not, and yer health is out of balance. Eating like that affects yer mind, and the next thing ye know ye're feeling irritable, fighting over possessions, and really off the beam. After that, the balance between energy and time goes and before ye know it, yer whole reality is out of focus. Ye end up not remembering how to feed yerself and then it really turns into a nightmare.

"The basis of yer reality is the world of nature. We all come from the world of nature. Lose that direct connection and ye will lose the whole reality because ye've lost yer base. Humans are at the top of nature's heap. Ye humans need everything that's in the heap under ye to support yer form of life. But nothing in the heap needs that human at the top. Ye humans are the most expendable of all—yet ye all think ye're indispensable!

"Picture the security of the human race right now as one lonely person riding a unicycle across a tightrope that is tied between two poles anchored in soup bowls floating on an ocean. Yer position is tenuous—at best!"

Then, without further comment, he put his hat back on his head, turned to the rest of the group, and off they went, leaving me and my hurricane at fever pitch.

CHAPTER 22 ❦

It was December 30, and 1993 was nearly over. The next day was New Year's Eve. Dinner had been eaten and cleared away. Jim was working in his shop, putzing as he called it, and I was wandering around my office, wishing the piles of papers, books, projects and general mess that had reappeared over the summer and autumn would clean themselves up. When they showed no sign of doing so, I went to make myself a cup of tea. I sat in the darkened kitchen, sipping the warm liquid and stewing about what it meant to develop Lily Hill.

In the first year of my association with the elves, they showed me a picture of what the farm could look like if we developed it. Occasionally, I had thought about this or that aspect of what I had seen, decided it was nice, and then went on about my business, never able to figure out why we would go to all that work or expense trying to make a place that looked like the Garden of Eden. It was beautiful, yes, but I didn't see how it would make us a living. Having once been very poor, I had a healthy respect for usefulness and practicality. I had climbed out of the pit of poverty through hard work and perseverance. The result was that I was fiercely skeptical of pretty dreams and frilly fantasies that lacked substance. A lot of people I knew who pursued spiritual development or the dream of making the world a better place did not believe that money, spiritual development, and meaningful work could go together; thus they were still struggling with that same pitiless poverty I had once believed in. I was not about to rejoin them by chasing some grand yet fruitless pursuit of better world work, all the while telling myself "it's a noble, worthy cause, therefore the gods or the universe will take care of any money problems." A beautiful farm was a nice idea, but for me it had to be more than that. It had to be practical, it had to be useful, and it had to take care of our physical needs—as well as serve some higher purpose.

When I finished the tea, I rinsed out my cup and put it in the sink. Not knowing what else to do with myself, I put on some of my favorite meditation music, seated myself in a large, comfortable chair, and dropped into a meditative state. Shortly, a series of amazingly clear pictures began to come to me. They were pictures of the farm and what was going on here.

It began when I saw myself just working with the grapes, trying to communicate love and energy to them.

The interest in plants and growing things continued to expand.

People began to come here for all sorts of reasons—mostly to learn how to heal themselves in physical, mental, emotional, and spiritual ways.

The house had become a sort of inn and we were living in an apartment above the completely finished barn, which had grown considerably in size and layout.

Some of those who came here rented a room in the house, getting clean, comfortable beds and baths; a regimen of vitamins, herbs, fruits, grains, and vegetables. There was massage therapy; music therapy; water therapy; lessons in how to cook to heal themselves; a personal growth and development plan; a personalized healing plan; the challenge to grow and learn; and a totally new experience of healing enhanced by being in a place of beauty filled with love, nature, peace, and good company.

Those who came for healing were encouraged to take an interest in and help heal others rather than be isolated in their illness.

The setting here provided multiple levels of support for healing and for personal development, along with clear, congruent information. This, combined with the obvious demonstration of balanced, healthy lifestyles had a massive effect on an individual's perception of how to live, or what was important in life.

There were also people who lived and worked here besides Jim and me. They worked in the gardens, and they helped take care of other people. Each had a special gift, an interest in health, and a desire for balanced living.

We provided some of these people who worked here with a home or room to stay in, good food, and an opportunity to make a balanced living by developing their own small, specialty businesses, which were either related or complementary to ours.

Sometimes these people who lived and worked here would take a special-interest case directly into their own home to earn extra money, study a particular pattern of illness, or develop a special therapy or form of nurture and support.

There was a house to the east, two houses to the west, two houses near the back pond, a house on Golden Mountain, and a house located about halfway to the back of the farm along old 32nd Street.

There were many, many trees and plants cultivated here on the farm.

There were patches of grains of all sorts in small quantities. We had some kind of cutting machine that looked like a rototiller but with a blade that stuck out in front or to the side. Jim, who loved inventing, had developed, or bought and then altered, this cutting machine to harvest small amounts of grain, an acre or two, grown organically, then harvested and shared with everyone here.

Some of the grain was stored in a large root cellar or basement here, then it was ground fresh just before being made into many kinds of breads that were eaten here or sold and shipped elsewhere.

We had a large, old-fashioned summer-kitchen that was used by nearly everyone here for eating, for cooking, for relaxing, for congregating, for teaching, for handling the large amounts of fruits, vegetables, grains, and herbs grown here.

The vegetable gardens were amazing and delicious places to browse for goodies to eat. Some of the vegetables I didn't even recognize.

There was a room in the corner of the North Barn that was nearly soundproof. In it a person could sit or lie down and be surrounded by therapeutic music while relaxing or meditating. Specific frequencies could be introduced as standing waves, and it was quite a powerful healing room.

There was another room that contained a large tank of water that people floated in and experienced a deep, healing form of meditation.

The grounds and the fields were also bathed in healing music in the early morning and again about dusk.

Over three hundred different herbs and leaves and roots and berries were grown here, dried here, and stored here.

There was an incredibly beautiful area of trees in a circle to the west of the house. There was another grove of trees toward the back near the pond. A firepit and meeting circle was in the middle of a third grove of trees nestled between the big hills just west of the lane.

The lane that went to the back of the farm had branched into several lanes and all were lined with fruit trees and hedges. There were small orchards in several places and a variety of delicious fruits were available.

There were a number of paths here and there that lead to small, beautiful, even romantic areas among the trees, flowers, or by one of the ponds. These places created serenity and peace in the soul of the visitor who happened to visit them.

There was a greenhouse used to grow special plants from other weather zones that would not ordinarily survive this far north. In the greenhouse was a Kirlian gadget that Jim had put together for diagnosing plant illness and disease.

There were sheep, goats, and chickens here! They lived in a small barn built for them near the cherry tree. They provided manure for renewing the soil, a few eggs for eating or baking, and some goat's milk for drinking and making yogurt. I had even learned to milk a goat and shear the sheep. They were more like pets and were not slaughtered; however, some were sold.

There was very little grass or lawn area at Lily Hill. Most of the land had been returned to habitat status or was used for gardens, herbs, or grains.

The west entrance of the barn was now a private entrance with a sloping sidewalk, a large screen-porch, and some beautiful flowers and plants. The main entrance and parking had been moved to the northeast side of the barn.

There were some short trees, about fifteen feet high, in the area that was currently used for parking. They provided shade in the summer and deep pink blossoms in the spring. The parking area looked more like a park with flowers and bushes and benches.

Almost the entire front yard of the barn was a beautiful herb and wild flower garden. Across the driveway, the land sloped down to a pond named Willow Pond beside which several beautiful willow trees grew.

We collected plants and seeds from everywhere we went. In fact, seeds, transplants, and cuttings were part of what we offered here. The fact that they were grown organically was quite an asset because they were extremely healthy and tolerant of all kinds of conditions.

There was quite a shipping and mailing operation here. People sent for seeds, herbs, books, bread, and other handmade, homemade items. They also ordered jams, jellies, sauces, mustards, juices, and other items made with our organically grown fruits and vegetables.

People came here in person to buy food—fruits, vegetables, herbs, eggs, yogurt, and grains—all organically grown, super-nutritious, and unparalleled in taste and keeping quality.

There was an herb growing and drying operation that was a large and continuous part of what we were doing. Some were sold to restaurants, some were dried and shipped elsewhere. Most of the appeal was the fact that they were organic, which gave them exquisite flavor.

We were teaching people to grow their own food and how to get from the soil to the stomach. This involved everything from composting to harvesting techniques, some preservation, and especially cooking from scratch rather than eating fake food out of boxes. We emphasized that growing your own food and cooking from scratch was a necessity, a right, a pleasure.

Many of the things we did here involving cooking, gardening, and healing were either audiotaped or videotaped, then edited and sold elsewhere to people who were interested in healthy, organic food and gardening.

Some of the techniques and music used in the music therapy room were also recorded and sold. In fact, there was quite a recording studio operation here.

The healing that went on here was based on a very simple philosophy: clean out the body and it would heal. Feed it healthy, nutritious food—and it would maintain good health. Help someone find a reason to live, and health became an important life goal. Clear emotional pain and mental garbage and the human being began to evolve toward his or her private, unlimited potential.

We were teaching how to project loving energy to people, plants, and animals. Most of all, we were teaching love; we were teaching peace. We were demonstrating how people could live together in an extended family lifestyle that supported the earth, the individual, the family, and the community.

There was a lot more that I saw besides just this. Some of it was personal, some was too unusual to mention. I was not sure how it all became part of our everyday reality, or even how it began, but it was clear that the growing and making of some very special food was a major part of what we were doing.

When the meditation ended, I sat for a long time sifting through the things I had seen and experiencing a state that could be described as a kind of where-did-all-that-come-from wonderment.

By New Year's Day, my resolution had been made. I spent the whole day cleaning my office and file room. Another six months' worth of clutter went into the trash bin. It was time to begin the transition to developing the farm. My ideas on how to actually get going were incomplete, but for the third time, I figured that cleaning out the old stuff was an appropriate step for now. The rest was based on trust.

CHAPTER 23

At the end of the first week of January, needing time off and determined to do something to help ourselves take a step in the direction of more natural and organic growing techniques, Jim and I decided to attend an agricultural conference offering a number of interesting seminars. This took us to Chicago where we spent several days at a conference on herb farming and specialty-grower markets that we had seen advertised in the *Fruit Growers News*. The program did not offer much in the way of support for organic growing, but as we wandered through the exhibits, we happened to talk to a fellow named Eric Gibson. He had written a book titled *Sell What You Sow*, and as I purchased a copy, he asked about our farm operation. When I told him that for the moment we were just trying to figure out how to grow anything without chemical poisons, he enthusiastically told us about a group called the Committee for Sustainable Agriculture. It was made up of people interested in all kinds of organic growing and they were having their Fourteenth Annual Ecological Farm Conference the very next week in Pacific Grove, California. We didn't really have the money for the registration and lodging fees, but on the spur of the moment, we decided to attend. Halfway there, I wondered if we were on a goose chase, but two weeks later we came home renewed and immensely relieved. The conference had been a godsend! Not only had we met and talked with agricultural specialists and consultants, farmers and ordinary people from all over the country who were cultivating large acreages without chemicals and poisons, we had found practical answers to our major questions on restoring the soil, managing pests, coping with fungus diseases, and dealing with weeds.

"Hang on, you're just in the transition phase," they told us. The elves had been right. Truly organic vineyards were a real possibility.

When we returned to Michigan the weather was still extremely cold. So far it had been a numbing winter with the temperature down as low as thirty degrees below zero on the thermometer accompanied by forty-mile-an-hour winds. I was concerned about our grapes. Concords could be severely injured and even killed at temperatures below minus twenty degrees. But my concern was highly tempered by my excitement about what we had learned on our travels. We had bought more books at the conference, over four hundred dollars worth of them, and both of us took up the study of non-toxic gardening and farming with a passion. For the next month, we wrapped ourselves in the theory and practice of sustainable agriculture.

The end of February was approaching, the weather was still cold and snowy, and for the first time in weeks I took a break from reading and study. I needed to do something different, so I got out my seed catalogs and began planning my garden.

When that was done I got out the notes detailing my conversations with the elves and decided to make another effort to pull them together. What happened as I did so was a huge and powerful coalescence of all that had happened in the past three years with all that I had learned in the past seven weeks. Suddenly, I could see where it had all been leading.

Three and a half years ago I went for a walk and wandered into a deal with the elves who offered me a hundred tons of grapes. That promise now seemed to have been a thinly veiled challenge cloaked in exactly the words that would hook my attention. Maybe I had needed a distraction from the fears that my son would be drawn into meaningless wars in frightening places. Perhaps it was because I wanted to do something exciting or something that would change or help the world.

Whatever it was, I had wanted to do something different, something besides educational consulting. I was looking for a change and the elves knew, or sensed, it. Perhaps they had even appeared in response to my need for change. But any way I looked at it, I had been hooked, quickly and completely. I liked the challenge they had presented on the surface. I thought it had to do with believing that eight or twelve or twenty tons of grapes per acre were possible. I even thought I knew what the outcome was going to be. It was going to be a Findhorn-style outcome with huge grapes and continuously high tonnage.

But the challenge turned out to be more than an effort to grow and harvest one hundred tons of grapes. The real challenge ended up confronting my entire belief system and our whole way of life. Offering me a chance to learn something about the nature of balance, they had led me down a path I would never have considered taking. I had taken on a lifestyle change of a major order. I had gone from something of a self-proclaimed expert on the brain/mind, perception, and consciousness to the lifestyle of a farmer, albeit a slightly reluctant one.

Several months into my dealings with the elves, I realized in some unspoken and unacknowledged way that increasing our grape tonnage might make it financially possible to leave educational consulting and begin doing the things I had always wanted—to garden all summer and write all winter. Suddenly, that hundred tons of grapes became the pot of gold that would allow me to garden and write without starving, freezing, or going bankrupt.

From that point on, I was seriously interested not only in the possibility of a hundred tons of grapes. I wanted that hundred tons to be consistent and I was willing to do whatever I could to help achieve it.

Once hooked, the elves kept pushing me to push Jim to avoid chemical sprays and fertilizers. They invited us to develop a working relationship with the gentle forms of intelligence that seemed to be the very essence of flowers, plants, and trees. We began to communicate with other forms of energy like the wind, the rain, our vines, and the many small critters that crawled, flew, or burrowed into our land. And over all, the elves kept asking us to develop Lily Hill Farm.

Thinking that this meant the decision to delve deeper into farming and return to the soil, we had taken a little time to try to learn about the land and the soil. We didn't know a lot, but we were beginning to feel like we had an outline of the basics. And the most basic of all was that dead soil produced increasingly nutrient-deficient vegetables and fruits, which left a trail of sick and dying people. Alvey's insistence that we stop spraying pesticides and other poisons was an attempt to make us understand the essential necessity of maintaining living soil. Soil, in a live, healthy condition, was a collection of crumbs! These crumbs were made up of particles of sand, dirt, clay, minerals, decaying matter, and the bodies (both living and dead) of millions of micro-organisms.

As these microscopic organisms lived, they excreted sticky substances; as they died and deteriorated they gave off other gooey stuff, all of which formed a sort of glue that held the particles of sand, clay, minerals, and dirt together in what was called the crumb structure of the soil. These crumbs, like marbles in a glass, formed a light, airy honeycomb of passages through which the roots of plants moved easily in their search for tasty nutrients, minerals, and moisture.

As the fine root hairs of growing plants worked their way through this kind of soil, they wrapped themselves tightly around the individual crumbs. Once the crumb was firmly in their grasp, they emitted a variety of humic acids. These plant-emitted acids combined with the gooey excretions of the bacteria and micro-organisms living in the soil. Together they turned into other mild acids—all of which reacted chemically with nutrients and trace minerals trapped in the soil crumb around which the root was wrapped. These acids helped break the soil crumb into its basic elements making them available for absorption by the plants.[9]

---

9 For further information see *The Rodale Book of Composting*, edited by Deborah L. Martin and Grace Gershuny, published by Rodale Press in Emmaus, PA.

I had always thought of soil as this messy, lifeless stuff that just held up the plants, but good soil was not only alive, it had form, structure, chemistry, and certain behaviors! When it rained, water falling on good, healthy soil would sink deeply into and through that same honeycomb of passages formed by the crumbs. Not only would the deep roots of plants be given a good drink, the water served to dilute the humic acids produced in the soil, thus preventing a chemical burn caused by nutrient overdose that also stunted plants. Healthy soil would absorb at least four times its weight in water before any kind of saturation point was reached, and rainwater dropping onto healthy soil sunk in immediately and quietly. It did not create mud that splashed all over the place or stuck to your boots!

By spraying poisonous chemicals on our fields and gardens, we killed the micro-organisms and bacteria that provided the glue that held the soil together in its crumb formation. With the death of the micro-organisms, the structure of the soil collapsed into a hardened mass that could literally turn into something like cement. It was called hardpan, and roots could not work their way through it. Rainwater rolled off of it instead of sinking deeply into the myriad passages and tunnels formed by the crumbs. Unexpected flash floods were not only a dangerous result, they carried whatever remained of precious topsoil off to be deposited in streams, lakes, rivers, and the living rooms of those who had built their homes in unfortunate places.

Of course, once the micro-organisms and bacteria had been killed, their work—which was to excrete humic acids that would break down mineral elements into nutrient forms the plants could use—did not take place! Plants needed nitrogen, phosphorus, and potassium, the standard ingredients in any NPK fertilizer, but they had a critical need for over fifty other mineral nutrients if they were going to be healthy and produce nutritious food. Destroying the soil left plants unable to take up the many nutrients they needed and the result was not only impaired function in the plant itself, but vegetables, fruits, and grains that were empty of nutrients that we humans needed.

Plants grown in poor, dying, or dead soil were not healthy enough to withstand cold, heat, periods without rain, or the normal range of pests, fungi, and viruses that lived in any soil. Our headlong rush to develop new hybrids or experiment with genetic engineering was driven by a misguided attempt to create plants that would adapt to conditions that they would have had no problem with if the soil had been healthy in the first place.

To my amazement, I discovered that plants radiated an electromagnetic field and that the antennae on bugs were exactly that—antennae! Healthy plants radiated a particular complex of electromagnetic signals that was different from the signal range given off by unhealthy plants. Insects and pests could pick up alterations in the electromagnetic signals from a diseased or dysfunctional plant and using their antennae as built-in radar would find the plant and attack it. Even when healthy and unhealthy plants were placed next to each other and their stems and leaves intertwined, the insects would ignore the healthy leaves and the plant would remain intact!

Healthy plants grown in good soil not only gave off a different electromagnetic signal, they maintained a very high level of natural sugars in their leaves, stems, and fruit—and this was the magic key to pest control! Logic would say that insects and pests would be anxious to get to the plants with the highest sugar brix. But it was only humans that were addicted to sugar. Insects munching on such plants would quickly get a paralyzing stomach ache and abandon the plant altogether. The high sugar also combined with the bugs' internal chemistry to produce an alcohol that quite effectively knocked out the delicate metabolism of insects and pests. Those insects who foolishly continued to eat would fall into the soil in a drunken stupor and end up as a tasty lunch for the micro-organisms and bacteria that lived in the soil![10]

The more I learned, the more hugely obvious it became that pesticides, herbicides, fungicides, and unbalanced chemical fertilizers were forces in a tragic, spiraling drama that few understood. The dead and collapsed soil we insisted on trying to grow foods in was just not capable of producing either healthy plants or healthy foods. Since insects and fungus were nature's garbage collectors, her way of cleaning up sick, diseased, or dysfunctional plants and removing them from the landscape because they were not fit for consumption, our continued use of poisonous sprays to protect worthless crops was nothing less than ridiculous, ignorant, and doomed.

Now I understood why the use of chemical sprays and fertilizers had become a bottomless pit once you started using them. I understood why our soil hadn't bounced back immediately. It was dead. We were having such difficulties in both garden and grapes because we were trying to bring the dead

---

10 From *Mainline Farming for Century 21* written by Dan Skow, D.V.M. and Charles Walters Jr., published by Acres U.S.A. Publishing in 1991.

back to life! We needed to reintroduce living micro-organisms into the soil and let them multiply over time, gradually restoring soil structure, known as tilth.

Fruits, vegetables, and grains that grew from dead soil were almost as dead as the dirt they came from. Even when they looked beautiful they lacked basic levels of proteins, sugars, and minerals. Worse, they contained chemical residues and other poisons. Healthy, normal amounts of protein in vegetables and fruits had to be at least 25 percent to support human life. Foods grown in the depleted soils of these United States had been at 3 percent or less for at least thirty-five years.[11] No wonder everyone I knew was sick, depressed, or falling apart.

I began to recognize the signs and symptoms of worthless food, signs that I had come to accept as normal when buying fruits and vegetables. Sweet corn, the kind whose kernels dented in on top when it was cooked then cooled enough to eat, was sick, anemic corn. Peaches and nectarines with split pits in the center were suffering from a lack of manganese, a factor in prostate and breast cancer. Broccoli or cauliflower with a hollow area that ran up the stem was deficient in boron, a trace mineral that allows us to absorb and use calcium. Lettuce, broccoli, brussels sprouts, and spinach that did not remain crispy, whether in or out of the refrigerator, were seriously deficient in calcium. When there was too much potassium in soil, the potassium would replace calcium in plants. This potassium-calcium mismatch in foods was not only the culprit behind soft, wilty vegetables, it was a major cause of heart disease and kidney disease in both animals and humans.[12] Lack of calcium was also a major cause of everything from osteoporosis and tooth decay, to many forms of depression and insomnia.

Natural sugars, also known as complex carbohydrates, were another story. "Fresh" fruit that rotted in only a few days did not have normal amounts of complex carbohydrates in it. In fact, fruits (or vegetables) that had the proper balance of natural sugars would not rot at all. Instead, it simply dehydrated, becoming a shriveled version of its former self, now dried and full of concentrated nutrition. Since plants used their natural sugars to make proteins, any deficiencies or anomalies in their sugar production often resulted in missing or low-grade proteins.[13]

---

11 *Science in Agriculture*, written by Arden B. Anderson, published by Acres U.S.A. Publishing in 1992.

12 *Mainline Farming for Century 21*, written by Dan Skow, D.V.M. and Charles Walters Jr., published by Acres U.S.A in 1991.

13 Ibid.

When phosphate was missing in the soil, nutrients would be taken into the plant, but they were never incorporated into the cells of the fruit, vegetable, or grain. Instead of good, healthy structure, the crop would be bloated, watery, and tasteless. Shortly after harvest, the shrinkage in these foods was unbelievable. It was the same with livestock and the meat obtained from them. Animals fed crops that were overloaded with nitrogen and potassium, but deficient in phosphorus, would produce cuts of meat that shrank away to nothing in the skillet or the broiler. They also tasted like cardboard because the minerals and nutrients needed for quality meat just weren't there.[14]

To make matters worse, these foods went straight from dead soils to huge food-processing plants, where the few remaining vitamins, fiber, nutrients and enzymes were removed via processing that would supposedly make it safe for public consumption. When we ate them, we not only ingested their original load of pesticides, fungicides, herbicides, and heavy metals, we also ended up filling our stomachs with strange preservatives in food that was only slightly more tasty and nutritious than the shrink-wrap it was packaged in.

I had never known until now how common the agricultural practice was of picking unripe vegetables and fruits, storing them in preservatives until they were out of season so they would bring a higher price, and then gassing them with chemicals to make them look ripe just before sale.[15] To help prevent evaporation of their water-logged flesh they were often waxed, and many of the waxes contained fungicides to prevent molds and mildews.

It was no wonder those fruits that looked so inviting brought such disappointment once you bit into them, no wonder that two days after purchasing a cucumber it had to go in the compost, and no wonder that lettuce was tasteless and turned to watery slime before I had a chance to use it up.

Only fruits and vegetables ripened on the vine would taste sweet or be juicy, because the picked-and-stored fruit could not make any more high quality sugars for itself. Only fruits and vegetables allowed to ripen before they were picked would have the full complement of nutrients necessary to sustain human life. And only fruits and vegetables with high levels of natural sugars would have a decent shelf life. The higher the natural sugar content, the longer

14 Ibid.
15 *Rainforest in Your Kitchen*, by Martin Teitel, published by Island Press in 1992.

the vegetable or fruit would last. What would people say and do if they knew they could get fresh peas[16] so sweet they would easily last two months, or watermelon[17] that was still juicy and delicious six months after being picked!

Other awarenesses began to click into place. I had never made the connection between poultry treated with all kinds of estrogens (to make plump, juicy chicken breasts) and the exponential rise of breast cancer in women. Or the practice of treating young beef cattle with growth hormones and the overall rise of cancer in the general population.[18] I thought the campaign against red meat was because the meat itself was bad for you, even though people had been eating meat and thriving on it for at least ten thousand years.

I discovered that most of the degenerative diseases—cancer, arthritis, allergies, constant ear, nose and throat infections, heart disease, lung disease, clogged arteries, strokes, high blood pressure, and diabetes—had been non-existent in primitive peoples.[19] True, they had suffered from infectious diseases, many of which had apparently been conquered with penicillins and sulfas. But, just as we began to think we had conquered infectious disease, we started giving away the job of growing our food to the farms of agri-business, and we started giving away the job of preserving our food to the food packers and processing plants.

To make agri-business work, we started using chemical sprays, not knowing what we were doing to our soil. We began dousing fields with salt-based fertilizers and chemical sprays, completely unaware that a major tactic of the early Roman army, when they had conquered some enemy, was to salt their lands, making it impossible to grow anything. This ruined their opponent's ability to feed their people, made them dependent on the Roman econ-

---

16 My personal experience with garden peas grown in healthy soil and nurtured with Sonic Bloom is that they easily last for weeks if not months in the refrigerator. Zucchini grown under the same system sat outside on the ground, without refrigeration, for approximately two and a half months and did not rot. Nor did the bugs seem particularly interested in it.

17 *Mainline Farming for Century 21*, by Dan Skow, D.V.M. and Charles Walters Jr., published by Acres U.S.A. in 1991.

18 See *Rainforest in Your Kitchen*, by Martin Teitel, published by Island Press in 1992.

19 See *Nutrition and Physical Degeneration*, by Weston L. Price, D.D.S., recently re-published by Keats Publishing, originally published in the 1940s.

omy, and ensured that they were too sick or hungry to mount an attack that would dislodge the invaders! [20]

In the ancient past as the land got crowded, the soil would get overused and crop failures would begin to appear, triggering waves of migration. These crop failures were usually accompanied by swarms of locusts that suddenly attacked the ailing and unhealthy plants, or perhaps the simple rotting of potatoes for no apparent reason before they could be harvested. When the land was depleted, people picked up and moved on, usually westward.

As the number of people worldwide increased, first the Industrial and then the Green Revolution seemed to promise that everyone could be well fed even while being enticed away from their farms and gardens and into factories and shops. The development of agri-business had seemed like a natural solution to the increasing demands for food.

Now we were running into serious problems. Dead or dying topsoil was collapsing and blowing away in the wind, and there was no more fresh, fertile soil or land left to migrate to. Too late we were recognizing we had all kinds of people to feed, and the promises of agri-business had turned out to be hollow. Worse, we had destroyed so many trees and forests that the climate was becoming less hospitable for any kind of dependable farming. High winds, prolonged droughts, and unusually heavy rains concentrated in isolated areas instead of scattered about were triggered by destruction of trees, and by soil that would not grow anything. Few people realized that the elements of wind, water, soil, and sun maintained a delicately balanced relationship, and when the balance was upset, the electromagnetic relationship collapsed into extremes.

Now it was obvious that the poor physical condition and mushrooming health crisis of our affluent United States was not due to natural or unknown causes, or even to that mysterious factor called aging. It could not be blamed on genes either. Genes were formed and triggered into action by the specific nutrients we ate. If there was not enough of a particular nutrient to either form or trigger a gene, it would not be activated and its capacity to build or heal the body would never be expressed.[21] How many natural immune system functions were never triggered into action because of missing nutrients?

---

20 See *Science in Agriculture,* by Arden B. Anderson, printed by Acres U.S.A. Publishing in 1992.

21 Ibid., page 49.

The other excuses for poor health that were heard everywhere from everyone—a "bug going around," "no time to exercise," "haven't been eating right lately," "too much stress," or "it runs in the family"—were our attempts to place the blame somewhere. The truth was that the sad state of our health was the result of years of eating foods that were empty, foods grown on dead soils, foods that were overprocessed until they, too, were dead. Our health problems were the direct result of the ways our food was grown and distributed, and most of these ways were quite sophisticated but terribly unnatural. They were useless as far as maintaining health went and destructive to true human happiness.

The meteoric rise of cancer and other degenerative diseases over the last seventy years corresponded almost perfectly to the abandonment of the family garden and the increasing practice of processing food into boxes and cans, thus removing the enzymes that were so essential to destroying cancer cells and tumor growth in human beings.

Rising health care costs were maintaining an inverse relationship to our demands for cheap food. It was turning out to be true, even with food, that you get what you pay for. Most of us were paying for cheap, poisoned foods grown in depleted soils and still complaining that it cost too much too eat. No one realized that what was saved at the grocery store was being spent at the hospital.

Fascinated by the similarities between the destruction of soil and our failing health, I searched for other information on nutrition. I came across a fifty year old book by Dr. Weston Price titled *Nutrition and Physical Degeneration* and read it from end to end. When I was finished, I put it down and sat in stupefied horror. With laser-like clarity I could see the result of poor nutrition working its way silently through our culture.

The first generation of people raised on dead or deficient foods in the twenties and thirties had suffered serious cavities, dental abscesses, and total loss of teeth at an early age. They struggled with diseases like tuberculosis, widespread mental and emotional disturbances, a tendency toward argument and alcohol. But we had covered these symptoms with fluoride, the rise of the dental industry, and drugs to kill their infections or elevate their moods.

The next generation of people raised with serious nutritional deficiencies in the forties and fifties had experienced a subtle worsening of bone and organ structures. There was a flood of infections in the ear, nose, and throat due to congenital deformities in the angle at which the Eustachian tubes grew and developed. Tonsillitis and appendicitis became epidemic due to the increase of toxins inside the body. Deformities such as club foot and a cleft palate began to appear. Poor bone structure resulted in underdevelopment of both upper and lower jawbones, which gave almost everyone crooked, overcrowded teeth. Underdevelopment of the pelvic cavity resulted in women who could not give birth without excruciating pain, or who needed a cesarean section in order to deliver at all. And an avalanche of degenerative diseases descended upon us; diseases such as arthritis, cancer, stroke, heart disease, migraine headaches, and other miseries began appearing in those who lived to be at least forty and beyond. We had covered these symptoms with further emphasis on drugs and the rise of the medical-pharmaceutical industry.

The third generation raised with serious nutritional deficiencies during the sixties and seventies had, in addition to inheriting the bad teeth, bone deformities and poor immune systems mentioned above, developed overwhelming allergies to the elements in nature. Their bodies, normally so efficient at disposing of irritating or harmful substances, were overwhelmed in trying to deal with the increasing load of toxic chemicals and preservatives taken in with their food. In addition, they were struggling with the inefficiencies of a metabolism that operated at a handicapped level because the body did not even get the necessary nutrients for maintaining normal daily functions, let alone rebuilding itself. Since all emotions and moods were the result of the body's chemical balance, mental and emotional problems increased, caused by the body's inability to manufacture various chemicals and neurotransmitters in the brain. The results were frightening increases in mental and emotional impairment, hyperkinetic behaviors, and attention deficit disorders at almost every economic level. We had tried to solve these problems by further specialization of the medical industry, by the tremendous expansion of public school and college remedial programs designed to "teach" people to do what the brain already did naturally—which was to learn.

The fourth generation raised with poor nutrition during the eighties and nineties was experiencing even more insidious troubles. In addition to poor bone structure, low immune response, and mental/emotional problems, they were beginning to exhibit such things as congenital brain and central nervous system anomalies; dangerously low birth weights, childhood cancers and arthritis; killer allergies and asthmas; and mental and emotional difficulties that left them unable to learn, unable to bond, and thus unable to be socialized in normal ways. We were trying to cover these symptoms by blaming our genes, and it was clear that if earlier trends were repeated, we would see a meteoric rise of the genetic engineering industry and a tremendous expansion of the criminal justice system as our next answer to the problems at hand—problems that were really nutritional at their heart.

No one seemed to appreciate that having something in your belly did not necessarily mean that you were feeding yourself well. No one seemed to understand that most of what appeared on grocery store shelves just did not supply the body with the raw materials it needed to function, or to heal and rebuild itself on a daily basis. Convenience foods, poor food combinations, and speedy meals laced with sugar, salt, caffeine, and unknown chemicals were gulped down without concern until the doctor pronounced some awful verdict and we found ourselves taking the chemicals directly—this time in the form of pills.

Many people I knew who were conscientious about eating right and exercising still ended up with a variety of diseases, some of them terminal. They often experienced a sense of anger and betrayal because they felt they had done everything right, this wasn't supposed to happen to them, and they had no idea what to do next or where to turn. It did not even occur to them that all those fresh fruits and vegetables they had been eating were not only seriously deficient in nutrients, they were laced with the heavy metals that were part of the pesticide recipes.

True healing seldom happened because no one ever got to the real source of the problem. Life became a race to stay alive, all the while feeling helpless and confused, certain in our minds that there must be an answer somewhere, and not realizing the answer was in our soils and our food.

I watched television commercials and was heartsick at the messages they poured out to children, teens, and adults. Magazine articles on health that I had once gobbled up, news reports on the latest in medical research that I had listened to so carefully and with such a sense of awe now seemed ridiculously irresponsible, scattered, and short-sighted. No one was even close to the truth.

Trips to the grocery store were even more discouraging. Non-food was everywhere and people were buying it because that was all there was, or because it was all they had time for. No one had time to grow their own food anymore. They were caught in the rat race for money so they could buy the food someone else had produced. The other basic joys of personal life expression in our culture—the making of clothing, the building of shelter, the design and making of furniture, the choice of transportation and even the arts—music, dance, painting, literature, and sculpture)—all had degenerated into businesses caught up in the rush for money. Those who joined this rush had no choice other than to allow someone or something outside of themselves to provide them with the necessities and the amenities of life. Old forms of interdependence were lost, to be replaced by new forms that lacked the pleasure and security of self-reliance and inner authority. People could no longer do things for themselves because they had sold their time and energy for a handful of dollars. They then kept their attention entertained with foods, fads, drink, sports, or sexual games in order to avoid the fact that they had sold an important birthright.

No one realized we were killing ourselves with food. We ate too much of it and bemoaned our weight gain, then cycled into colds and sinus troubles, depression and lethargy when we tried to cut back. Feeling miserable, we ended up eating too much again, then berated ourselves for not being able to maintain the discipline of our diet. Throughout the cycle, we remained unaware that we kept wanting more to eat because food was supposed to provide fuel in the form of energy and nutrients. The nutrients allowed us to both use the fuel value to the maximum, and to maintain our bodies in top working condition. But the foods we were eating had very little value as a fuel any more, and most of it was worthless when it came to the care, maintenance, and repair of a human body. When it came to worthless foods, we didn't know we had to eat a lot more of it to get enough fuel and nutrient value just to keep going at minimum levels, and all that extra food caused weight gain. No one realized that dead food or empty fruits, vegetables, breads, and meats meant overweight, sick, and degenerating people.

Then I saw a lecture given by a young medical doctor in New York[22] who had been helping people to heal terminal cancers (pancreatic, liver, uterine) for over ten years. When I realized that he was doing it by analyzing an individual's personal metabolism, replacing missing vitamins and minerals, designing

---

22 For further information on enzymes and their role in literally dissolving cancer and tumors, see a six-hour, taped seminar by Nicholas Gonzales, M.D. in New York. For audiocassettes of the seminar, call Willner's Pharmacy, (212) 682-2817 or 1-800-633-1106. For videocassettes, call Dr. David Luce in Boulder, Colorado, (303) 444-5689. The World Research Foundation also has information on enzyme therapies at (818) 907-5483.

protocols that cleansed the body of all toxic materials and wastes, and insisting they find and eat raw organic foods that were high in nutrition and enzymes, I knew that our attempts here at Lily Hill Farm to learn to grow fresh, super-nutritious, organic food were not only possible, they were absolutely necessary.

A bright light went on inside me, and I realized that the pot of gold at the end of the rainbow did not have one hundred tons of grapes in it at all. Instead it held living, healthy soil, water that we could drink right out of the earth, vegetables and fruits that were sweet and fully nutritious. It held perfect health and quick healing for us and for our families, and an abiding security that came from our connection to the earth.

Alvey was terribly right, the world was seriously out of balance—from the desert sands of Iraq and Kuwait to the clay-loam vineyards of Lily Hill Farm, from the polluted air swirling about our heads to the missing crumb structure of the soil under our toes.

In a moment of unexpected vision, I saw that my whole experience with the elves was not about getting that hundred tons of grapes. It truly was learning to embrace the nature of balance—balance in our minds and hearts, balance between our need to make a living and the choice of meaningful work, balance between our need to eat and the fact that we had nowhere left to run. This was it. Here we were, with our land, our water, and the other living creatures, large and small, plant and animal, who shared that same air, water, and soil, and who made it possible for us to be here, alive and well.

It is as Alvey said. We humans are at the top of the heap. We need everything in the heap underneath us, but nothing in the heap needs that human at the top.

COMMUNICATING WITH ELVES AND DEVAS &

Anyone who is interested, even if only a little bit, in the idea of communicating with elves, devas, or elementals would benefit in making an effort to contact this generally unseen world of helpers and wonder workers. If you have any amount of curiosity and can remain open to new experiences, communicating with the many forms of life that may be sharing your property with you can be a life-changing experience for several reasons.

First, trusting yourself to recognize and respond to these subtle forms and their messages has a transforming effect on the whole issue of trust. Second, the expansion of your world to include these other forms of intelligence has a healing and balancing effect that ranges all the way from a sense of no longer being alone, to a sense of specialness, to an attitude of rediscovering the world, to a deep reconnection with nature, to taking better care of yourself, and many other personal benefits.

Third, the delicate truths and sensitive communications that characterize any relationship with elves, devas, and elementals often affect the rest of your life, transforming relationships at home and at work, renewing your interest in life, and reviving your creativity in living it.

After deciding to contact elves or devas, it is a good idea to put some thought into when, where, and how to go about it. When to make your first effort is dependent on a combination of factors. Are you ready, or do you have too much doubt? Should you find someone with more experience and talk or work with them first? And if you were successful in contacting an elf or deva, would you just end up scaring yourself silly?

I don't think that doubt is a big issue for elves, devas, nature spirits, or elementals. It was more of an issue for me than for them, and it was my experience that the devas were very willing to make contact any time with anyone who was willing to make the effort to communicate. Their concern over the destruction taking place in the natural world and the increasing difficulty with which they energize the many plant forms they are responsible for tending (your flowers, trees, vegetables, fruits, grains, grasses, and every kind of plant and even animal life) seemed to make them very anxious to communicate with humans and hopefully influence their consciousness in order to make them more aware of what is happening.

Choosing a good time for you, a time when you can sit quietly and settle yourself and your mind, is really the most important factor. There are advantages and disadvantages of being fresh into your day. On the one hand, you will be alert and attentive; on the other you may find it more difficult to settle yourself because of real or potential interruptions, or a sense of having too many things to do. Choosing a time at the end of the day may make it easier to settle yourself into deep quiet, but you may also be too tired to pay attention and may even end up going to sleep.

Also important in choosing the right time is a very individual and unpredictable factor that can only be described as a sudden urge or inner sense that tells you, "Now... now is the time... just send your message to...!" And you stop right there, make your first impromptu call, and get an immediate answer.

Otherwise, to begin, I would suggest choosing a time that fits your personal preferences and a place that is quiet and peaceful. Although the elves did come into my office a few times, they definitely seemed to prefer a place outdoors where nature was relatively quiet and undisturbed. It also helps to be away from other people at first because you might feel quite silly or uncomfortable trying to talk to elves—even mind-to-mind—when there are people and lots of activity going on around you.

If you wish to begin by contacting the elves, I found a good place to sit is under a tree. For devas, most places are okay, but the best place is in a vegetable or flower garden.

For the wind spirit, it always seemed best to wait for a windy day or night to make contact. I found the wind especially easy to make contact with. The result was that I ended up turning to the wind most often for both big and little things, and we became good friends.

If you have chosen to start by making contact with the water spirit, you can begin by sitting beside a small pond, creek, or lake. Of course, anything from a mud puddle to an ocean is okay, but I found that for me, the best time is when it's raining.

To contact the fire elemental you have a couple of choices. Either sit comfortably in the sun, or settle yourself in front of a fireplace, a woodstove, a campfire, or any place that a wood fire is burning.

To contact the earth elemental, who may sometimes be referred to as the soil deva, the landscape deva, or the rock spirits, an excellent place to begin is on a hillside or a mountain, near a large rock, or in a quiet cave.

Once you have decided which form you need to contact, and when and where to go about it, it is infinitely helpful if you have a very real need or question to ask, or a decision to be made.

If you're just curious about making contact and all you have to say is "hello," you will probably get exactly that in response—a quiet hello—and end up wondering if you imagined the whole thing.—especially if you don't see anyone or anything and only hear the response in your head. Of course, you can always make contact just to let devas and nature spirits know that you have become aware of their existence and hope to cooperate with their efforts. These kinds of messages are always heard, and there is often just a thank-you, but sometimes they will come back with a response that asks what you intend to do to cooperate with them. If you haven't thought this far, it would be polite to ask them what most needs to be done, and then you must do it, no matter how plain, how difficult, how useless, or how unnecessary it seems! This is their way of testing your intentions and deciding how honorable and reliable you are.

If you have a real request, your first communication may be much more satisfying. For instance, suppose you want to plant some radishes in your back yard and you're not sure where to put them. Or, maybe you know where you want them, but you'd like to get the radish deva to work with you to protect them or to make them especially healthy and nutritious.

First you settle yourself in a quiet spot, even your living room will do, and state your intention clearly, either aloud or in your mind. Then, take about a half-dozen slow, deep breaths, holding each for a moment or two, then letting the air out slowly but completely. After these six breaths, breathe in your own natural way and turn your attention to creating a picture of a healthy, living, intelligent radish in your mind's eye. This is a very individual, creative effort. Your radish might have eyes and a smile, or a single leg, some clothing, or a particular color—pink, red, even blue, green, or brown and white! Creating the picture of a radish takes a minute or two, but once it is created, hold the picture of it clearly in your mind and then, with the intention of communicating with the intelligence that forms all radishes, send a greeting (always—this can be either aloud or in your mind) and ask if she would be willing to communicate because you would like to work with her.

The responses can be many, just as when you're dealing with people—from no immediately recognizable response, to an auditory response from your radish picture, to the disappearance of the radish picture altogether and the substitute picture of seeing the beautifully growing radishes in a particular spot (sometimes right where you wanted them, sometimes somewhere else). Sometimes you may see or find yourself in the back yard having a conversation with no one in particular, just a clear voice in your head, discussing where to plant the radishes. The voice may warn you that the spot you have in mind will make for soft, wormy radishes, or that the chosen spot is right where the neighbor's cat likes to go to the bathroom at night (which will certainly disturb any carefully planted seeds and burn any young sprouts). It may suggest another spot requiring more work, and when you object, it may raise questions as to the honor of your intention to grow radishes.

This whole conversation could easily be dismissed as just arguing with yourself, but this is not quite correct. You are having a discussion with yourself, but it is not with the ordinary, everyday you. Instead, you are talking with the part of you that "knows." When you are just arguing with your everyday self, you will generally experience a series of arguments and rebuttals that leave you feeling stuck and undecided. But when you are talking to the part of you that "knows," you are talking to the part of you that is connected to everything that exists (including nature spirits and devas) and the discussion will have a slightly more dynamic flavor. All sorts of useful information will come up and the discussion does not generally end in your feeling stuck. You may feel relieved, you may feel challenged to rethink the whole issue, but you seldom feel stuck.

It is also possible that you are actually having a conversation with the radish deva using mental telepathy—and there are very subtle differences here. During mental telepathy, the conversation is even more dynamic, effortless, and quite spontaneous as far as the voice you are listening to is concerned. In fact, the voice may start the conversation without you, and if you don't answer, the voice may prod you for a response. The voice may also have unusual inflections, or an accent. The conversation can become so engrossing that after it is over and you think back on it, it can seem more real than some of your conversations with "real" people. The conversation may have unusual energy to it, and the ideas and information suggested can be really foreign to your way of thinking and doing things, or can range into areas that you have very little knowledge of and yet present you with highly sophisticated concepts. Sometimes your created picture takes on a life of its own and redesigns itself spontaneously into a different form, but one you are familiar with, and then proceeds to communicate in an extremely clear, coherent, and congruent manner. For instance, my created picture of the wind was frequently transformed into a small form that appeared to be composed of two or three clouds, my created maple tree form quickly and consistently became a face on a maple leaf, and my small picture of a mole consistently became a creature as big and cumbersome as a dinosaur.

Sometimes, however, all of your created pictures will fade away to be replaced by a magnificent form that is the actual deva or elemental. The first time I saw one of the devas in its true form, I was speechless. They do not always appear this way, but if they do, don't be surprised. I still feel a little stiffer, perhaps more awkward, and my communication is more careful when I am confronted with these regal forms, but that may just be me.

In any case, state your greetings and make your request, then pay close attention to the details of whatever response you get. Do not be afraid to ask clarifying questions, or bring up problems that you think may occur as a result of what they are asking you to do. Also, do not hesitate to let them know that you appreciate their work, as well as the fact that they made the effort to communicate with you. When you have communicated everything that you needed to, and carefully noted everything the deva has said to you, say a final thank-you and a good-bye. The deva, elemental, or nature spirit will usually fade from view or simply leave. It is a good idea at that point to have a small notebook or pad of paper handy to write down the date, what you asked, and what the response was. Quite often, the communications are ongoing and your notes become a valuable record of who said what and when it was said. And their consistency can sometimes be amazing!

Many people, when first making an effort to do something as unfamiliar as make contact with elves or communicate with any of the intelligences in nature, end up with a hundred more questions than they started with. The original question of where to plant the radishes has been replaced by questions like "I saw this form... do you suppose that it was really a deva? She looked like this... is that what a deva looks like? What did she look like when you saw her?" or "I heard someone say something like... what do you think it means? Should I follow that?" or "I didn't see or hear anything, but I have this feeling I should put the radishes right over here. What do you think?" At this point it is only more experience that will give you a secure base from which to grow in your understanding and ability to work with the many forms and intelligences in nature.

A couple of years after I began working with Alvey and his group of elves, someone told me there was an old adage that said contact with elves was supposed to bring wisdom, wealth, and good health for a long life. Aggravating them was supposed to bring sickness and bad luck. I'm not sure about the wisdom and wealth yet, but I can agree about the health part. Both my husband and I feel that we have been brought to the door of understanding that opens into a life of good health.

Recently, on discovering that I had been dealing with elves and nature spirits, one of my clients told me a story that came from her daughter living in New

Mexico. I don't know whether it's true or not but it seemed to hold an important message.

A wealthy, successful architect had moved to New Mexico where he bought a piece of land on a rocky hillside with a beautiful view. He decided to build a large house on his property and brought in the equipment to move some very large rocks and begin the excavation for the foundation.

Not long after his house was finished, the man began to lose contracts and suffer in his business. Struggling to make ends meet he began to feel more and more tired, ill, and apathetic. After several trips to the doctor, he was diagnosed with some kind of cancer. He and the medical doctors fought the cancer unsuccessfully for two years, and finally they told him there was nothing more they could do.

In desperation, he looked around for alternatives and finally found an old Indian healer who was reputed to have helped others. He went to the healer who agreed to work with him. The old Indian began a series of chants and meditations, and during one of these he happened to contact the nature spirit of the earth. They talked at length and when the meditation was over the healer turned to the architect and asked if he had recently built a house. The architect affirmed that he had. The healer then asked him if he had moved one or two especially large rocks in order to build it. The architect said that he had. Then the healer told him that he had spoken with the nature spirits of the earth and the rocks. They were very angry that he had moved those particular rocks. Evidently, they were made of a particular mineral that somehow picked up and amplified positive, healing electromagnetic frequencies coming out of the earth at that particular spot, and by moving them, the architect had upset a very delicate balance of energies in that region. Not only was the architect himself now suffering from the effect of fewer positive energies, the nature spirits were very upset with him and had showered him with their angry projections, causing the cancer.

"If you want to heal," the old Indian told the architect, "put the rocks back where they were."

When the architect argued that his house was right where the stones had been, the Indian simply repeated the message given to him by the nature spirits, "If you want to heal, put the rocks back where they were."

The architect went home and surveyed the house he had so carefully designed. Sitting down at his drawing board, he played around with the idea of putting the rocks back, which was approximately where his living room and dining area came together. By moving this wall, changing that shape, gradually he rearranged the space to accommodate the huge rocks. A building crew removed the front wall of his house and the rocks were returned to their original position. Shortly afterward, the architect's cancer disappeared and his business returned to a successful condition. He still lives in New Mexico and his house is far more interesting and beautiful than it was before with the unusual addition of the two large rocks to his living space.

This whole story embodies something that both Alvey and the Great Mole hinted at. It has to do with our assumption that we can do anything we feel like doing as far as Mother Nature is concerned. Can we do anything we want? Should we? The immediate reaction most of us would make if we were told we had to get permission from Mother Nature to do anything would probably be an arrogant "Humph!" followed closely by the fear that she would not give her permission at all, and compounded by a sense of impatience at having lost some vague freedom or having more details to worry about.

If you really think it through, asking permission from Mother Nature does not necessarily mean we have lost our supremacy and are now subject to some force that is as selfish as we have been. You can't ask Mother Nature for permission if you are coming from a loser's position. If you do, you will simply end up trying to get back on top, to dominate, or to skin your way past what you have learned from her. Instead, we must ask Mother Nature to collaborate with us and listen carefully when she warns against something. We are not the only intelligence on this planet, and working with Mother Nature's very considerable power can open the door to new possibilities that may be even better than the ones we are already living with. Certainly, there is a serious drain on our energy caused when we find ourselves working against her.

However you look at it, the result of contacting these intelligences is an expansion of your reality—whether the contact is once or becomes a regular visit. You may think that there is nothing that you could do or say that would make much difference in restoring the delicate balances here on earth, but this is simply not true. You might even think you know just what they might ask you to do—but don't be so sure.

If you do make contact and your intentions are at all honorable, you may find a whole group of devas, elves, and fairies ready, even anxious to work with you. They are very perceptive of who you are and thus make tremendous efforts to teach or guide you gently. Even so, somewhere down the road you will find that the impact on your life and the life of those around you is enormous and is not at all what you thought it was going to be.

Steps for good communication:

1. Make the decision to contact elves or devas, nature spirits or elementals.

2. Decide on a good time.

3. Choose a place.

4. State your intention.

5. Take a half-dozen deep, slow breaths.

6. Create a mental picture of the intelligence you want to contact.

7. Ask your question or state your need.

8. Listen carefully to any response, answers, or advice that comes to you.

9. Carefully note any images that come to you.

10. Thank the form of intelligence for communicating.

11. Say good-bye.

12. Follow through with the answer or advice given.

USEFUL TERMS ✍

Many of the following terms and concepts are included in the fore-going pages. A few do not appear in the text but are useful additions to a more complete understanding. It should also be noted that these are not dictionary definitions. I have tried to define the terms as they are used and understood by the common man or woman, not by university standards. This means that all of them suffer the necessity of being filtered through my own perception and interpreted by me.

I am also keenly aware of several serious problems in the use of the word "chemical." Everything in this world has a chemical basis of some sort. Some fertilizers, insecticides, fungicides, and herbicides are considered organic, but they still work on the basis of their chemistry. The common use of the word chemical—in combination with chemical fertilizers and sprays—is often taken to mean "poisonous," "unbalanced," "salt-based," or "petro-chemical," and therefore is inherently inaccurate.

In the agricultural industry, strict organic certification will not allow for use of any unnatural or chemically synthesized products. But there are synthetic products that are perfectly acceptable organics, and some perfectly natural products that are dangerous poisons and thus make excellent pesticides.

AGRI-BUSINESS—the term used to describe the main form of agriculture in the First World countries. The common image of agri-business is one populated by large farms run by corporations (using petro-chemicals and treated hybrid seeds) whose first goal is to make a profit regardless or in spite of destruction to the soil, water, and air.

ANTIBIOTICS—potent anti-bacterial drugs routinely fed to poultry, cattle, hogs, sheep, and goats to prevent infections and keep them alive long enough to get to slaughter.

BIODIVERSITY—a state or condition within any ecosystem that maintains and supports the widest possible range of plants, animals, and natural life in order to maintain a gene pool containing a huge number of options for adapting to the changing conditions of life.

BIODYNAMIC—a system of organic growing developed by Rudolph Steiner back in the 1920s that uses only natural organic soil amendments and produces fruits, nuts, grains, vegetables, and herbs of superior nutritional quality while restoring the land to healthy, integrated usage.

BLACK ROT—a fungus disease that appears in hot, humid weather and infects the grapes, causing the fruit to mummify into hard, dark, shriveled berries.

BLOOM—in the fifth stage of grapevine growth each year, bloom is when hundreds of tiny stamens appear on the visible clusters of grapes. *See* stages of grapevine growth.

BRIX—a term used to denote one percentage point of sugar, or complex carbohydrates, in fruits and vegetables. A bunch of grapes having sixteen brix of sugar is a bunch of grapes whose percentage of sugars and complex carbohydrates is 16 percent.

BUD BREAK—in the second stage of grapevine growth each year the swollen buds on the canes break open to form a small, pinkish rosette of leaves. *See* stages of grapevine growth.

BUD SWELL—in the first stage of grapevine growth each year the buds on the canes begin to swell as the sap begins to rise in the plant. *See* stages of grapevine growth.

BULK BOX—used in commercial grape production, a large wooden box of standard size, which holds approximately 2,000 pounds of fruit.

CANES—the woody part of the grapevine from which both leaves and clusters are suspended. Good grapes only grow on one-year-old canes.

CANOPY—the total leaf and cane production of a vine.

CERTIFIED ORGANIC—a farm or farm product that has been off "chemical" fertilizers, pesticides, fungicides, and herbicides for at least three years, has been inspected on-site, and has filled out the necessary paperwork to become a certified grower. Some certifying organizations can certify for both regional or overseas marketing.

CHEMICAL BURN—exposure of growing plants to fertilizers or humic acids, insecticides or herbicides that are too strong, that fry delicate root hairs and result in stunted plants, dried yellow leaves, and sometimes death.

CHEMICAL-FREE—a farm (or farm product) that is not using chemical fertilizers, pesticides, fungicides, or herbicides, but has not been inspected on-site or filled out the paperwork to register as a certified organic grower.

CLAY—a heavy, densely packed form of soil that lacks the balancing effects of sand, silt, decayed matter, and micro-organisms. Clay often becomes waterlogged, blocking the passage of both air and water, and plants and seeds growing in it tend to succumb to fungus. Although clay is good for growing some things, it is not the preferred growing medium.

COLLAPSED SOIL—soil that has lost its living micro-organisms and is unable to maintain its crumb structure will collapse into a tight, hard-packed soil.

CONCORD GRAPES—also known as Vitis lambrusca, are an old variety of blue-black, slip-skin grape found growing in America from Maine to Florida by the early colonists. They are used to make jellies, juices, and wines. As a result of the severe weather changes, Concords growing along Lake Michigan have such a unique flavor or "bouquet" that they have been officially recognized as the "Lake Michigan appellation."

COMPOSTING—a method of converting all manner of waste materials into living soil. Everything from grasses and leaves, to manure, to kitchen garbage, to sewage, to commercial waste can be used to make compost. The fact is that every single material good we have or can make comes from the earth and can be returned to the earth in a healthy condition. Even radioactive waste can be digested by worms and returned to the earth clean and pure.

CORDON TRIMMING—a type of trimming in which two to four canes are left permanently on the trellis, one stretching left, the other right on the upper wire, the other two on the lower wire, and from which grow a number of new, much shorter canes. Using the Cordon system, the canes do not have to be tied to the trellis each year.

CRUMB STRUCTURE—refers to the crumbs, made up of particles of sand, silt, clay, humus, and micro-organisms, that characterize healthy soil and the way these crumbs fit together allowing air, water, and nutrients to move easily through the soil.

DEAD FOOD—food that does not have all the vitamins, minerals, enzymes, trace elements, and nutrients that Mother Nature intended. Usually this includes anything out of a can, bag, or box, many things that have been cooked to death, anything made with white flour, white sugar, or white rice, as well as coffee, tea, and alcohol.

DEAD SOIL—soil that no longer has a living population of soil organisms such as bacteria, azotobacters, actinomycetes, fungi, and protozoa.

DEGENERATIVE DISEASE—serious diseases caused by long-term nutritional deficiency.

DEVA—a form of intelligence that manages and cares for a specific kind of plant. For instance, there is a Grape Deva, a Lily Deva, a Rose Deva, a Maple Tree Deva, et cetera. They are sometimes referred to as "nature spirits" because they embody or represent the particular forms found in nature and are responsible for the maintenance of the form in the physical world.

DEVELOPING FRUIT—in the seventh stage of grapevine development each year, developing fruit grows in size and weight to become large clusters of grapes. *See* stages of grapevine growth.

DISEASE—a state or condition of "dis-ease," ill health, or less than optimum functioning of an organism due to physical, mental, emotional, or spiritual factors.

DOG DAYS—according to the Farmers' Almanac, the dog days of summer usually begin about the first week of July and end about the first week of August. They are the hottest, most humid days of the year.

DOUBLE CURTAIN—a form of trellising that uses two top wires and one bottom wire instead of one top and one bottom wire. A vineyard that is trellised in a double curtain arrangement will produce significantly higher tonnage per acre, but is harder and more expensive to maintain.

DOWNY MILDEW—a fungus that grows on the leaves and fruit of grapes during humid weather and ruins the berries by destroying first the outer casing and then the entire grape.

DROPS—*see* long arms.

ELECTROMAGNETIC (EM) FIELDS—known as EM fields, these are generated every time there is electrical current moving through a substance. Since all living things run on the self-generated electricity offered by life itself, everything is surrounded by EM fields of varying frequencies, colors, and sizes.

ELEMENTALS—this term refers to the forms of intelligence that are embodied in the elements of weather. Sometimes referred to as nature spirits, elementals include the intelligence known as the wind, the spirit of water, the fire or sun elemental, and the earth elemental.

ELVES—small human-like forms, sometimes referred to as "nature spirits," that live both on the land and in buildings, but occupy a different range of frequencies which make them invisible unless you are adept at shifting the frequency your brain normally operates at. Elves are usually quite friendly and have a great sense of humor bordering on the mischievous. They are helpful, energetic, and if you befriend them, they will intercede for you any time help is needed.

EMOTIONAL HEALTH—emotional health is a state or condition characterized by a steady, generalized relaxation and calm, clear perception. Emotional health is highly dependent on physical health. Emotions are the result of chemicals generated in the limbic area of the brain and it is important to understand that all specific feelings are caused by specific neuro-chemicals. If the body does not have the nutrients it needs to generate the neuro-chemicals of relaxation and peacefulness, emotional health can be out of reach. Or, if the limbic area of the brain is constantly pushed into a "fight-or-flight" mode by various threats and upsets, the nutrients that help maintain emotional balance will be depleted and feelings can be dominated by other powerful chemicals that cause depression, fatigue, et cetera.

EMPTY FOOD—*see* dead food.

ENVIRONMENTAL POLLUTANTS—are found in food, air, water, and soil and end up in the human body. The most serious are: the heavy metals of lead, cadmium, and mercury; things such as strontium 90 and radioactive iodine left over from early tests of atomic weapons; DDT, which comes in from other countries; carbon monoxide found in plentiful supplies along major highways during rush hour; x-rays used by doctors, dentists, and industries; nitrates and nitrites used in the preservation of processed foods; and a wide variety of manufactured drugs that cause serious side-effects.

ENZYMES—tiny chemical powerhouses that act as catalysts for the hundreds of chemical transformations that go on during metabolism in our body day after day.

ESTROGENS—hormones often used in raising poultry to force the chicken or turkey breast into a plump fullness, but often resulting in meat that is tough and tasteless.

FOLIAR FERTILIZER—the fertilizing of plants using nutrients sprayed on leaves, stems, and fruits rather than put into the soil to be taken up by the roots.

FRUIT SET—in the sixth stage of grapevine development each year, the stamens on the tiny grape clusters are fertilized and development of each grape berry is set into motion.

FUNGICIDE—a poisonous chemical spray used to kill fungus organisms and prevent them from gaining access to fruit and rotting it.

FUNGUS—a micro-organism that propagates by releasing spores, and whose life purpose is to finish decomposing dead, diseased, or defective organic matter.

GASSING—the use of ethylene gas to force unripe fruit to move quickly to a softer stage approximating ripeness.

GENE—a single set of instructions carried in the chromosomes of a plant, animal, or human, and defining a particular physical characteristic, ability, trait, or metabolic function of the organism. Genes determine everything from eye color and bone structure to metabolism and immune capabilities.

GENETIC ADAPTABILITY—the ability of an organism to activate certain genes that might be needed to survive in a changing world. The rule of survival for all biology is "change or die."

GENETIC ENGINEERING—although it encompasses much more, genetic engineering is usually thought of as the attempt to transfer genes having a needed set of traits or characteristics from one plant, animal, or person to another.

GREEN REVOLUTION—a period in recent history, around the 1940s and 50s, when it was believed that agri-business and the chemical fertilizer industry would transform farming into a feast that would feed the entire world on much less acreage and with much less effort, worry, or work.

HARDPAN—a cement-like layer of soil that starts below the surface of the soil, usually six to eight inches, and extends down as deep as four feet. Hardpan is often caused by the compacting effect of heavy equipment moving over the fields, and is seriously compounded by the remains of salt-based fertilizers that are applied to the soil.

HEAVY METALS—these include things such as lead, mercury, cadmium, and others commonly used as a base for chemical fertilizers.

HEIRLOOM VEGETABLES OR FLOWERS—vegetables and fruits having an original set of genes that will reproduce themselves in an unbroken line and that will adapt to a wide set of environmental growing conditions. Heirloom fruits and vegetables often have superior taste and texture, and ripen gradually, not over-burdening the gardener with too much produce at once.

HERBICIDE—a powerful chemical that either burns away green plant matter or is taken up by the plant's leaves and leads to systemic poisoning that destroys the root.

HUMUS—as critical as humus is, it is still not completely understood even today. Humus and humic acids are the results of composting organic waste matter and are extremely important in maintaining good soil health. A living population of soil micro-organisms is required to break down organic matter and create humus.

HYBRID—a plant or seed that has been cross-pollinated by other species or varieties. A hybrid can have a number of variations from the original, some improvements, some not, but often with the result of sterile seeds that will not reproduce.

INTEGRATED PEST MANAGEMENT—to the organic gardener IPM is a system of using natural predators and micro-organisms to control pests in a garden, field, or greenhouse. To the university researcher or the chemical salesman, IPM is the use of chemical sprays for insects and fungus organisms but only when the insect or fungus is active rather than as part of an ongoing, preventive-spray program. Often organic IPM techniques do a much better job than pesticide sprays and do not leave poisonous residues on the crop, especially in greenhouses.

IRRADIATION—the practice of subjecting foods to strong radiation in order to kill germs and bacteria.

KNIFFEN TRIMMING—a style of trimming that removes all old canes each year, leaving four to six new canes on the trunk of the vine in a sort of umbrella arrangement. These canes must be tied to the trellis for support or the weight of the grapes could tear the cane off the vine.

LEAVES BEGIN—in the third stage of grapevine growth each year, leaves begin to open all along the canes where new shoots will eventually grow, some becoming as much as twenty feet long. See stages of grapevine growth.

LIME—a soil amendment that helps move a too-acid soil toward alkalinity and greatly improves plant health and nutrition.

LOAM—a rich, dark soil with a well-balanced composition of sand, clay, silt, and humus. This is the preferred soil for growing anything.

LONG ARMS—a long cane, about ten to fifteen feet in length, that is used to replace missing vines. The long arm is carried along the ground to the place where you want a new vine to grow, then a hole is dug and a section of the cane is buried so that at least three buds along the cane are underground. These buds will produce roots, forming a new plant which can then be cut away from the mother vine in a year or two.

MENTAL HEALTH—is highly dependent on physical health. If the body does not have adequate supplies of essential vitamins and minerals, then thinking, speech, and conversation, or the ability to perceive and sequence both perception and action will suffer because neurotransmitters, which are required in all mental operations, cannot be synthesized if the necessary ingredients are not present. This interferes with higher functioning such as planning, communication, and creative activities, and without these functions, relationships at all levels will flounder.

METABOLIC WASTES—the waste matter left inside the body after metabolism has converted everything it can into useable nutrients. Often what it cannot use ends up being stored in fat cells and connective tissue, causing a variety of serious diseases.

MICRO-ORGANISMS—these microscopic critters are the basic ingredients of life in the soil and include bacteria, actinomycetes, fungi, and protozoan organisms.

MINERALS—these are among the most important of nutrients (for plants, animals, and people) as they must be present for many of the chemical reactions that involve the uptake of vitamins and trace elements. Remineralization of soils has become a major thrust in organic growing.

NPK FERTILIZING—a common term used to refer to the use of simplistic and unbalanced forms of fertilizer that supply only nitrogen, phosphorus and potassium, ignoring the need of plants to have at least four dozen other nutrients as well.

NATURE SPIRIT—this term refers to the many, usually invisible forms of intelligence in Nature. For each kind of plant or animal that exists, there is a nature spirit, sometimes called a deva, whose work is to nourish and maintain that specific plant form or animal. There is also a nature spirit for the wind, the rain, fire, and the soil but these are usually referred to as the elementals. It is with the nature spirit of the plant that you would communicate if you were a plant breeder and were trying to develop a special strain or characteristic in that plant, or if you wanted special assistance in protecting an important crop. It is said that when nature spirits want to present themselves to humans they usually do so in the form of elves.

NIAGARA GRAPES—a variety of white grape used to make white wines and grape juices. Niagara is a popular grape and ripens several weeks earlier than Concords.

NITRATE—an excess of nitrogen fertilizers used on our fields leaches down into the water table and ends up polluting our water with nitrates. It is also used as a preservative in processed foods. Nitrates (and nitrites) destroy Vitamin A in the body, cause high blood pressure and heart problems, and a number of cancers.

NITROGEN—an important nutrient needed in many forms by plants, animals, and human beings to build sturdy cell walls. When nitrogen, which is used to make protein, is not available, cell construction is undermined. This is the beginning of degenerative disease.

NON-TOXIC PRODUCE OR FARMING—another term used to indicate a grower or gardener that is not using "chemical" fertilizers, insecticides, herbicides, or fungicides, but has not registered as an organic grower.

NEGATIVE ENERGY—the range of electromagnetic frequencies given off by the body/mind system when one is tense, angry, worried, tired, irritable, fearful, depressed, enraged, et cetera.

NUTRITIONAL DEFICIENCY—when an organism does not have access to or is unable to assimilate necessary nutrients, either vitamin or mineral, it will suffer from nutritional deficiency, a condition which usually precedes serious disease or dysfunction.

OPEN-POLLINATED—a term describing the ability of a vegetable, fruit or flower to reproduce itself whether it has been pollinated by a member of its own variety or another variety altogether.

PESTICIDE—a powerful poison sprayed over fields and orchards to kill insects and various pests and worms and their offspring.

PETRO-CHEMICALS—chemicals, often poisonous, that are synthesized from petroleum products.

PHOMOPSIS—a fungus disease that is spread through the canes by raindrops falling onto infected canes and splashing fungal spores in every direction. The fungus infects the stem of the grape cluster, and grapes either fall off the vine before they can be harvested, or, being so loosely attached, they cannot tolerate mechanical harvesting.

PHYSICAL HEALTH—the state or condition in which a plant, animal, or human has access to, and is able to assimilate all required vitamins, minerals, proteins, and trace elements to rebuild and regenerate the physical body, as well as to quickly and continuously eliminate toxins and metabolic waste. Excellent physical health is a basic requirement for mental, emotional, and spiritual health.

POSITIVE ENERGY—the range or matrix of electromagnetic frequencies given off by the body/mind system when one is relaxed, happy, thoughtful, rested, calm, joyous, cheerful, pleased, composed, tranquil, peaceful, et cetera.

POTASSIUM—another important nutrient needed for good health—but in the right proportion to calcium. If too much potassium is available, plants will uptake potassium instead of calcium. In animals and humans, an excess of potassium leads to diseased kidneys and arthritis.

POWDERY MILDEW—another fungus that grows on both leaves and fruit of the grapevine, spread by rain, and ruining the berries by rotting them right on the vine.

PRE-EMERGENT HERBICIDE SPRAY—usually a herbicide sprayed on the ground before weeds have emerged to kill weed seeds and thus prevent their germination.

REFRACTOMETER—a small device, dimly resembling a microscope, into which you put a drop of juice from a vegetable or fruit. You then hold it up to the light and look into it to see where the line of light, which is refracted by the amount of dissolved solids in the juice, intersects the gauge inside the refractometer. This will indicate the amount of sugar in the vegetable or fruit you are measuring.

RUN-OFF—when chemical fertilizers, pesticides, etc. are applied to the soil in excessive amounts and then it rains, the excess chemicals run off the field into ditches, ponds, creeks, and rivers or lakes, often killing or sickening the water and the many organisms that live in it or drink from it.

SAND—a coarse, loose form of soil, lacking humus and composed mainly of minerals, which has little ability to hold water. Although sand is preferred by a few plants, it is generally not the preferred growing medium.

SHELF LIFE—a term used to denote how long a fruit or vegetable will last in storage. A common myth is that nothing will last without processing and preservatives, but this is not true. The healthier the plant is, the higher the percentage of complex carbohydrates will be in the fruit or vegetable, and the higher the complex carbohydrates, the longer the shelf life. Many things will even keep outside the refrigerator for long periods of time.

SHOULDERS—a small cluster of berries attached to the upper stem of a large cluster of grapes that adds to the fullness of the cluster. It is said that if every cluster has a "shoulder" there will be one extra ton of grapes per acre.

SOIL SCIENCE—although many university departments would define this term differently, in sustainable agriculture it is often used generally to mean the study of the soil as a living system of important creatures whose biochemistry is crucial to the health of plants, animals, and humans, and the practice of renewing soils of all kinds, thus returning them to a healthy condition.

SONIC BLOOM—a registered, trademarked system of plant nutrition that combines special sound frequencies and a rich organic nutrient sprayed on the plants.

SONIC DOOM—a registered, trademarked system of weed control that combines special musical frequencies and a minimal amount of herbicide to eliminate weeds without saturating the soil with poisons.

SPIDER—a mechanical hoe that attaches to the tractor and has eight metal "fingers" that spin around, quickly removing weeds and unwanted growth from between vines.

SPIRITUAL HEALTH AND DEVELOPMENT—spiritual health does not depend on going to church, in fact it has little to do with church. Spiritual health and development is characterized by the evolution of meaning in an individual's life. If you cannot decide for yourself what your life is about and what you want to do with your time here then you are still a spiritual child. Deciding what is important to you; what is intrinsically right and good and how you intend to incorporate these values into your life; and your choices of people, work, even words—all these are high points of spiritual development. As meaning continues to develop throughout life, the entire perception of reality and what it is about begins to change.

SPRAY RECORD—a complete record of every single pesticide, herbicide, and fungicide sprayed on vegetables or fruit, the date sprayed, the amount used, and the reason for using it.

STAGES OF GRAPEVINE GROWTH—a grapevine moves through the following stages of growth each year in its effort to produce grapes: bud swell, bud break, leaves begin, visible clusters are seen, bloom, fruit set, developing fruit, veraison (coloring), sweetening, and harvest.

STOMATA—the microscopic openings on the underside of plant leaves through which they breathe, take in carbon dioxide and give off oxygen, and through which they absorb nutrients such as nitrogen from air and foliar feeds sprayed onto them.

SUGAR—the term used to refer to the complex carbohydrates contained in vegetables and fruits. *See* brix.

SUGAR TEST—consists of putting grapes from a number of areas in the vineyard into a large blender, mixing well, then putting a few drops of the juice into a refractometer and getting a sugar brix reading.

SUSTAINABLE AGRICULTURE—consists of agricultural practices that help build and maintain excellent health and welfare for people, plants, animals, and the earth. This includes avoiding the use of "chemical" products and sprays, restoring natural habitats, and the use of beneficial insects.

SWEETENING—in the ninth stage and last stage of grapevine development each year, sweetening develops the sugar content in each grape berry. Top-notch sugar brix is 24 percent for grapes. As soon as acceptable sugar is reached the grapes are harvested. *See* stages of grapevine growth.

TILTH—the term used to describe a soil that has humus, good structure, and a plentiful population of soil microorganisms. Soil with good tilth is often thought of as healthy soil.

TRANSITION PHASE—this is a three-to-five year period during which a farm, gardener, or greenhouse abandons the use of "chemical" supports and poisons, works to restore the soil, and learns new techniques of growing food.

TRELLIS—any system of fencing, slings, or posts and wires arranged to support fruits, vegetables, or flowers.

TYING—the practice of using twist-ties to fasten the long canes of vines to the trellis for support. Eventually the vines put out their own natural ties, but in order to maximize sunlight, canes are tied horizontally to the trellis until they are able to grasp the wires themselves.

VERAISON—the eighth stage of grapevine development is when the grapes turn from dull, dark green to a rich, translucent purple. After veraison, Concords are no longer susceptible to black rot. *See* stages of grapevine growth.

VISIBLE CLUSTERS—in the fourth stage of grapevine development each year, visible clusters form and tiny grape buds can be seen with the eye. *See* stages of grapevine growth.

INDEX

G

gassing fruits, 205

gene expression, 207

genetic engineering, 202, 209

Golden Mountain, 23, 41, 57, 90–92,
100, 104–105, 110, 118, 126,
134–135, 190, 194

golden world, 8, 16, 108

H

hardpan, 202

harvest

1991 tonnage, 86

1992 tonnage, 125

1993 tonnage, 176

estimating tonnage, 9–10, 103, 110

history of tonnage in vineyard,
9–10, 20, 86–88, 103, 110–112,
123, 125, 168, 176–177, 200

Harvey

advises us to grow fruit, 28–29

becomes dragonfly, 91

dims the lights, 51

first meeting with, 18

helps trim vines, 19–20

on trip to Detroit, 31

Hazel Hills Experimental Nut Farm,
138

heart disease, 204, 206, 209

heavy metals, 205, 210

humic acids, 201–202

hyperkinetic behaviors, 209

I

insects and pests

cutworm, 37

leafhopper, 37

J

jawbone, underdevelopment of, 208

K

kidney disease, 204

Kniffen method, 9

kundalini, x–xi, 47, 58

L

learning disabilities, 77, 209

light patterns

complementary light patterns,
28–29

geometric light patterns, 52

Lily Hill Farm

buying, 3, 9, 35, 115, 138, 150,
152, 204, 210

naming the farm, 32

rightful ownership, 40–41

STAY IN TOUCH...

Llewellyn publishes hundreds of books on your favorite subjects.

On the following pages you will find listed some books now available on related subjects. Your local bookstore stocks most of these and will stock new Llewellyn titles as they become available. We urge your patronage.

ORDER BY PHONE

Call toll-free within the U.S. and Canada, 1–800–THE MOON.

In Minnesota call (612) 291–1970.

We accept Visa, MasterCard, and American Express.

ORDER BY MAIL

Send the full price of order (MN residents add 7% sales tax) in U.S. funds to:

> Llewellyn Worldwide
> P.O. Box 64383, Dept. K382-4
> St. Paul, MN 55164–0383, U.S.A.

POSTAGE AND HANDLING

- $4.00 for orders $15.00 and under
- $5.00 for orders over $15.00
- No charge for orders over $100.00

We ship UPS in the continental United States. We cannot ship to P.O. boxes. Orders shipped to Alaska, Hawaii, Canada, Mexico, and Puerto Rico will be sent first-class mail.

International orders: Airmail—add freight equal to price of each book to the total price of order, plus $5.00 for each non-book item (audiotapes, etc.). Surface mail— Add $1.00 per item.

Allow 4–6 weeks delivery on all orders. Postage and handling rates subject to change.

GROUP DISCOUNTS

We offer a 20% quantity discount to group leaders or agents. You must order a minimum of 5 copies of the same book to get our special quantity price.

FREE CATALOG

Get a free copy of our color catalog, *New Worlds of Mind and Spirit*. Subscribe for just $10.00 in the United States and Canada ($20.00 overseas, first class mail). Many bookstores carry *New Worlds*—ask for it!

MOTHER NATURE'S HERBAL

Judith Griffin, Ph.D.

A Zuni American Indian swallows the juice of goldenrod flowers to ease his sore throat…an East Indian housewife uses the hot spices of curry to destroy parasites…an early American settler rubs fresh strawberry juice on her teeth to remove tartar. People throughout the centuries have enjoyed a special relationship with Nature and her many gifts. Now, with *Mother Nature's Herbal*, you can discover how to use a planet full of medicinal and culinary herbs through more than 200 recipes and tonics. Explore the cuisine, beauty secrets and folk remedies of China, the Mediterranean, South America, India, Africa and North America. The book will also teach you the specific uses of flower essences, chakra balancing, aromatherapy, essential oils, companion planting, organic gardening and theme garden designs.

1-56718-340-9, 7 x 10, 448 pp., 16-pg. color insert, softcover $19.95

ANIMAL-SPEAK

The Spiritual & Magical Powers of Creatures Great & Small

Ted Andrews

The animal world has much to teach us. Some are experts at survival and adaptation, some never get cancer, some embody strength and courage while others exude playfulness. Animals remind us of the potential we can unfold, but before we can learn from them, we must first be able to speak with them.

In this book, myth and fact are combined in a manner that will teach you how to speak and understand the language of the animals in your life. Animal-Speak helps you meet and work with animals as totems and spirits—by learning the language of their behaviors within the physical world. It provides techniques for reading signs and omens in nature so you can open to higher perceptions and even prophecy. It reveals the hidden, mythical and realistic roles of 45 animals, 60 birds, 8 insects, and 6 reptiles.

Animals will become a part of you, revealing to you the majesty and divine in all life. They will restore your childlike wonder of the world and strengthen your belief in magic, dreams and possibilities.

0–87542–028–1, 400 pp., 7 x 10, illus., photos, softcover $17.95

PSYCHIC EMPOWERMENT

A 7-Day Plan for Self-Development

Joe Slate, Ph.D.

Use 100% of your mind power in just one week! You've heard it before: each of us is filled with an abundance of untapped power—yet we only use one-tenth of its potential. Now a clinical psychologist and famed researcher in parapsychology shows you how to probe your mind's psychic faculties and manifest your capacity to access the higher planes of the mind.

The psychic experience validates your true nature and connects you to your inner knowing. Dr. Slate reveals the life-changing nature of psychic phenomena—including telepathy, out-of-body experiences and automatic writing. At the same time, he shows you how to develop a host of psychic abilities including psychokinesis, crystal gazing, and table tilting.

The final section of the book outlines his accelerated 7-Day Psychic Development Plan through which you can unleash your innate power and wisdom without further delay.

1-56718-635-1, 6 x 9, 256 pp., softbound $12.95